P9-CRX-383

Dedicated to
Oscar and Phoebe

Published in 2010 by Stewart, Tabori & Chang
An imprint of ABRAMS

Library of Congress Cataloging-in-Publication Data
Lang, Hillary.
Wee wonderfuls / Hillary Lang ; photographs by Jen Gotch.
p. cm.
ISBN 978-1-58479-858-3
1. Soft toy making. 2. Dollmaking. I. Title.
TT174.3.L365 2010
745.592'4--dc22 2009035050

Editors: Melanie Falick and Liana Allday
Designer: Onethread Design, Inc.
Production Manager: Anet Sirna-Bruder
Technical Editor: Chris Timmons

The text of this book was composed in Verlag and Chronicle Text.

Printed and bound in China
10 9 8 7 6 5 4 3 2

115 West 18th Street
New York, NY 10011
www.abramsbooks.com

Wee Wonderfuls

24 Dolls to Sew and Love

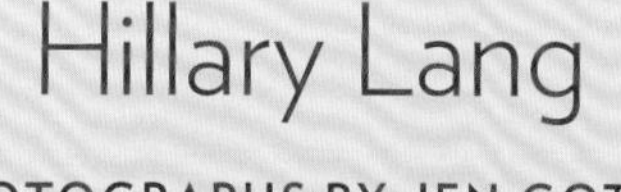

Hillary Lang

PHOTOGRAPHS BY JEN GOTCH

STC CRAFT | A MELANIE FALICK BOOK   STEWART, TABORI & CHANG | NEW YORK

Table of Contents

INTRODUCTION...6

EVELYN INCHWORM...9

PIXIE...13

KOJI...17

MARIE ANTOINETTE...21

MARGOT...25

BETSY...31

MERMAIDEN...37

ELLIE BAG...41

PANDA BUNS...45

WEE TOWN TROLLEY...49

SLEEPOVER PALS...53

EDDIE...57

TAG-A-LONG DOLL...61

I HEART YOU...67

WES, THE BABY GIRAFFE...71

KATIE KITTY...75

MELVIN AND MARIAN...79

BJORN BJORNSON...85

LITTLE MISS STORYBOOK...89

DOXIE NECKLACE...95

PATCHWORK PENNY...99

BONNETED BABY...105

HAUS SWEET HAUS...109

HANSEL AND GRETEL...113

WEE WONDERFULS BASICS...118

WEE WONDERFULS PATTERN PIECES...129

RESOURCES...167

ACKNOWLEDGMENTS...168

Introduction

SUPER CUTE! DARLING! HOW ADORABLE IS THAT?!

When I sew I like to get a big reaction. And nothing in my 25 years of sewing has ever been as satisfying as making toys. I made my first stuffed animal when my son Oscar was born and I was immediately hooked! My flexible schedule as a stay-at-home mom allowed me to fully embrace my crafty side, and quickly I realized I had a certain knack for it. As a kid I had surrounded myself with beloved friends like Holly Hobbie, My Friend Mandy, and Ginny dolls. I'd also spent hours reading stories about the secret lives of toys, like the Lonely Doll, Velveteen Rabbit, and Corduroy. This early initiation was coming in handy.

In 2004 I started a blog called Wee Wonderfuls to document my toy-making and other crafty efforts. I was no expert. Though I knew my way around a sewing machine and patterns, I was new to toy-making. But the supportive community on my blog gave me the confidence to keep at it when I struggled through a project, and reminded me to still have fun. When readers started asking for my patterns, I began to publish them. It was so exciting to see how someone else could follow my directions and create a doll that was both like mine and had its own unique personality. And all of that led me to create this book in which I present my first collection of 24 toys together. In it I have included everything from a topsy-turvy doll like the one I coveted as a child to a fiercely cute monster with spikes to an elephant purse—and all manner of characters in between.

My favorite part of writing this book was when I sat down with my sketchbook and began dreaming up all of the toys you see here. You won't find 24 variations on the same idea—I set out to create a diverse gang with as many interesting and unique personalities, construction techniques, and details as possible. There are projects sewn by hand and by machine. Designs that call for appliqué, embroidery, and quilting. Some dolls sit, some stand. Some are poseable, while others like to flop around. And the hair! There's ribbon hair, yarn hair, felt hair, fur hair, buns, braids. There is a toy for every member of your family and circle of friends, boys and girls of all ages—nobody's left out.

All of the projects in the book are suitable for beginner sewers. Some are more involved, but few contain complex concepts, so a basic knowledge of sewing is sufficient. If you are new to sewing or toy-making, you should definitely take a look at Wee Wonderfuls Basics, which begins on page 118, before you start a project. There I introduce the materials and methods I used for sewing all of the toys. You'll find there is a lot of wiggle room when making toys: uneven seams, wonky embroidery, lumpy stuffing...still cute. With handmade toys, imperfection is part of the charm.

Start with the toys here and see where your imagination takes you. Before long you may be improvising and designing toys of your own, ones that take you back to your childhood, or match the quirky personality of your little one today. Get ready to submit yourself to the addictive power of cute. Now go! Make some lovable, destined-to-be-treasured toys for your kids, and the kids in all of us.

Hillary

BUTTON
BUTTONHOLE
20c

Evelyn Inchworm

I am addicted to making up tiny critters from wool felt, and the latest addition to the menagerie is this little scrunched-up, green inchworm, Evelyn. She is named after my dear grandmother Evelyn, who was long on style but short on hustle. While Ev may be pokey, the sewing—all by hand—is surprisingly quick and easy. You can make her up on your daily commute or while watching your favorite tv show. Try working without pins and I think you'll find, as I do, that it's very easy (and much safer on public transit).

FINISHED SIZE
4″ long

PATTERN PIECES (see page 129)
Body (A); Gusset (B); Kerchief (C); Sunglasses (D)

MATERIALS
6″ x 13″ (1⁄4 yd. or fat quarter) wool felt for body
5″ x 6″ scrap of cotton print for kerchief
Scrap of wool felt for sunglasses
Two 3⁄8″ buttons for eyes
Matching and coordinating thread
Embroidery floss for body and mouth
Stuffing

STITCHES USED (see pages 125–128)
Whipstitch, tacking stitch, backstitch.

NOTE
Unless otherwise noted, all seam allowances are 1⁄4″ and built into the patterns.

1. Cut Out Pattern Pieces

Cut out all the pattern pieces from the designated fabrics, cutting the number of pieces called for on each pattern piece. For more information on cutting out pattern pieces, see page 125.

2. Sew One Side of Body to Gusset

Pin one side of the Body (A) to one side of the Gusset (B), aligning the gusset's small pointed end with the body's tail end and pinning the gusset up the body and around to the back of the head (alternatively, instead of pinning, you might prefer to just hold the small gusset in place as you sew). Hand-sew the gusset in place with six strands of matching embroidery floss and a whipstitch (see diagram).

RIGHT SIDE | WRONG SIDE

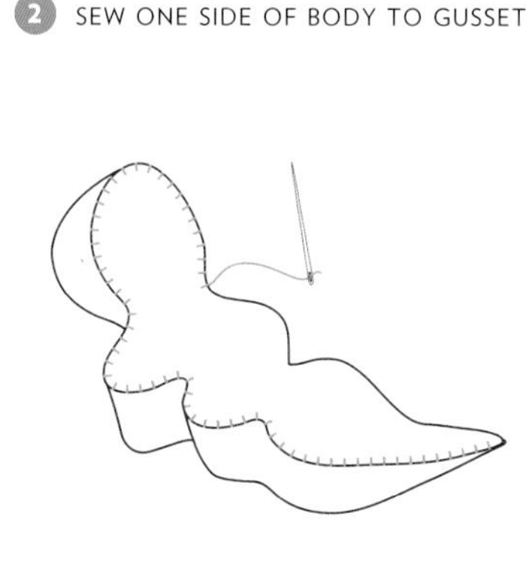

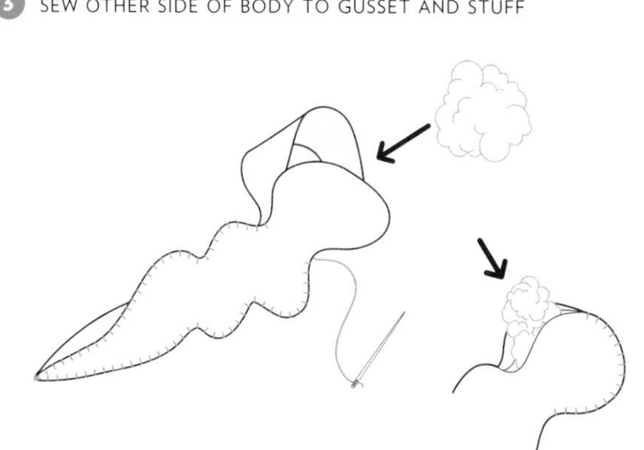

3. Sew Other Side of Body to Gusset

Pin the other side of the Body (A) to the body's first side along the back. Whipstitch the back seam, beginning at the tail and knotting off at the back neck where the gusset begins (see diagram). Next sew the free side's bottom edge to the gusset, starting at the tail and stopping at neck. Pause sewing here to stuff the tail and the body firmly (see page 121). Then continue sewing the gusset up and around the head, pausing again for stuffing the head firmly (see diagram). Then finish sewing up the gap.

4. Attach Eyes and Accessories

Using the marking method in the Basics section on transferring faces to fabric (see page 124), the face template on the Body (A), and the diagram as a placement guide, hand-sew the button eyes with thread, repeating the stitches until the eyes are secure. Attach the sides of the Sunglasses (D) with tacking stitches, and tack-stitch the Kerchief (C) in place under the neck (see diagram), repeating the stitches until the accessories are secure. Using three strands of contrasting floss and a backstitch, embroider the mouth.

Pixie

Pixie was the first toy I designed for this book, and I was so encouraged when her little ball of a body, fluffy mop of curls, and long, skinny pixie legs turned out just like my sketch. Pixie's perfectly round, lovably squishy body is made from a pair of knee socks and stuffing. Her happy puffy hair is made by tying off loops of mohair yarn, a method that has become a fast favorite of mine. Add a cute gathered frock tied off with a big satin bow for wings, and a pair of embroidered ballet slippers, and you are sure to fall in love with Pixie at first sight—just like I did.

FINISHED SIZE

19″ tall

PATTERN PIECES (see page 130)

Arm (A); Leg (B)

MATERIALS

1 pair of adult knee socks, preferably cotton blend
16″ x 6½″ (¼ yd. or fat quarter) cotton print for dress
12″ length of 1½″-wide ribbon
1 skein of mohair or angora yarn
Matching and coordinating thread
Embroidery floss for shoes and facial features
Stuffing

STITCHES USED (see pages 125-128)

Gathering stitch, ladder stitch, whipstitch, edgestitch, satin stitch, backstitch, tacking stitch.

NOTE

Unless otherwise noted, all seam allowances are ¼″ and built into the patterns.

1. Begin Constructing Body

Trim off the top cuff of one sock and cut a 9″ length of sock for the body, measuring from the trimmed edge. Turn the sock wrong side out, and hand-sew a gathering stitch around one edge ½″ from that edge (see diagram). Pull the gathers taut, and tie off the thread with a double or triple knot (depending on the tightness of your sock's weave) that's big enough not to pull through the weave. Turn the sock right side out.

2. Stuff and Complete Body

Begin to stuff the body (see page 121), balling the stuffing in the gathered end to form the head. When the head is plump, stop stuffing and sew up the neck as follows: Hand-sew a gathering stitch about 2½″ from the top of the head, pulling the thread taut without completely closing off the neck while forming the stuffed head into a nice, round shape (see diagram). Tie off the gathering stitches at the neck with another big knot.

Continue stuffing the body until it's nice and plump. Then sew a gathering stitch ½″ from the bottom end of the body, and pull the opening taut, tucking the opening's raw ends inside the body. Tie off the thread with a big knot (see diagram).

3. Cut and Sew Limbs

Turn the second sock wrong side out, to sew and cut out two Arm (A) and two Leg (B) pieces from the sock. Since it's difficult to trace on the sock, pin the pattern pieces to the sock and sew right around them as follows: Align and pin each pattern piece, so one of its straight sides is positioned along one of the sock's folded edges (see diagram). Sew around the pinned pieces, leaving the flat, top edge unsewn; then cut out the pieces with a 1/8″ seam allowance. Since the stretchy sock is very forgiving, don't worry if your sewing is not precise.

4. Stuff and Attach Limbs

Turn the limbs right side out and stuff them, taking care not to overstuff them and pop the seams. Use the eraser end of a pencil or a stuffing fork to push little clumps of stuffing, one clump at a time, down into each limb. When each limb is plump, roll it between your hands to shape it. Pin the legs and arms to the body, as shown in the diagram, with the limb's raw edges tucked inside; and hand-sew each limb in place using a ladder stitch or a whipstitch, repeating the stitches until each limb is secure.

5. Begin Constructing Dress

With right sides together, sew the short ends of the dress fabric together and press the seam allowances open. Press the top and bottom edges of the sewn fabric 1/4″ to the wrong side. Turn the fabric right side out and edgestitch the top and bottom edges.

6. Stitch Dress in Place

Hand-sew a gathering stitch around the dress's top folded edge, but don't pull the gathers taut yet. Pull the dress up over Pixie's legs and arms, and tighten the gathering stitches around her neck. Tie off the gathering thread with a knot.

Feel through the dress to find where each arm meets the body, and, at those two points, cut 2½″ slits in the dress for armholes (see diagram). Pull the arms through the slits, tuck each slit's raw edges to the wrong side around each arm, and sew the dress to each arm using a ladder stitch. Sew a gathering stitch around the dress's bottom folded edge. Pull the gathering stitches taut until the gathers hit the legs, and tie off the thread with a knot (see diagram).

7. Embroider Shoes

Using a satin stitch and six strands of floss, embroider ballet shoes on the bottom of the legs, following the diagram, and bury the thread tails (see page 128) of the floss inside each leg.

8. Start Making Hair

Pixie's fluffy mop is made by tying clumps of 5″-long yarn loops together on a string. Here's how: Start by cutting a 12″-long piece of yarn on which you'll tie the clumps. Next wrap the remaining yarn around your fingers ten times, holding your fingers as wide apart as needed to make loops about 5″ wide (see diagram). After wrapping a clump, cut the yarn; and, starting at one end of your 12″ piece, tie the yarn around the middle of the clump. Make four more clumps, and tie the yarn around each of them, positioning them about 1″ apart (see diagram).

9. Attach Hair

Pin the clumps through their tied-off centers to the stuffed head, flipping the loops as needed so that they create a nice, full hairdo (see diagram). Hand-sew the clumps to the head through their centers with matching thread, stitching from one clump to the next without knotting off until you reach the end and repeating the stitches until each clump is secure.

10. Embroider Facial Features

Using a backstitch and six strands of floss, embroider Pixie's facial features following the diagram. Start by making a huge knot in your floss that won't pull through the sock's weave. To hide this knot, start stitching under the fluffy hair, and bring the needle out on the face. When you've finished embroidering the face, stitch back under the hair, and tie another big knot, being careful not to pull too tightly to keep from denting Pixie's face. Wrap the ribbon around Pixie's neck twice, so its ends fall in back, and tie the ends in a big bow to make fairy wings. Sew a few tacking stitches through the bow's knot to secure it.

RIGHT SIDE	WRONG SIDE

1 SEW GATHERING STITCH TO CREATE BODY

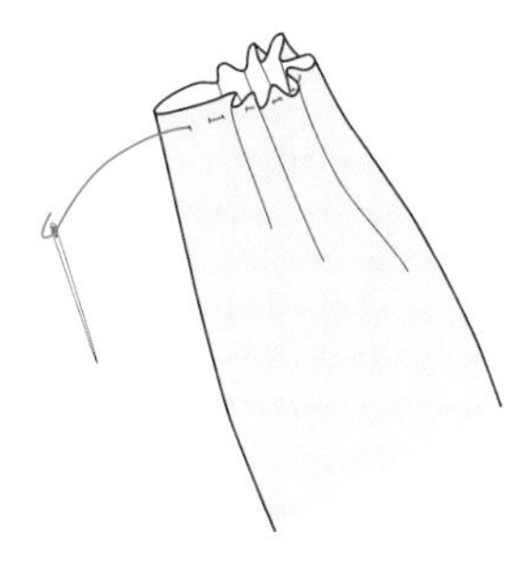

2 STUFF AND COMPLETE BODY

3 CUT AND SEW LIMBS

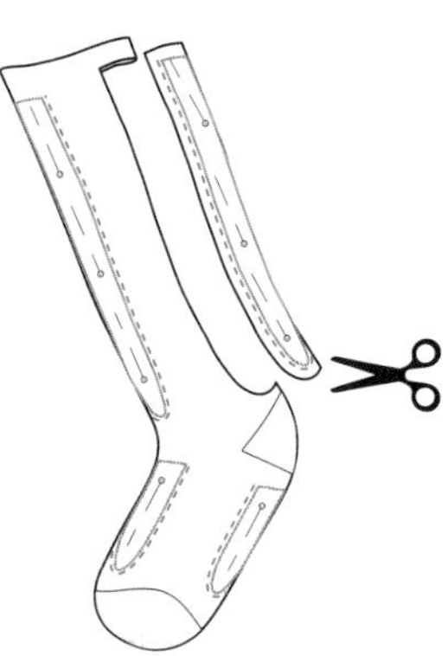

4 STUFF LIMBS AND ATTACH TO BODY

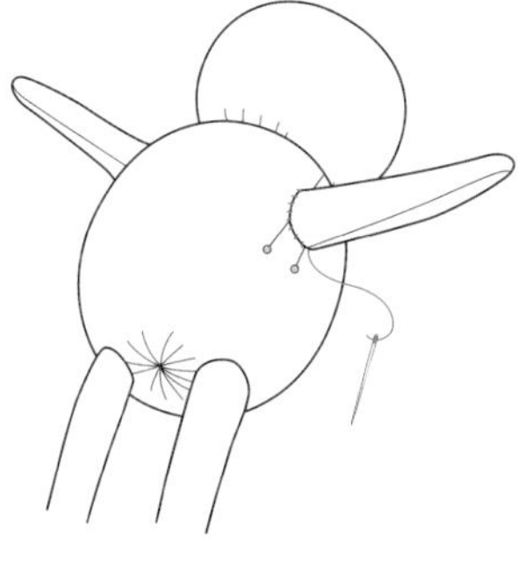

6 STITCH DRESS IN PLACE

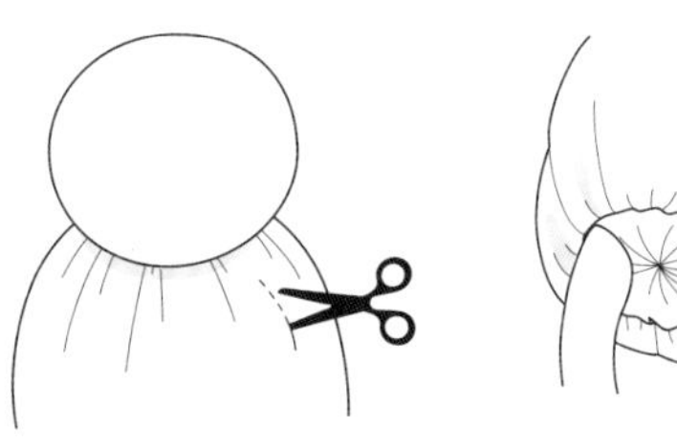

7 EMBROIDER SHOES

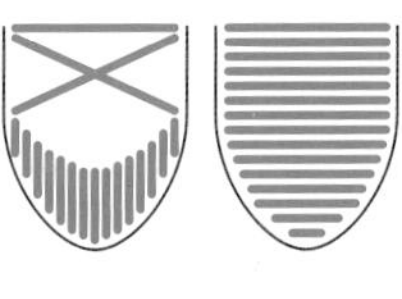

8 START MAKING HAIR

9 ATTACH HAIR TO HEAD

10 EMBROIDER FACIAL FEATURES

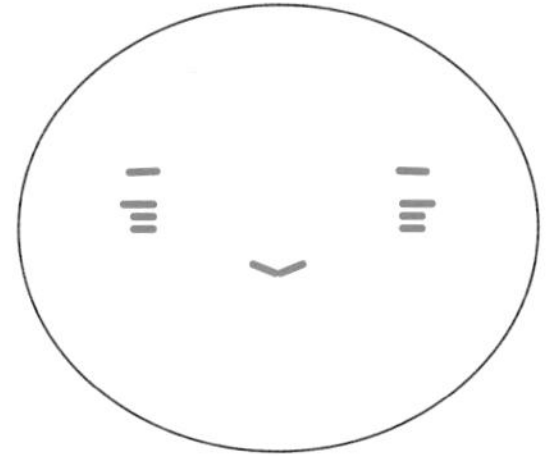

Koji

Can a doll be both cute and creepy at the same time? I should think so. A sturdy little block of fun, Koji is equally good for hugging or mischief making. Pick a fun corduroy print for your monster's thick skin. The impressive spikes are the perfect finish for your little monster. They are very easy to make using one of my favorite materials—wool felt.

FINISHED SIZE

8″ tall

PATTERN PIECES (see pages 131–132)

Body (A); Body Gusset (B); Body Bottom (C); Underbelly (D); Tail (E); Tail Bottom (F); Mouth (G); Spikes (H)

MATERIALS

15″ x 30″ (1/2 yd.) corduroy for body
5″ x 10″ scrap of cotton print for belly
4″ x 12″ (1/4 yd. or fat quarter) wool felt for spikes
1″ x 3″ scrap of wool felt for mouth
Matching and coordinating thread
Embroidery floss to match spikes and mouth (and to contrast with wool felt beads or circles if you're using them for eyes)
Wool felt beads, buttons, or 1/4″ circles of wool felt for eyes
Chalk pencil
Stuffing

STITCHES USED (see pages 125–128)

Edgestitch, ladder stitch, whipstitch.

NOTES

In cutting dimensions, the rectangle's width is always given first, followed by its height.

Unless otherwise noted, all seam allowances are 1/4″ and built into the patterns.

1. Cut Out Pattern Pieces

Cut out all the pattern pieces, except for the Spikes (H), from the designated fabrics, cutting the number of pieces called for on each pattern piece and transferring all pattern markings to the cut pieces. In addition, cut two 12″ x 2″ strips from wool felt for the spikes, which you'll cut for the spikes as explained in Step 7. For more information on cutting out patterns and transferring pattern markings, see pages 122–123.

2. Sew Underbelly to Body Gusset

With right sides together, align and sew together the two Underbelly (D) pieces along the sides and top, leaving the bottom edge open. Turn the underbelly right side out, and press it flat. Pin the underbelly to the Body Gusset (B), centering it on the gusset and aligning the bottom edges (see diagram). Edgestitch the underbelly to the gusset along the three sewn sides, again leaving the bottom edge unsewn.

3. Attach Body Gusset

With right sides together, align and pin the body gusset to one side of the Body (A), aligning the arms and legs (see diagram). Sew the gusset to the side of the body, beginning at the dot at the bottom edge. Repeat the above process for other side of the body.

4. Finish Sewing Body

With right sides together, pin the Body Bottom (C) to the body, aligning the center-front dot at the bottom with the center of the underbelly. Sew the bottom in place, leaving the back end open for

turning and stuffing (see diagram). Clip the bottom seam where it meets the side seams. Also clip under the arm curves. Turn the body right side out and stuff it firmly (see page 121). Hand-sew the gap closed with a ladder stitch.

5. Sew and Attach Tail

With right sides together, sew the sides of the Tail (E) along the top edge. Open up the tail's sides and, with right sides together, sew them to the edges of the Tail Bottom (F) (see diagram). Clip the points, turn the tail right side out, and stuff it. Fold the tail's top edge 1/4″ to the wrong side; pin the tail to the body, as shown in the diagram; and hand-sew the tail into place with a ladder stitch.

6. Sew Facial Features

Hand-sew the felt Mouth (G) to the face with a whipstitch and three strands of matching floss, using the diagram as a placement guide and hiding the knots (see page 128) under the mouth. If you're using wool felt beads for eyes, sew them in place using a contrasting color of embroidery floss, pushing the needle all the way through the center of the bead and then back through the head. If you're using buttons for the eyes, sew them securely in place. Note that if this toy is intended for a child under the age of three, do not use any detachable parts or trim.

7. Stitch Up Some Spikes

First, cut a full-size paper pattern piece for the spikes by placing the Spikes (H) pattern on folded paper. Next use a chalk pencil to trace the full-size spikes pattern on one of the 12″ x 2″ felt strips you cut in Step 1. Place the two felt strips together, with the traced strip facing outward and the strips' edges aligned, and sew the layers together along the traced line. Trim the seam allowances to 1/8″ (see diagram).

To sew the spikes to the body, press open the bottom 1/4″ of the spikes, and pin these seam allowances flat along the monster's forehead and back, starting at mid-forehead and running to the end of the tail. Hand-sew the spikes in place with a whipstitch (see diagram) and three strands of matching floss.

RIGHT SIDE | WRONG SIDE

2 SEW UNDERBELLY TO BODY GUSSET

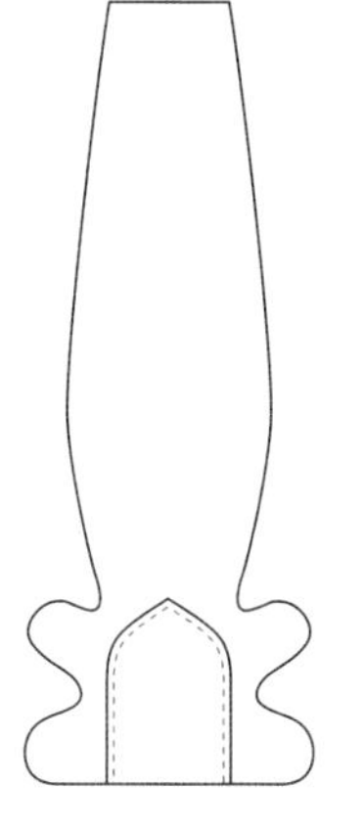

3 ATTACH BODY GUSSET

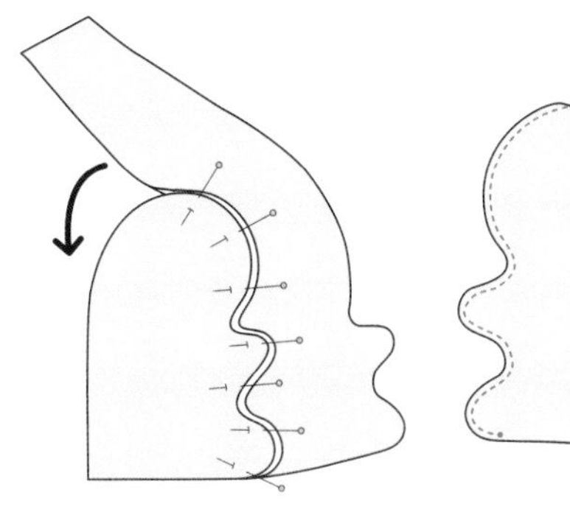

4 SEW BODY BOTTOM TO REST OF BODY

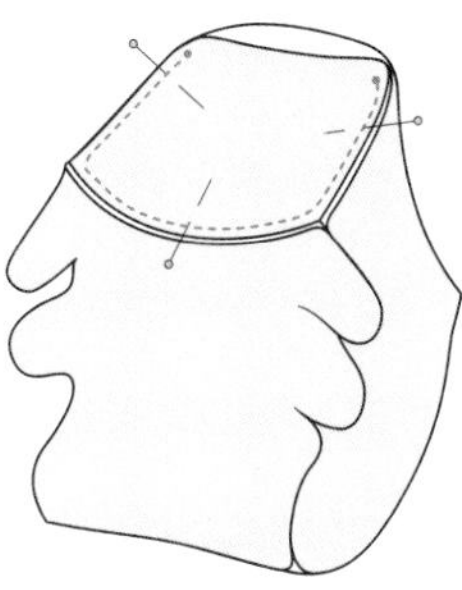

5 SEW TAIL AND ATTACH TO BODY

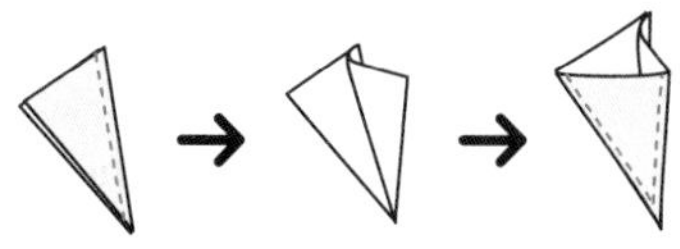

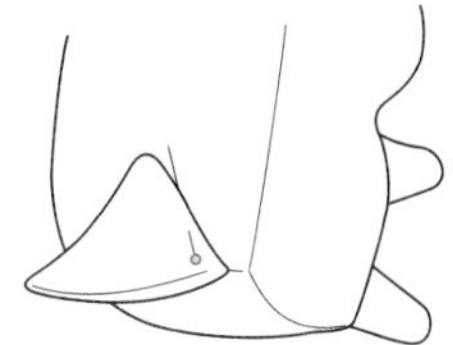

6 SEW FACIAL FEATURES

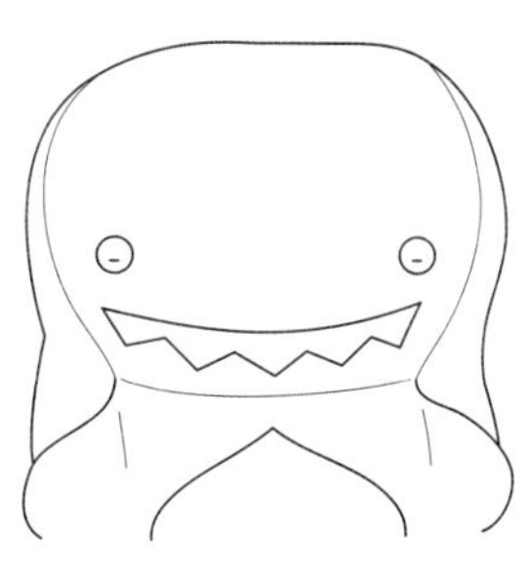

7 SEW AND CUT OUT SPIKES AND ATTACH TO BODY

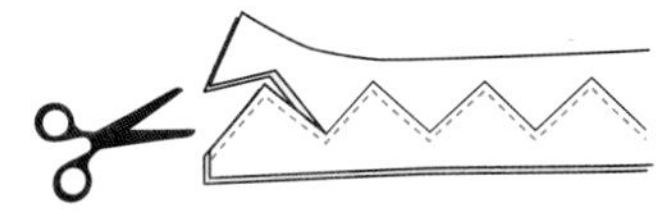

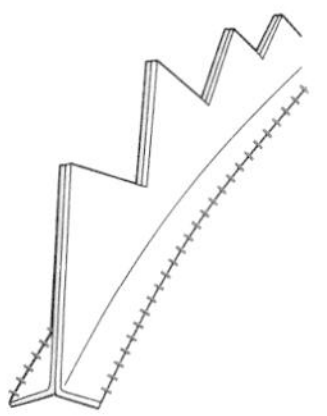

Marie Antoinette

Sometimes you just have to go all-out girly, and who better for this royal treatment than Marie Antoinette? Done up in pastels, she is a true confection and the perfect opportunity to overindulge—more colors, more textures, more embellishments. If you've never embroidered before, do not be discouraged. All you need to learn are a few easy stitches and you'll be set.

FINISHED SIZE
11″ tall

PATTERN PIECE (see pages 133–134)
Marie Antoinette

MATERIALS
16″ x 16″ (1/2 yd.) wool or linen for body
8″ x 12″ (1/4 yd. or fat quarter) cotton for backing
Wool felt scraps for embellishments
Scrap of pleated or plain ribbon for fan
Matching and coordinating thread
Embroidery floss
Rainbow Gallery's angora floss (see Resources on page 167)
Transfer pencil
Tracing paper
12″ embroidery hoop
Stuffing

STITCHES USED (see pages 125–128)
Split stitch, backstitch, ladder stitch, tacking stitch.

NOTE
Unless otherwise noted, all seam allowances are 1/4″ and built into the patterns.

1. **Transfer Embroidery Design to Fabric**
Center the pattern's embroidery design on pages 133–134 on the 16″ fabric square, and use a transfer pencil to trace and transfer the design onto the fabric following the instructions on the pencil's packaging or as follows: Trace the embroidery design on a piece of tracing paper with a regular pencil. Next trace over the design on the opposite side of the paper with a transfer pencil. Then, with the transfer-pencil side of the paper facing down, center the design on the 16″ fabric square and, with iron on hottest nonsteam setting, iron the design on the fabric to transfer it.

2. **Embroider Traced Design**
Using three strands of fluffy angora floss for Marie's hair; three strands of embroidery floss for her body, face, and dress; and a 12″ hoop, embroider the traced design with a split stitch, substituting a backstitch for the tiny details. Wait until Step 4 to embellish the doll after sewing and stuffing it.

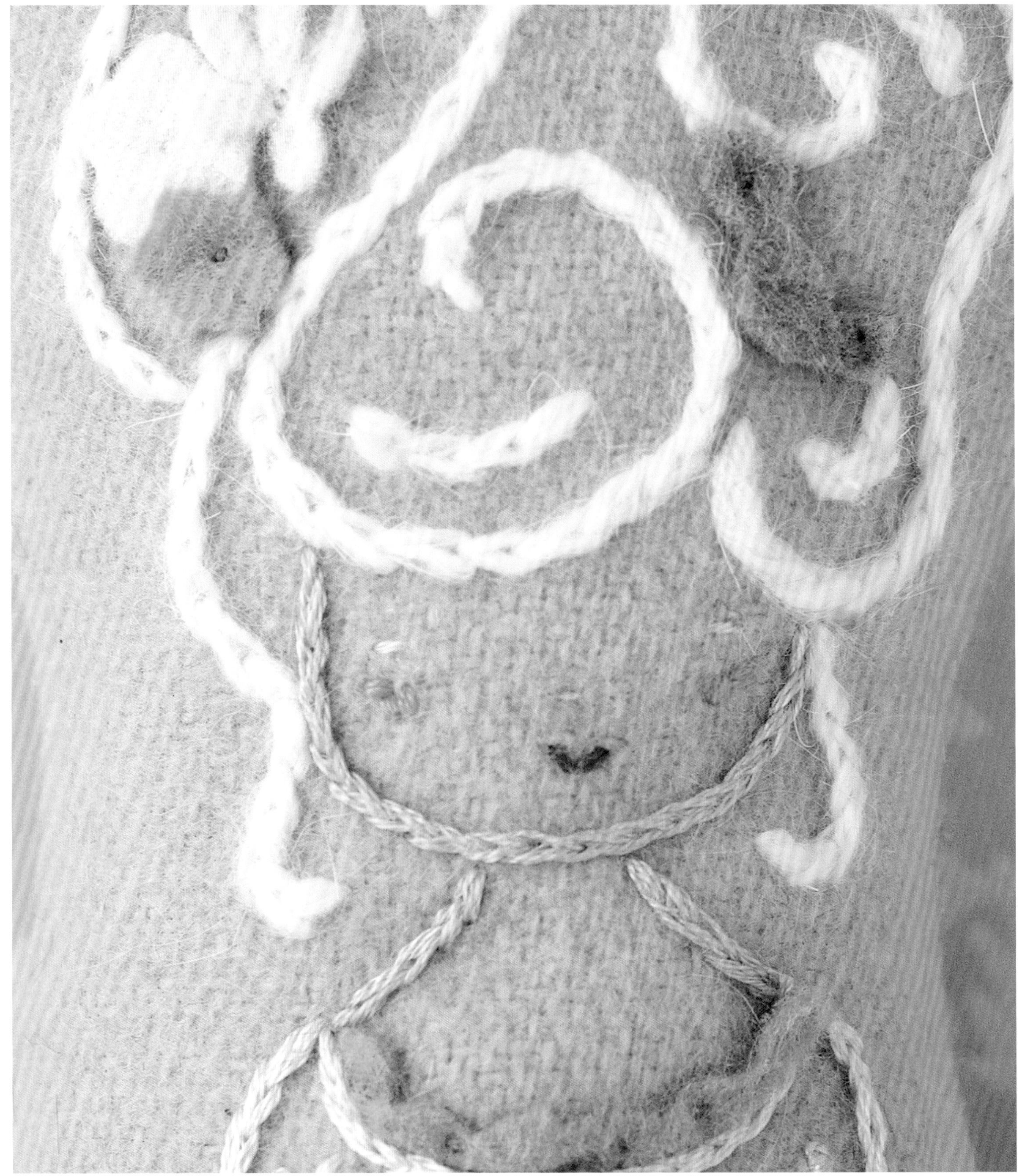

RIGHT SIDE

WRONG SIDE

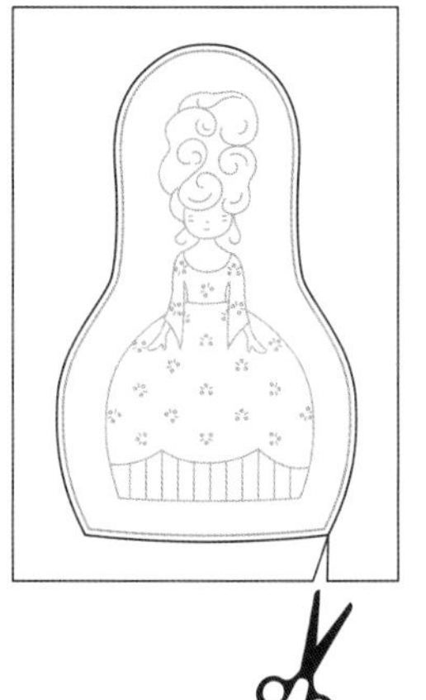

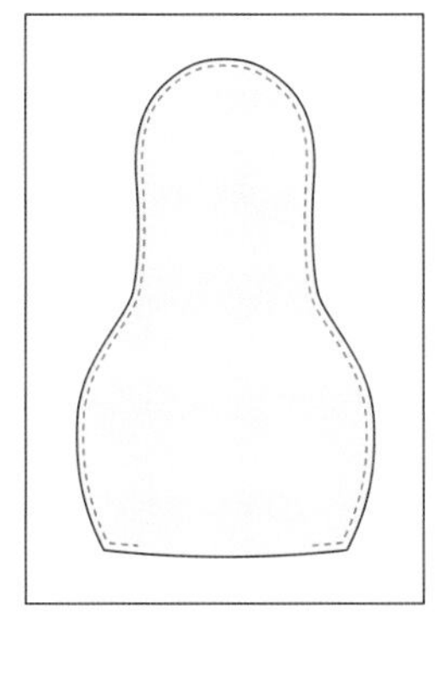

3. Cut, Sew, and Stuff Doll

With the fabric's embroidered side facing up, center and pin the doll pattern's silhouette over the embroidery; and cut the fabric to shape (see diagram). Then place the backing fabric right side up and the embroidered doll front right side down on top of the backing. Sew the doll front to the backing fabric with a 1⁄4″ seam, leaving a 3″ opening along the bottom edge for turning and stuffing (see diagram). Cut around the doll front, and turn and stuff the doll until it's firm but still somewhat flat (see page 121). Use a ladder stitch to sew the opening closed, tucking in the opening's edges as you sew.

4. Embellish Doll

Cut out the embellishments on the pattern—flowers and birds for her hair, scallops for her neckline and sleeves, and bows for her skirts—from the wool felt scraps and hand-sew them to the stuffed body with small tacking stitches (see diagram), using thread or one strand of floss, and the photo as a placement guide. As you sew, hide the knots under the embellishments (see page 128), and finish off the doll by gathering the pleated ribbon into a fan and sewing it to Marie's hand.

Margot

I never had a topsy-turvy doll as a girl and was always in awe of the doll whose skirt flips up to reveal...an entirely new doll! So for my daughter Phoebe's first Christmas, I had to try my hand at making one. Instead of a two-character topsy-turvy, Margot is one gal, twice the fun. Dressed-Up Margot wears her hair in festive buns and sports a party dress with a scalloped hem while Dressed-Down Margot feels right at home with her apron and braids. Simply change the color of the yarn hair if you want to split your doll's personality. I made two Margots for the photo at left. To see both halves of Margot together, see the photo on page 28.

FINISHED SIZE

13″ tall

PATTERN PIECES (see page 135)

Body (A); Top Front (B); Top Back (C); Collar (D); Scallops (E)

MATERIAL

9″ x 36″ or 18″ x 18″ (1/4 yd. or fat quarter) solid-color cotton or flannel for body
22″ x 16″ (1/2 yd.) cotton print for Dressed Down's dress
11″ x 7″ scrap of cotton print for Dressed Down's apron
22″ x 16″ (1/2 yd.) cotton print for Dressed Up's dress
11″ x 22″ (1/2 yd.) accent fabric for Dressed Up's waistband, collar, and scalloped hem
4″ length of 1/2″-wide ribbon
Matching and coordinating thread
Embroidery floss for facial features
Doll needle
1 skein Lamb's Pride Worsted yarn
Red ink pad
Small paintbrush
Stuffing

STITCHES USED (see pages 125–128)

Ladder stitch, whipstitch, backstitch, tacking stitch, edgestitch, gathering stitch.

NOTES

In cutting dimensions, the rectangle's width is always given first, followed by its height.

Unless otherwise noted, all seam allowances are 1/4″ and built into the patterns.

1. Cut Out Pattern Pieces

Cut out all the pattern pieces, except for the Body (A), Collar (D), and Scallops (E), from the designated fabrics, cutting the number of pieces called for on each pattern piece and transferring all pattern markings to the cut pieces (you'll cut the body as explained in Step 2, the collar as explained in Step 11, and the scallops as explained in Step 12). In addition, cut the following:

From each of Dressed Down's and Dressed Up's dress fabrics, a 22″ x 10″ rectangle.

From Dressed Up's accent fabric, a 22″ x 7″ rectangle for the skirt's scallops, a 9″ x 3 1/4″ rectangle for the waistband, and a 4″ x 2 1/2″ rectangle for the collar.

From Dressed Down's apron fabric, an 8″ x 6″ rectangle for the apron skirt and a 3″ x 6″ rectangle for the apron's bib.

For more information on cutting out patterns and transferring pattern markings, see pages 122–123.

2. Cut Out and Sew Body

With right sides together, fold the body fabric in half to get a piece 18″ x 9″. Pin the Body (A) pattern to the fabric, and trace around it (see page 122). Flip the pattern piece over, align and pin the flipped pattern's bottom edge with that of the traced pattern, and trace the doll's second side (see diagram). Sew on the traced line, leaving a 3″ opening at the side for stuffing the doll. Cut out the sewn pattern with a ¼″ seam allowance, and clip the curves (see page 125). Turn the piece right side out through the opening, and press it flat.

3. Transfer Facial Features to Body

Referring to the Basics section on transferring faces to fabric (see page 124), transfer the face template to both of Margot's faces. Because the doll's faces face opposite directions, you'll need to trace one face on one side, and then flip the doll upside down and over in order to trace the other face.

4. Stuff and Close Body

Stuff the body firmly, starting with the arms and heads, and then stuff the center of the body. Hand-sew the opening closed with a ladder stitch or a whipstitch, tucking in the opening's edges as you sew.

5. Embroider Faces

Using a backstitch and three strands of embroidery floss, embroider the traced face on each stuffed head. Begin by knotting your floss and inserting your needle from the back of the head and through and out the front (you'll later hide the knots with hair). After embroidering the features, paint on rosy cheeks by first dabbing a small dry paintbrush on a red ink pad. Dab the brush on a cloth to remove excess ink, and start with very light dabs on the face to make a circle for the cheek. Fill in the cheek, applying ink slowly and lightly (remember you can always add more, but you can't remove it) and always dabbing the brush on a cloth to remove excess ink every time you recharge it.

6. Embroider Hair

Both the Dressed-Up and the Dressed-Down dolls have the same basic hairstyle. Using a doll needle and unknotted 20″ lengths of yarn, hand-sew the yarn on the head as if you were embroidering very large stitches. Following the diagram, start embroidering the back of the head, leaving tails of the yarn to be clipped at the surface after you're done. After embroidering the front and back of the head, add filler stitches along the seam line to cover bald spots (see diagram).

7. Create Dressed Down's Braids

For Dressed Down's hanging braids, cut nine 12″-long strands of yarn, fold them in half, and tie the bundle around the middle with a 6″-long piece of yarn. Create three sections of six strands each, and braid the yarn for 2″-3″ before tying it off with another piece of yarn. Trim the braid's ends to 1″, and repeat the process for a second braid.

Using the diagram as a placement guide, attach the braids to the head by sewing one 3″-long end of the yarn you tied around the bundle into the head and back out in a small tacking stitch. Tie this end with the other and knot it securely. Bury the thread tails of the yarn inside the stuffed head (see page 128).

8. Create Dressed Up's Buns

For Dressed Up's buns, cut six 16″-long pieces of yarn. Tie the pieces together at one end; and, using three sections of two strands each, braid the yarn. Leave a short ½″ tail on the braid, and tie it off with another short piece of yarn. Repeat the process to make a second braid.

Coil one braid into a bun, and pin it to the head, using the diagram as a placement guide. Sew the bun to the head with matching thread, as follows: Push the needle through the braids, stitch in and out of the head under the bun, and then stitch back up through the bun near where the needle exited. Continue sewing this way, taking small, barely visible stitches to secure the bun to the head—10 to 15 stitches should do the trick. It may seem like you're sewing air together, but after finishing, gently tug at the bun, which should feel secure. Tie a bow from ribbon, and sew it to one side of the head near the bun.

9. Sew Dressed Down's Apron Bib and Top

With right sides together, fold the 3″ x 6″ bib fabric in half, matching up the short sides to get a 3″ x 3″ piece, and sew around three sides, leaving one 3″ side open. Clip the fabric at the corners, turn the piece right side out, and press it flat. Align and pin the bib's bottom unsewn edge to the bottom edge of Dressed Down's Top Front (B), and edgestitch the bib in place around its three sewn edges (see diagram).

With right sides together, sew the long-sleeve Top Front (B) to the Top Backs (C) at the side seams (see diagram). Clip the curves under the arm and at the shoulder, turn the top right side out, and press it flat. Press the neck and sleeve edges and one center-back edge ¼″ to the wrong side.

RIGHT SIDE

WRONG SIDE

2 CUT OUT AND SEW BODY

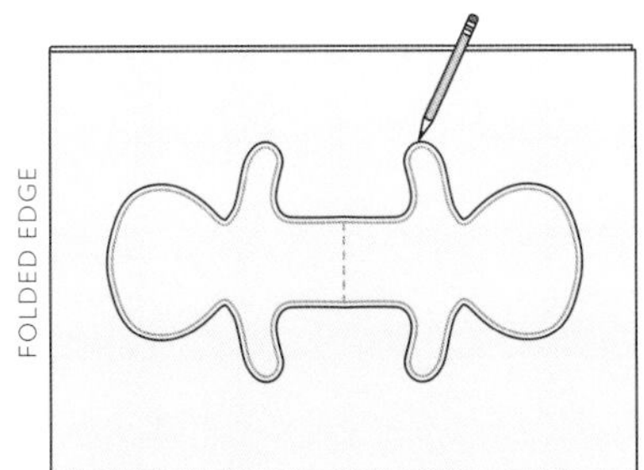

6 EMBROIDER HAIR

7 CREATE DRESSED DOWN'S BRAIDS

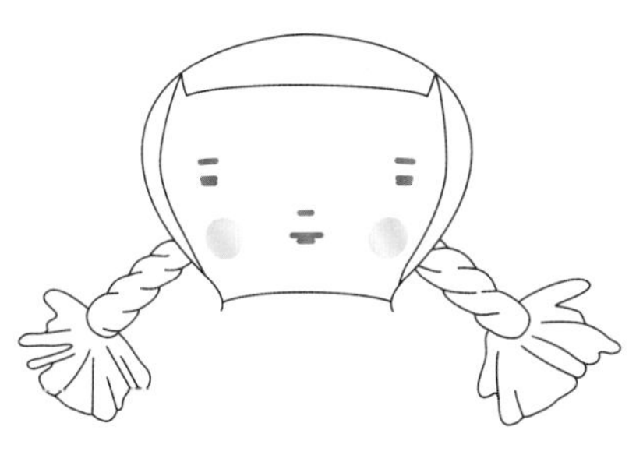

8 CREATE DRESSED UP'S BUNS

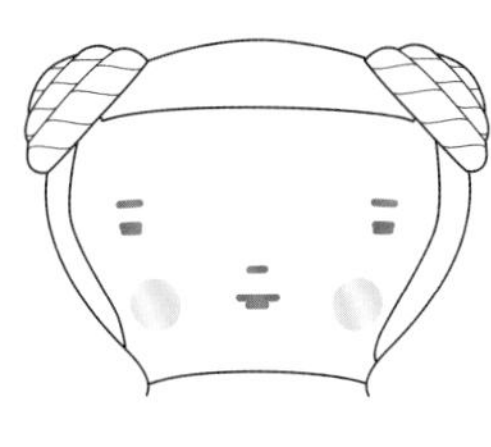

9 SEW DRESSED DOWN'S APRON BIB AND TOP

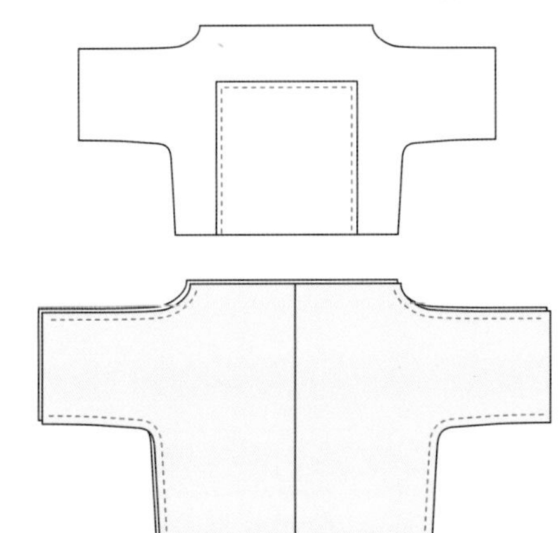

10. Attach Dressed Down's Top

Put the top on Dressed Down; and, with the folded-under edge on top at center back, use a whipstitch and thread to hand-sew the back of the shirt shut and to the body (see diagram). Then whipstitch the shirt to the body at the neck and sleeve edges.

11. Sew and Attach Dressed Up's Top

Flip the doll, and repeat steps 9 & 10, omitting the apron bib but sewing the top to Dressed Up (see diagrams).

12. Attach Dressed Up's Collar

With right sides together, fold the 4″ x 2½″ rectangle of accent fabric in half, matching up the sides to get a 2″ x 2½″ piece. Pin and trace the Collar pattern (D) on the fabric with its straight edge aligned with fabric's raw edges. Sew along the traced line, leaving the raw edges open. Cut out the collar, leaving a ⅛″ seam allowance, and clip the curves at the center. Turn the collar right side out, and press it flat. Then turn the open edges ¼″ to the wrong side, and press them flat. Pin the collar to Dressed Up's top, aligning its top straight edge with the top's neckline. Hand-sew the collar in place with a whipstitch (see diagram).

13. Attach Dressed Up's Skirt Scallops

With right sides together, fold Dressed Up's 22″ x 7″ rectangle of accent fabric in half, matching up the sides to get a 22″ x 3½″ piece. Then, with the pattern's straight edge aligned with the fabric's bottom fold, trace the Scallop pattern (E) three times in a row, as shown in the diagram, omitting the pattern's seam allowance on the center piece and flipping the pattern to trace it for the third time, so the seam allowance faces to the right.

Sew the two layers of fabric together along the traced line and cut out the sewn piece with a ¼″ seam allowance. Clip the seam allowances between the curves, turn the scallops right side out,

RIGHT SIDE | WRONG SIDE

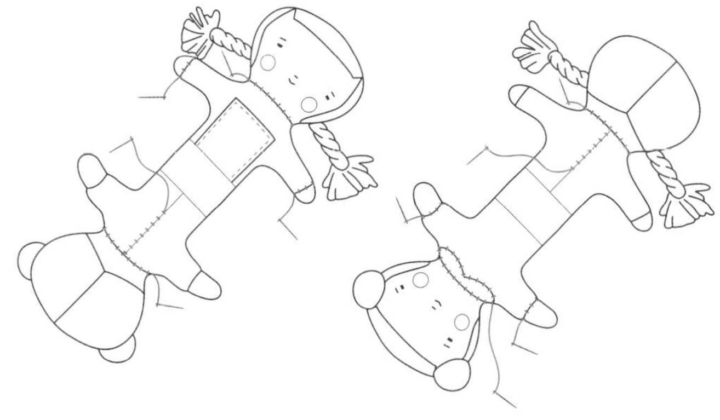

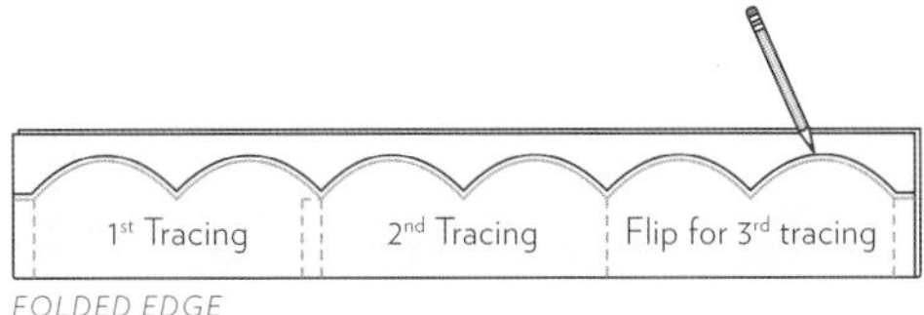

17 SEW SKIRT BOTTOMS OF TWO DOLLS TOGETHER

and press them flat. Align and pin the bottom edge of the scallops to the bottom edge of the 23″ x 10″ skirt fabric for Dressed Up. Edgestitch along the top edge of the scallops to attach them to the fabric.

14. Sew Dressed Up's Skirt

Fold the skirt fabric in half, with right sides together, sew the short ends together with a ½″ seam, and press the seam allowances open. Press the skirt's top and bottom edges ¼″ to the wrong side. Sew a gathering stitch around the top folded edge. Place the skirt on Dressed Up, and pull the gathers taut around the waist, with the top of the skirt overlapping the bottom of the top by about ¼″. Ladder-stitch the gathered edge of the skirt to the doll's waist.

15. Attach Waistband

With right sides together, fold the 9″ x 3¼″ rectangle of accent fabric in half, matching up the long sides to get a 9″ x 1⅝″ piece; and sew the long edges together to make a tube. Turn the tube right side out, and press it flat. Then press one short edge ¼″ to the wrong side.

Wrap and pin the waistband around Dressed Up's waist, overlapping the top of the skirt by about ¼″ and positioning the ends so they overlap at center back, with the folded end on top. Sew the ends of the waistband together with a whipstitch. Then whipstitch the waistband to the doll along both the top and bottom edges.

16. Sew Dressed Down's Skirt and Apron

Repeat Step 14 to sew Dressed Down's skirt and attach it to the body, omitting the scalloped trim. For her apron, press all edges of the 8″ x 6″ rectangle ¼″ to the wrong side. Edgestitch around three of the fabric's edges, leaving one 8″ edge unsewn. Sew a gathering stitch across the unsewn edge along the fold. Pull the gathers so that the top of the apron is the same width as the bottom of the apron bib. Pin the apron to the skirt, aligning the gathered top edge with the bottom of the bib, and hand-sew the apron in place with a ladder stitch.

17. Sew Skirt Bottoms Together

Pin the bottom folded-under edges of the two skirts together, matching up the skirts' side seams. Hand-sew the skirts' folded-under bottom edges together with a ladder stitch (see diagram).

Betsy

Like a paper doll come to life, Betsy is dressed in real fabric as well as real buttons, bows, ribbons, and lace. I was inspired to make her by a friend's childhood dress-up-doll-on-a-pillow that came with great '70s-style felt outfits. Here I've taken the concept one step further and sewn collaged fabric outfits to a backing of wool felt, so the outfits have the super-stickability of felt but also all the color and pattern of favorite fabric scraps. And so that no tiny shoes go astray, Betsy's wardrobe is conveniently tucked away in the pillow's back pocket. See Betsy's complete wardrobe on page 34 and the pillow's back pocket on page 33.

FINISHED SIZE

Pillow: 10″ x 10″

PATTERN PIECES (see pages 136–137)

Body (A); Head (B); Hair (C); Ponytail (D); Outfit templates

MATERIALS

9″ x 6″ scrap of wool felt for body
4″ x 8″ scrap of wool felt for hair
22″ x 11″ (1⁄3 yd.) flannel for pillow
15″ x 9″ (1⁄4 yd. or fat quarter) cotton print for pillow's back pocket
Scraps of cotton, corduroy, and wool felt for outfits
1½ yds. of ¾″-wide pleated ribbon or ruffled trim
11″ length of ½″-wide elastic
Matching and coordinating thread
Embroidery floss for hair and facial features
Miscellaneous trim, buttons, beads, pom-poms, and bits of felt for embellishing outfits
Stuffing

STITCHES USED (see pages 125–128)

Edgestitch, split stitch, backstitch, gathering stitch, ladder stitch, zigzag stitch, whipstitch.

NOTES

In cutting dimensions, the rectangle's width is always given first, followed by its height.

Unless otherwise noted, all seam allowances are 1⁄4″ and built into the patterns.

PILLOW

1. Cut Out Patterns

Cut out the Body (A), Head (B), Hair (C), and Ponytail (D) from wool felt, cutting the number of pieces called for on each pattern piece and transferring the face template on the cut Head (B). Also cut two 11″ squares from the pillow fabric and one 15″ x 9″ rectangle from the pocket fabric. You'll cut out the templates and fabric for Betsy's clothes after finishing the doll. For more information on cutting out patterns and transferring the face template, see pages 123–124.

2. Sew Body to Pillow

Center the Body (A) on one of the 11″ squares of pillow fabric, with Betsy's feet 2″ from the bottom edge (see diagram). Pin the body in place, and edgestitch around it with matching thread.

3. Embroider Hair

Using the diagram as a guide, a split stitch, and six strands of floss, embroider "swooshes" on the Hair (C) and Ponytail (D).

4. Attach Hair and Head

Place and pin the hair on the head, aligning the top edges. Overlap the head and the ponytail, as shown in the diagram, and pin the head in place. Place the head and hair on the body on the pillow front, overlapping the top of the neck. Edgestitch the pieces in place with thread in matching colors, stopping to change thread colors when you move from stitching the hair to stitching the face.

RIGHT SIDE

PILLOW

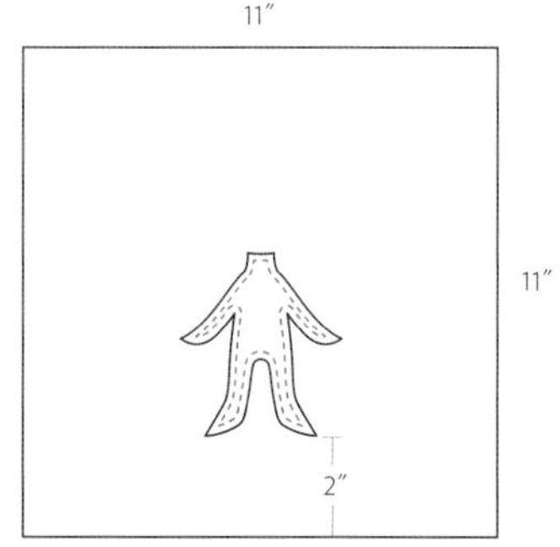

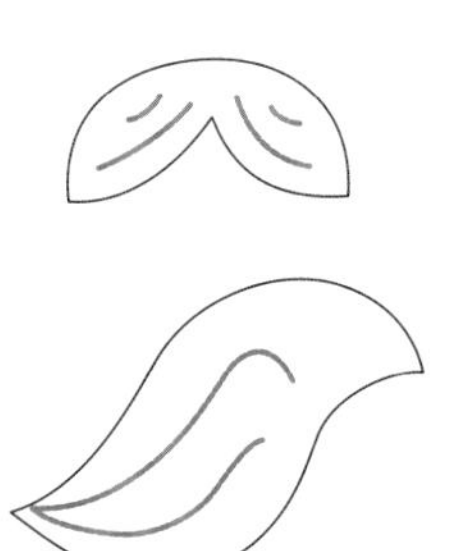

4 ATTACH HAIR AND HEAD

5 EMBROIDER FACIAL FEATURES

6 ATTACH PILLOW TRIM

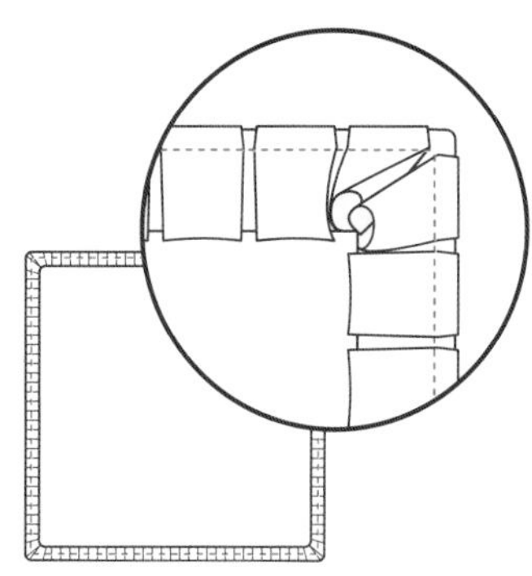

7 SEW POCKET ONTO PILLOW

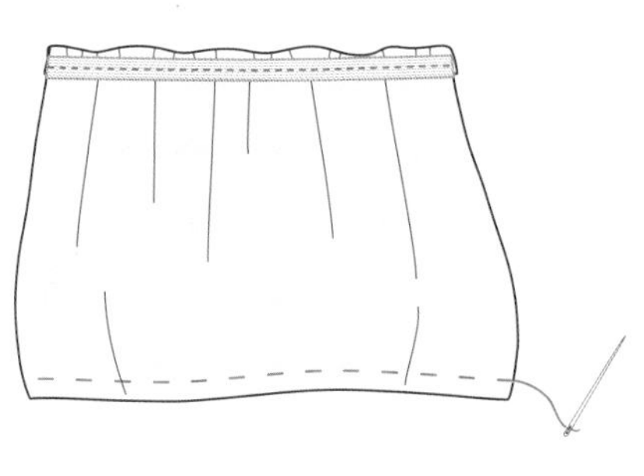

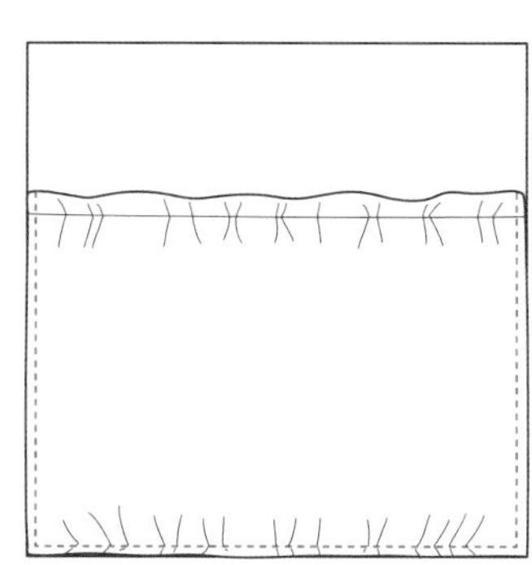

RAINCOAT

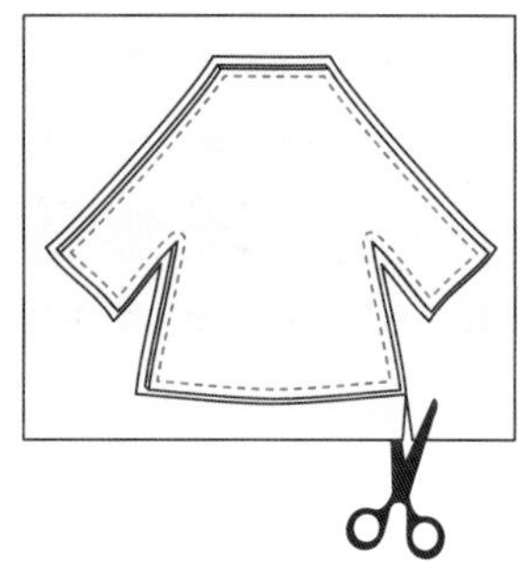

RAIN HAT

EMBELLISH HAT WITH NARROW ZIGZAG STITCH

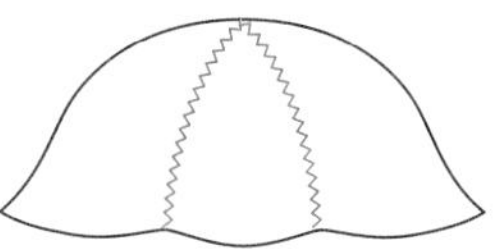

5. **Embroider Facial Features**

Referring to the Basics section on transferring faces to fabric (see page 124) and using the diagram as a guide, embroider features on the face with six strands of floss and a backstitch.

6. **Attach Pillow Trim**

Pin the pleated ribbon or trim facing inward around the pillow front's edge, folding the trim at the corners into mitered corners (see diagram). Edgestitch the trim in place (this stitching will be caught within the 1/4" seam when you sew the pillow together, so it will not show on the finished pillow).

7. **Sew Pocket**

Press one long edge of the 15" x 9" pocket fabric 1/2" to the wrong side. Sew the 11" length of elastic along the fold, stretching the elastic as you sew (see diagram). Hand-sew a gathering stitch along the long bottom edge, and pull the gathers up, so the side measures 11" long.

Lay the pillow back right side up, and place the pocket right side up on top of it, aligning the bottom edges. Pin the pocket in place, and edgestitch it to the pillow back along the side and bottom edges (see diagram).

8. **Sew Pillow Together**

With right sides together and the edges aligned, pin the pillow front to the pillow back. Sew the two sides together with a 1/4" seam, leaving a 3" gap at the bottom for turning. Clip the corners (see page 125), and carefully turn the pillow right side out. Stuff the pillow so that it's firm but not overstuffed (see page 121). Hand-sew the opening closed with a ladder stitch, tucking in the opening's edges as you sew.

BETSY'S OUTFITS

All of Betsy's outfits are constructed the same basic way: You'll cut a felt template for each piece, edgestitch the felt template to the fabric, and then cut the fabric away around the felt. The three-step directions for Betsy's raincoat below further explain this basic construction. To make the other outfits listed after the raincoat, follow these general three-step instructions but with the variations noted for each individual piece. (Note that all the garment hems are left raw and that you can use Fray Check on any edges that fray.)

RAINCOAT

(Basic Directions for All Outfits)

1. **Cut and Sew Felt Template to Fabric**

Cut the Raincoat template from wool felt. Then cut the fabric for the raincoat with slightly larger dimensions than the template. Lay the fabric right side down and the felt template right side down on top of it. Edgestitch the template (note that you're stitching on the back of the garment), making sure your bobbin thread is the stitch color you want to see on the garment's right side (see diagram).

2. **Trim Fabric to Felt's Silhouette**

Trim the fabric to the edge of the felt, and, voilà, an outfit whose felt backing will stick to the felt doll (see diagram).

3. **Add Embellishments**

Turn the raincoat right side up, and use a very narrow zigzag stitch in a contrasting thread to sew the collar and "placket" details (see diagram). You'll embellish the other garments with different trim and details.

RAIN HAT

Cut the Rain Hat template from felt and, using the same fabric as for the raincoat, follow the general instructions above. Embellish the hat with a zigzag stitch, as shown in the diagram.

UNDERSUIT

Cut the Undersuit template from felt and, using cotton fabric, follow the general instructions above. Embellish the undersuit with a little bow by sewing a bit of floss at the center neck and tying it in a bow.

BLOUSE

Cut the Blouse template from felt and, using cotton fabric, follow the general instructions above.

T-SHIRT AND CORDS

Cut the T-Shirt and Cords templates from felt and, using cotton fabric for the T-shirt and corduroy for the pants, follow the general instructions above. Use the Apple template to cut an apple appliqué from felt. Hand-sew the apple appliqué on the center of the T-shirt with two strands of floss and a whipstitch, or edgestitch it in place.

PAJAMAS

Cut the Pajamas template from felt. For the pants, cut a 4″ x 3″ piece of pajama fabric, and align it as shown in the diagram. Edgestitch the fabric in place, and trim it to the template's edge.

For the top, cut a 4″ x 3″ piece of pajama fabric. Fold over 1⁄4″ in the center of the fabric's longer side, press the fold flat, and edgestitch it. Align this piece with the felt template, as shown in the diagram, centering the fabric's fold. Edgestitch the pajama top on the template and trim the fabric to the template's edge. Hand-sew bits of 1⁄4″ baby rickrack to the back of the template at the neck and pants edges, so the rickrack peaks out on the front (see diagram). Sew beads along the front placket for buttons.

PARTY DRESS

Cut the Party Dress template from felt for the base of the dress, which will also become the dress's top. Cut a 3″ x 1 3⁄4″ piece of lace for the dress's underskirt, and lay it over the dress, as shown in the diagram. Sew the lace in place along the waist; then trim the lace to the template's side edges. Cut a 4″ x 1 1⁄2″ piece of skirt fabric, and hand-sew a gathering stitch 1⁄8″ from the raw top edge. Pull the gathers until the fabric fits the waist of the dress, and sew the skirt in place on the dress (see diagram). Make a bow from 1⁄4″-wide grosgrain ribbon by folding it into two loops and wrapping a separate piece of ribbon around the center; then hand-sew the ribbon in place across the waist (see diagram), hiding the stitching.

JUMPER

Cut the Jumper template from felt and embellish it, as shown in the diagram, with a backstitch and six strands of floss.

SUNDRESS

Cut the Sundress template from felt and, using dress fabric, follow the general instructions above. For the skirt, cut a 3 1⁄2″ x 1″ piece of dress fabric. Fold pleats across the skirt's top edge until the skirt is about 1 1⁄2″ wide. Press the pleats flat and sew the skirt to the dress across the dropped waist (see diagram). Hand-sew or edgestitch a piece of 1⁄4″-wide ribbon across the waist.

SOCKS

Cut the Socks template from felt and embellish each sock, as shown in the diagram, with a backstitch and six strands of floss.

BOOTS AND SHOES

Cut the various boot and shoe templates from felt. Sew tiny pom-poms on to Betsy's slippers.

RIGHT SIDE | WRONG SIDE

PAJAMAS

SEW THEN CUT PAJAMA PANTS

FOLD AND STITCH CENTER OF PAJAMA TOP FABRIC

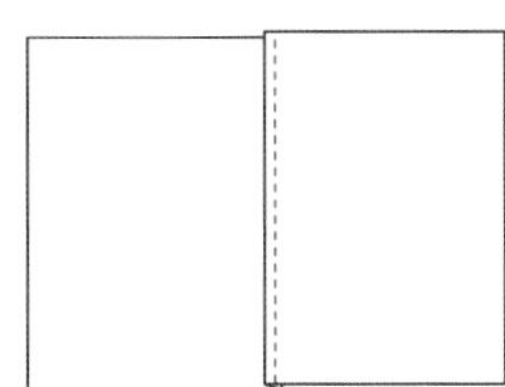

SEW THEN CUT PAJAMA TOP

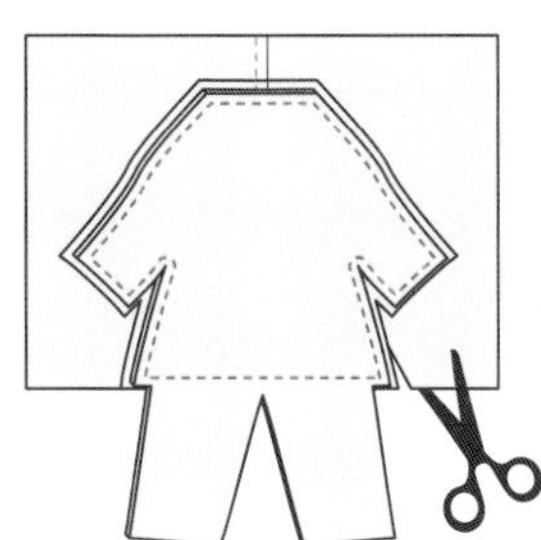

EMBELLISH PAJAMAS WITH RICKRACK

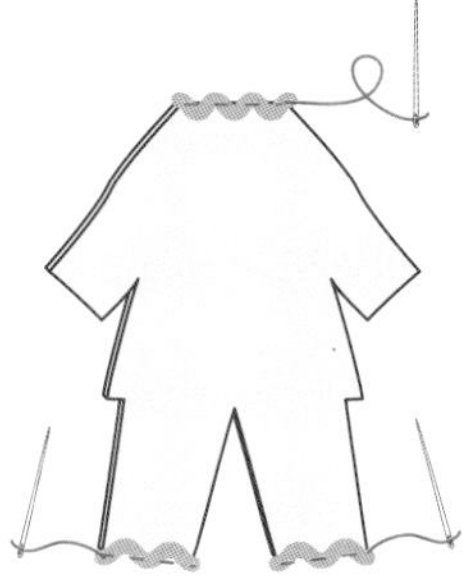

PARTY DRESS

SEW LACE TO DRESS TEMPLATE

ATTACH SKIRT FABRIC WITH GATHERING STITCH

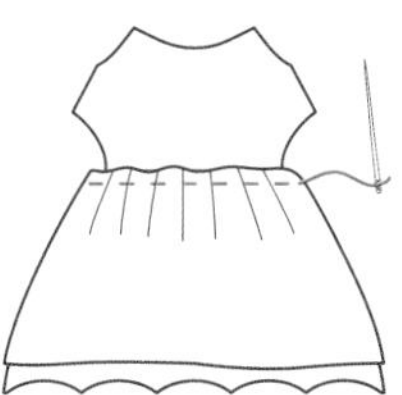

SEW RIBBON TO SKIRT WAIST

JUMPER

EMBELLISH JUMPER WITH BACKSTITCHES

SUNDRESS

FOLD AND PRESS PLEATS AND SEW SKIRT FABRIC TO WAIST

SOCKS

EMBELLISH SOCKS WITH BACKSTITCHES

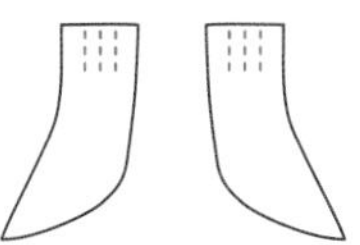

Mermaiden

Who says mermaids have to glitter and sparkle? This cozy Mermaiden with her soft, quilted feel is sure to win over even the most die-hard sparkly princess fans. Once you get the hang of the free-motion quilting, Mermaiden sews up quickly. Her hair and fin are flat, quilted fabric without batting, so they're textured but not bulky. Kids love Mermaiden's fun, small size and will want one for every pocket.

FINISHED SIZE

7″ tall

PATTERN PIECES (see page 138)

Body (A); Fin (B); Hair Front (C); Hair Back (D)

MATERIALS

6″ x 10″ scrap of solid-color cotton or flannel for body
12″ x 10″ (1/4 yd. or fat quarter) corduroy or velvet for hair
12″ x 10″ (1/4 yd. or fat quarter) cotton print for fin
3″-length of 1/2″-wide rickrack
Matching and coordinating thread
Embroidery floss
Stuffing

STITCHES USED (see pages 125–128)

Ladder stitch, backstitch, edgestitch, tacking stitch.

NOTES

In cutting dimensions, the rectangle's width is always given first, followed by its height.

Unless otherwise noted, all seam allowances are 1/4″ and built into the patterns.

1. Trace, Sew, and Cut Out Body

With right sides together, fold the 6″ x 10″ piece of cotton or flannel, matching up the short sides to get a 6″ x 5″ piece. Trace the Body (A) on the folded fabric, and sew along the traced line, leaving a 1 1/2″ opening at the bottom for turning and stuffing (see diagram). Cut out the body with 1/4″ seam allowance. Clip the body's curves (see page 125), turn it right side out, and stuff it (see page 121) so that it's full but still rather flat. Hand-sew the opening closed with a ladder stitch, tucking in the opening's edges as you sew.

2. Embroider Facial Features

Referring to the Basics section on transferring faces to fabric (see page 124) and using the diagram as a guide, embroider the eyes and mouth on the face with three strands of floss and a backstitch. Tie off the floss tails at the back of the head, being careful not to pull them too tightly to prevent denting Mermaiden's face.

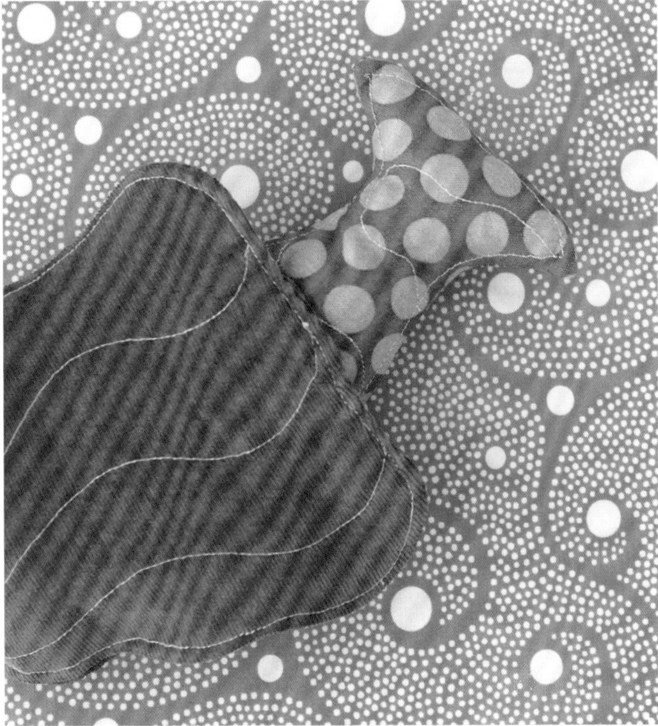

3. Sew Hair

With right sides together, fold the 12″ x 10″ piece of corduroy or velvet in half, matching up the short edges to get a 6″ x 10″ piece. Place the Hair Front (C) and Hair Back (D) on the folded fabric, trace around the patterns, and sew along the traced lines, leaving a 1½″ opening at the bottom of the hair back and a ¾″ opening at the top of the hair front for turning the pieces (see diagram). Cut the pieces out with a ⅛″ seam allowance, but leave a ¼″ seam allowance along the openings. Turn the pieces right side out, and press them flat, tucking in the edges at each opening. Edgestitch both pieces with a contrasting thread and, using the diagram as a guide, machine-sew decorative stitching inside the edgestitching.

4. Make Fin Front and Back

With right sides together, fold the 12″ x 10″ piece of cotton print in half, matching up the short edges to get a 6″ x 10″ piece. Trace the Fin (B) twice on the folded fabric and sew along the traced lines, leaving a 1½″ opening at the side for turning (see diagram). Cut out the fins with a ⅛″ seam allowance, but leave a ¼″ seam allowance along the openings. Turn the pieces right side out, and press them flat, tucking in the edges at each opening. Edgestitch both pieces with a constrasting thread and, using the diagram as a guide, machine-sew decorative stitching inside the edgestitching.

5. Sew Fins and Hair Together

Align the front fin on top of the back fin with wrong sides together; and, using matching thread and a ladder stitch, hand-sew the outside edges of the pair together, leaving the rounded top open (see diagram). Align the top edge of the hair front and hair back with wrong sides together, and hand-sew the pair together along the top edge with a ladder stitch (see diagram).

6. Assemble Mermaiden

Pull the hair down over the top of the head until it fits snugly. Stuff the bottom of the fin lightly, and pull the fin up over the body until it's snug (see diagram). Using matching thread and a ladder stitch, hand-sew the hair and fin to the body, repeating the stitches until the attached parts are secure.

7. Sew Rickrack Flower

Make a rickrack flower by hand-stitching along the bottom curves of a 3″-long piece of rickrack and pulling the thread taut to draw in the rickrack (see diagram). Hand-sew a few tacking stitches to keep the flower in place, and knot off the thread. Hand-sew the flower to Mermaiden's hair with a tacking stitch.

RIGHT SIDE

WRONG SIDE

1. TRACE, SEW, AND CUT OUT BODY

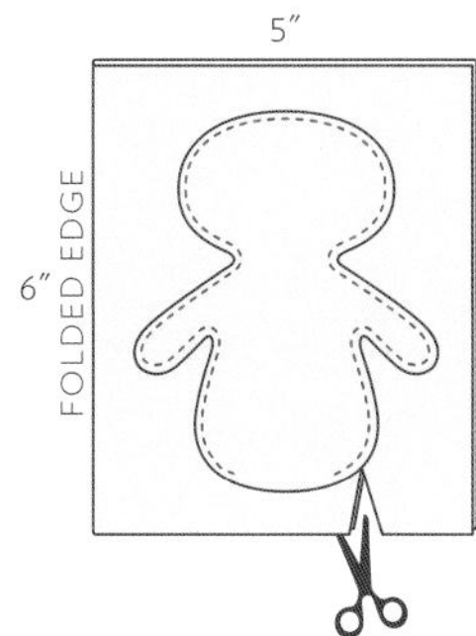

2. EMBROIDER FACIAL FEATURES

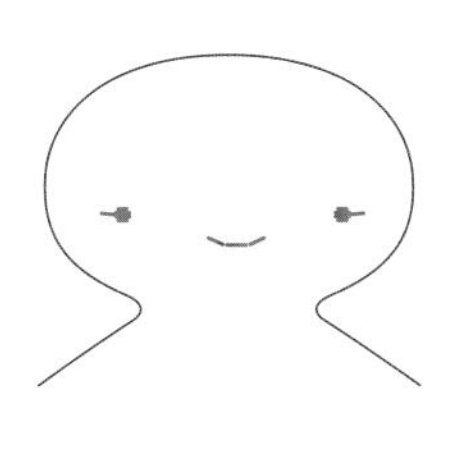

3. SEW HAIR, CUT, TURN RIGHT SIDE OUT, AND EMBELLISH WITH STITCHES

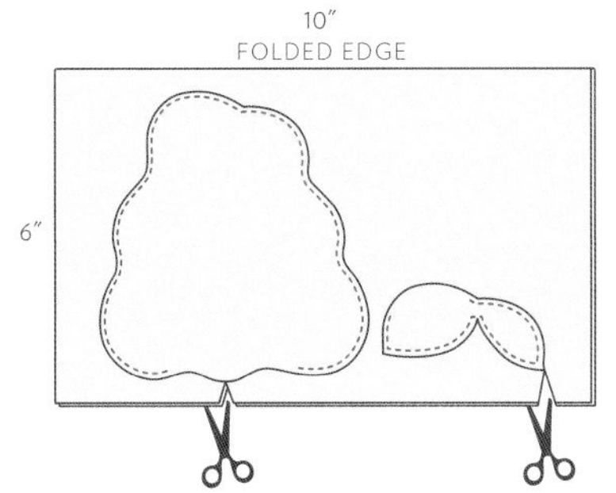

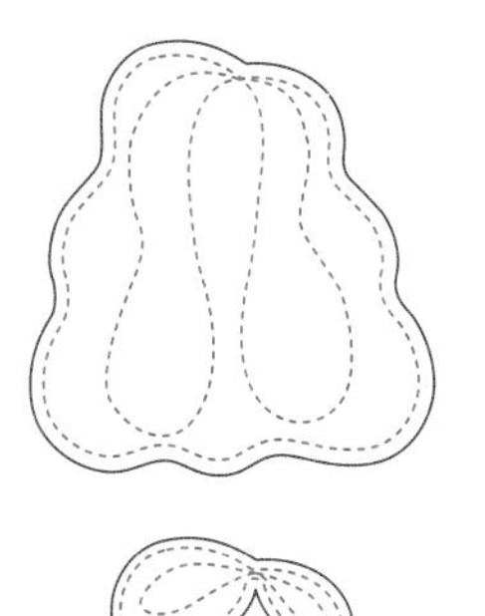

4. SEW FIN FRONT AND BACK, CUT, TURN RIGHT SIDE OUT, AND EMBELLISH WITH STITCHES

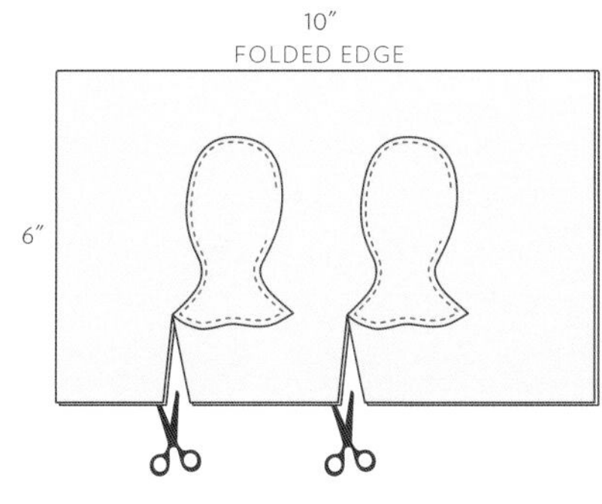

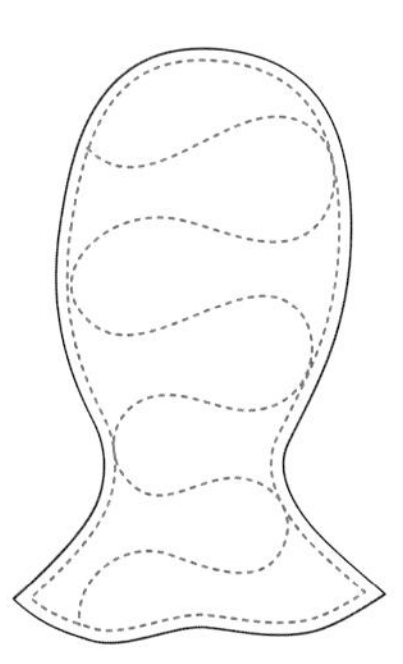

5. SEW FINS AND HAIR TOGETHER

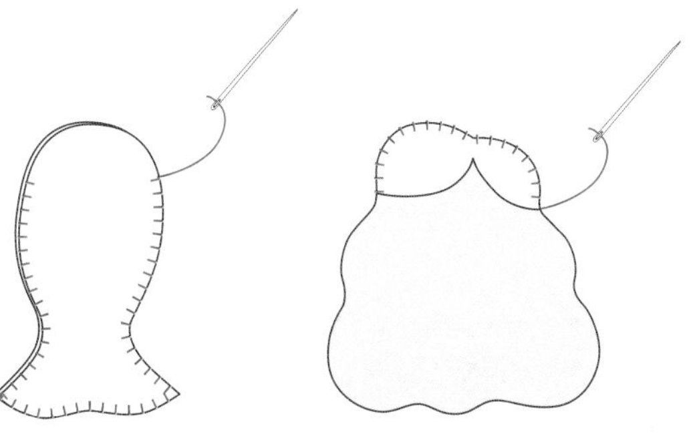

6. STUFF MERMAIDEN AND ATTACH HAIR AND FIN

7. SEW RICKRACK FLOWER FOR HAIR

Ellie Bag

I am a sucker for stuffed-animal bags. It takes all my restraint not to ditch my sensible mom bag for a new one with ears and a smile. Use a fuzzy but sturdy fabric, such as shaggy felt, for a bag that is both huggable and durable. Match it with a cute thick ribbon for a strap and a lively print for the ears, and finish it off with a sweet little ribbon tied around her head.

FINISHED SIZE
8″ tall

PATTERN PIECES (see pages 139–140)
Ear (A); Head (B); Body Front (C); Body Back (D); Bag Lining (E); Foot Pad (F)

MATERIALS

18″ x 36″ (1/2 yd.) shaggy felt, faux fur, or other heavyweight fabric for body
9″ x 20″ (1/4 yd. or fat quarter) cotton print or midweight fabric for ear lining
8″ x 16″ (1/4 yd. or fat quarter) cotton print or midweight fabric for bag lining
4″ x 4″ scrap of wool felt for foot pads
38″ length of 2″-wide ribbon for strap
25″ length of 1/4″-wide ribbon for head tie
Matching and coordinating thread
Embroidery floss for sewing foot pads
Two 3/4″ buttons or 3/4″-diameter circles of wool felt for eyes
Velcro closure
Stuffing

STITCHES USED (see pages 125-128)
Ladder stitch, whipstitch, tacking stitch.

NOTE
Unless otherwise noted, all seam allowances are 1/4″ and built into the patterns.

1. Cut Out Pattern Pieces

Cut out all the pattern pieces from the designated fabrics, cutting the number of pieces called for on each pattern piece and transferring all pattern markings to the cut pieces. For more information on cutting out patterns and transferring pattern markings, see pages 122–123.

2. Sew Ears

With right sides together, sew one Ear (A) and ear lining together, leaving the straight edge open. Turn the ear right side out and press it flat. Press the open edge 1/4″ to the wrong side. Repeat for the other ear.

3. Sew and Stuff Head

Sew the darts on the Head (B) front and back. With right sides together, sew the front and back heads together, leaving an opening between the darts for stuffing (see diagram). Clip the curves and corners on the head and trunk (see page 125). Turn the head right side out, and stuff it firmly (see page 121). Hand-sew the opening closed with a ladder stitch.

4. Attach Ears to Head

Fold one ear as marked on the pattern, and pin it to the back of the stuffed head, using the diagram as a placement guide. Using thread and a ladder stitch or a whipstitch, hand-sew the ear sturdily in place, repeating the stitches until the ear is secure. Repeat with the other ear. Then secure the ears further out towards the back of the head with a few tacking stitches, as shown in the same diagram, burying the thread tails in the head (see page 128).

5. Sew and Stuff Body

Sew the darts on the Body Front (C). With right sides together, sew the Body Front (C) to the Body Back (D). Clip the corners, and turn the body right side out. Stuff the body, stuffing the limbs firmly and leaving the body itself more loosely stuffed so that it leaves room for "hollowing out" the purse's interior and dropping in the bag lining in Step 7.

6. Tack Limbs and Add Foot Pads

Fold the stuffed limbs forward, and hand-sew them to the belly with a few tacking stitches (see diagram). Add each Foot Pad (F) by pushing in the ends of the arms and feet so that they're squat and a little bit concave. Pin the felt pads to the bottoms of the now shorter, wider limbs, and hand-sew the pads in place with a whipstitch and three strands of embroidery floss (see diagram), hiding the knots (see page 128) under the pads.

7. Sew and Attach Lining

With right sides together, sew the Bag Lining (E) pieces together, leaving the top open. Press the open top edge 1/4″ to the wrong side. With the lining still wrong side out, slide it into the body (see diagram). Pin and hand-sew the top edges of the bag and lining together with a ladder stitch (see diagram).

8. Putting It All Together

Pin the head to the body at the back neck, as shown in diagram, and hand-sew with a ladder stitch only the body's upper back edge to the back of the head, repeating the stitches until the head is secure.

9. Attach Ribbon Strap

With the ribbon's right side facing the front, tuck the ends of the ribbon inside the ears' folds. Hand-sew the ribbon in place with a sturdy ladder stitch or whipstitch (see diagram).

10. Finish Your Bag

Sew the button eyes in place with thread (alternatively, for a child under the age of three, whipstitch felt eyes on the elephant with three strands of floss). Sew the Velcro closure to the trunk's underside and to the belly where it matches up. Wrap the ribbon around the head, and tie it with a bow. Sew the ribbon in place with a few tacking stitches through the bow and a few along its length.

RIGHT SIDE | WRONG SIDE

3 SEW AND STUFF HEAD

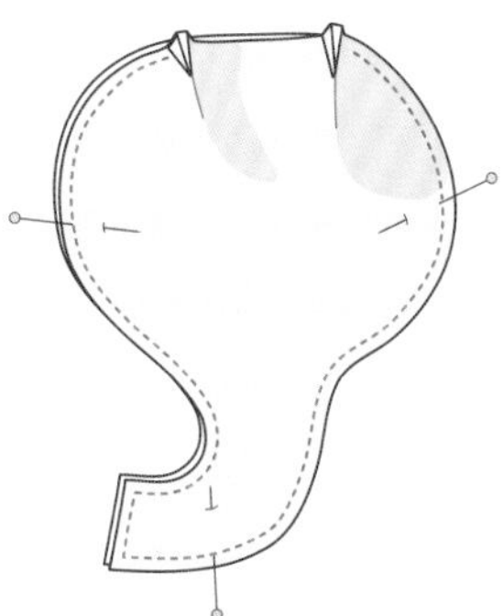

4 ATTACH EARS TO HEAD

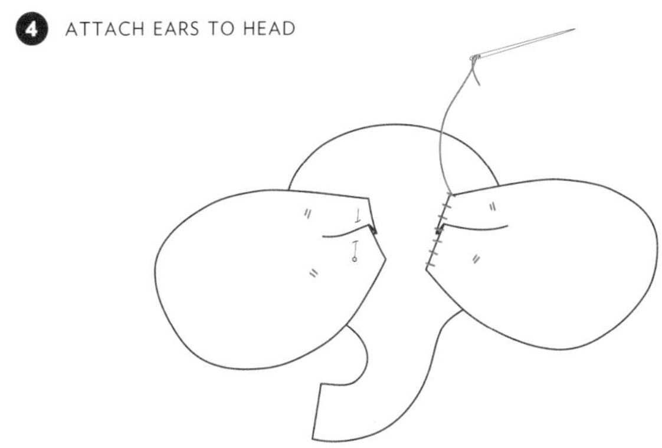

6 TACK LIMBS AND ADD FOOT PADS

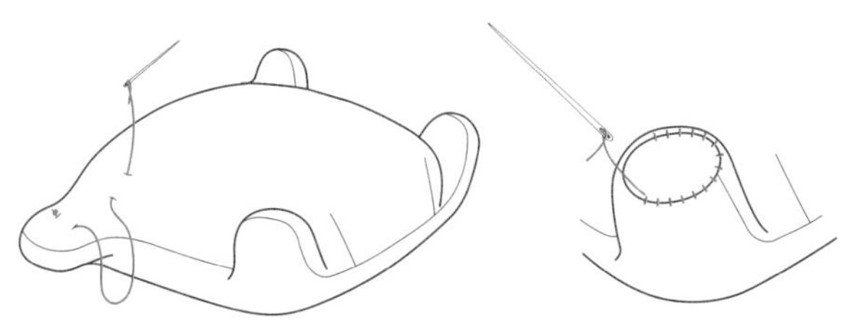

7 SEW LINING AND ATTACH INSIDE BODY

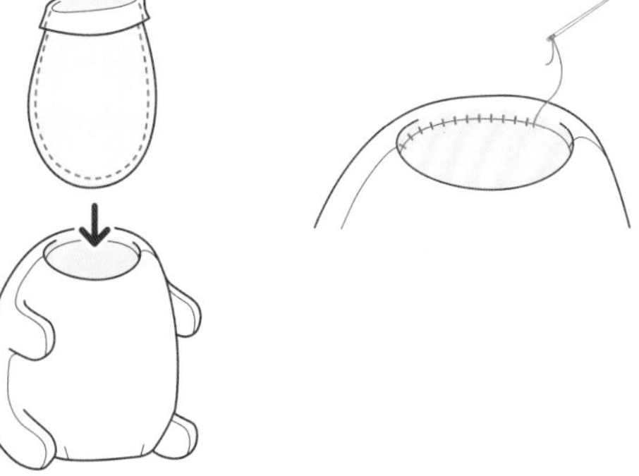

8 ATTACH HEAD TO BODY

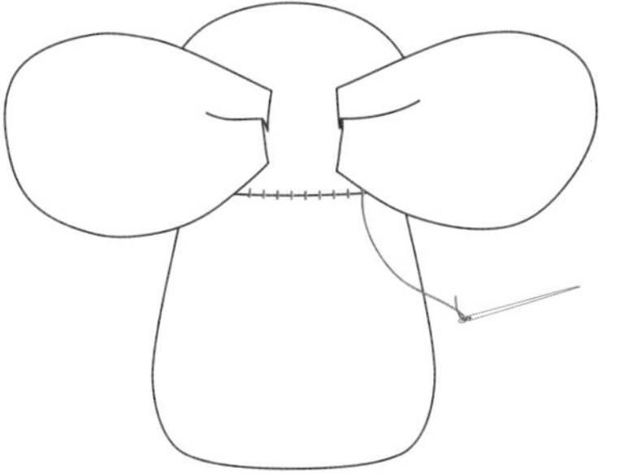

9 ATTACH RIBBON STRAP TO BAG BODY

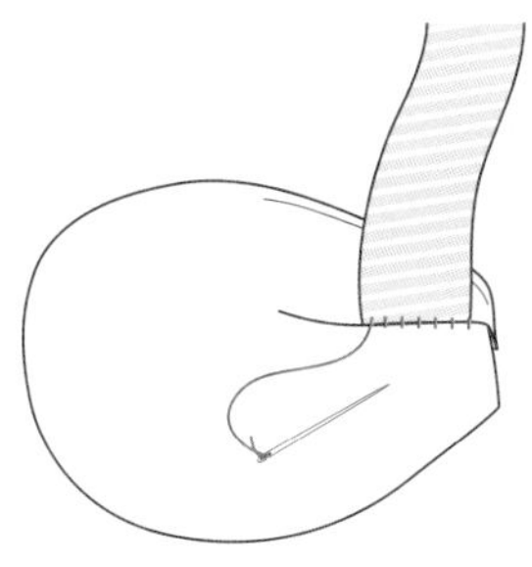

KUSMI TEA
PARIS

Panda Buns

Giggles and squeals of delight follow Panda Buns wherever she goes. Is it her irresistible Chinese pajamas (which, by the way, look great in either a slinky silk or a soft cotton Asian print)? Her lively hair-do (which indulges my ardent love of buns)? Or maybe her removable slippers or her sweet little face? Whatever the case, just remember the ancient Chinese proverb: Big pandas, big wisdom; little pandas, little wisdom.

FINISHED SIZE
14″ tall

PATTERN PIECES (see pages 141–142)
Panda Head (A); Panda Eye (B); Panda Ear (C); Body (D); Hair Front (E); Hair Back (F); Eye (G); Leg (H); Pajama Top Front (I); Pajama Top Back (J); Pajama Pants (K); Shoe (L)

MATERIALS
12″ x 40″ (1/3 yd.) solid-color cotton for body and legs
9″ x 14″ (1/4 yd. or fat quarter) black wool felt or fleece for hair and panda buns
4″ x 6″ scrap of white wool felt or fleece for panda buns
8″ x 38″ (1/4 yd. or fat quarter) cotton print for pajamas
8″ x 6″ scrap of wool felt for shoes
Scraps of wool felt for eyes
1 package of 1/4″-wide bias tape to coordinate with pajama fabric
8″-long piece of 3/8″-wide elastic
Matching and coordinating thread
Embroidery floss for facial features
Stuffing

STITCHES USED (see pages 125-128)
Edgestitch, French knot, ladder stitch, whipstitch, backstitch, zigzag stitch, topstitch.

NOTE
Unless otherwise noted, all seam allowances are 1/4″ and built into the patterns.

1. Cut Out Pattern Pieces
Cut out all the pattern pieces from the designated fabrics, cutting the number of pieces called for on each pattern piece and transferring the face template to the cut Body (D). For more information on cutting out patterns and transferring the face template, see pages 123–124.

2. Make Panda Buns
Construct each panda bun as follows: Using the diagram as a placement guide, edgestitch the black felt Panda Eye (B) pieces on the white Panda Head (A). Using six strands of embroidery floss and the same diagram as a guide, embroider a French knot in each eye. With right sides together and the edges aligned, sew two Panda Ear (C) pieces together, leaving the bottom open (see diagram). Turn the ear right side out. Repeat for the other ear. Pin the ears facing inward on each side of the front of the head (see diagram). With right sides together, sew the back and front panda heads together, leaving a 1 1/2″ opening at the bottom for turning and stuffing (see diagram). Turn the head right side out, and stuff it firmly (see page 121). Hand-sew the opening closed with a ladder stitch, tucking in the opening's edges as you sew.

3. Sew on Hair and Embroider Facial Features
With right sides facing up and the top edges aligned, edgestitch the Hair Front (E) to one Body (D) piece along the hair's bottom edge. Then similarly edgestitch the Hair Back (F) to the second body piece (see diagram).

Referring to the Basics section on transferring faces to fabric (see page 124) and using the diagram as a placement guide, hand-sew the felt eyes on the face with three strands of matching floss and a whipstitch. Again using three strands of floss, embroider the nose and mouth with a backstitch.

4. Sew Body

Sew the darts in the hair on the body front and back. With right sides together and the edges aligned, sew the body front and back together, leaving a 2½″ opening at the bottom for turning and stuffing (see diagram). Clip the corners and curves (see page 125), and carefully turn the body right side out. Stuff it firmly, and hand-sew the opening closed with a ladder stitch, tucking in the opening's edges as you sew.

5. Attach Buns

Pin the stuffed panda buns to the sides of the stuffed body, using the diagram as a placement guide. Hand-sew the buns in place using a ladder stitch, repeating the stitches until the buns are secure.

6. Make and Attach Legs

With right sides together and the edges aligned, sew two Leg (G) pieces together, leaving the top edge open for turning and stuffing. Turn the leg right side out and stuff it so that the stuffing is firm in the feet and thins toward the top of the legs. Fold the open top of the leg so that what was the side seam now faces front. Fold the leg's top edge ¼″ to the wrong side and hand-sew the opening shut with a whipstitch. Repeat for the other leg. Next pin the stuffed legs to the body, centering them on the body and using the diagram as a placement guide. Ladder-stitch them in place, repeating the stitches until the legs are secure.

7. Sew Pajama Top

With right sides together and the shoulder edges aligned, sew the Pajama Top Front (I) pieces to the Pajama Top Back (J) at the shoulders and press the seam allowances open (see diagram). Enclose the edge of the sleeves with bias tape, stitching the tape in place with a zigzag stitch and matching thread (see diagram). Next, with right sides together, sew the front and back pajama top together under the arms (see diagram). Clip the curves, turn the top right side out, and press it flat.

Beginning at the center-back neck and using a zigzag stitch and matching thread, enclose the pajama top's raw edge with bias tape, sewing it around the neck, down one front, across the bottom edge, back up the other front, and around the remaining neck edge (see diagram). Cut two 7″ strips of bias tape, and zigzag stitch down the center of these strips to close them and make ties.

Sew the edge of one tie to the left side under the arm and the other tie to the front right side of the top (see diagram).

8. Sew Pajama Pants

Sew bias tape to the bottom edges of the Pajama Pants (K) pieces with a zigzag stitch and matching thread (see diagram). With right sides together, sew the pants' front and back seams (see diagram). Next open out the pants, keeping the right sides together and aligning the edges and seams, and sew the pants' inseam (see diagram). Clip the curve under the legs, turn the pants right side out, and press them flat.

To create a casing for the elastic waistband, press the pants' top edge 1″ to the wrong side and topstitch the casing ¾″ from the fold, leaving a ½″ opening at the back waist for inserting the elastic (see diagram). Using a small safety pin or bodkin attached to one end of elastic, thread the elastic through the casing and sew the elastic's ends together. Topstitch the opening closed.

9. Make Shoes

With right sides together and the edges aligned, sew two Shoe (K) pieces together around the outer edge, leaving the top curved edge unsewn (see diagram). Turn the shoe right side out. Repeat for the other shoe.

RIGHT SIDE | WRONG SIDE

2 A SEW PANDA EYES TO PANDA HEAD

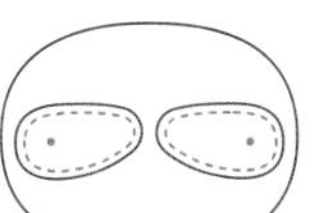

B SEW PANDA EARS

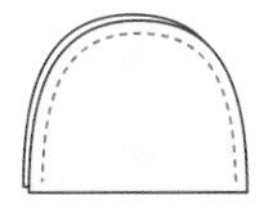

C PIN EARS TO HEAD

D SEW BACK AND FRONT PANDA HEADS TOGETHER

3 SEW ON HAIR AND EMBROIDER FACIAL FEATURES

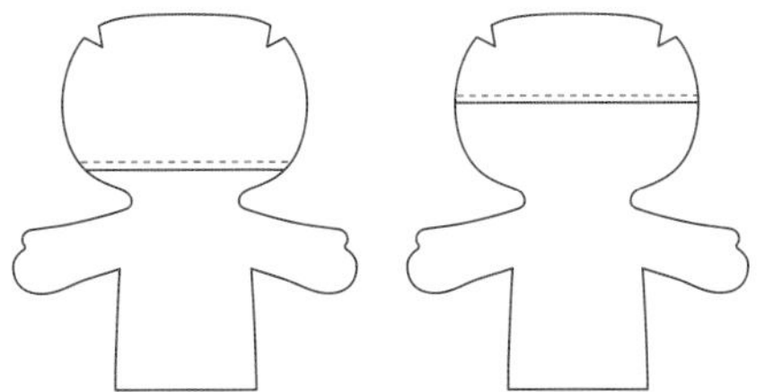

4 SEW BODY

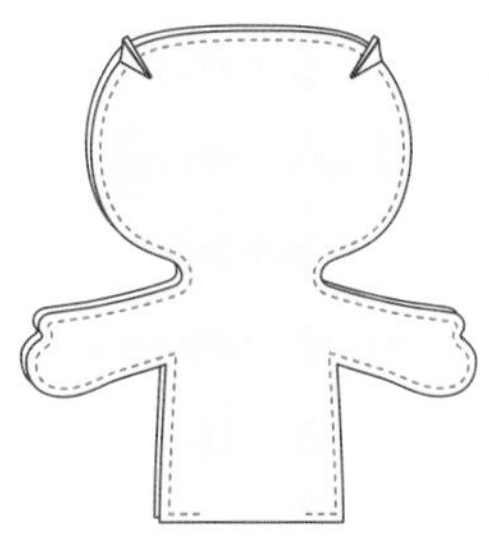

5 ATTACH PANDA BUNS TO HEAD

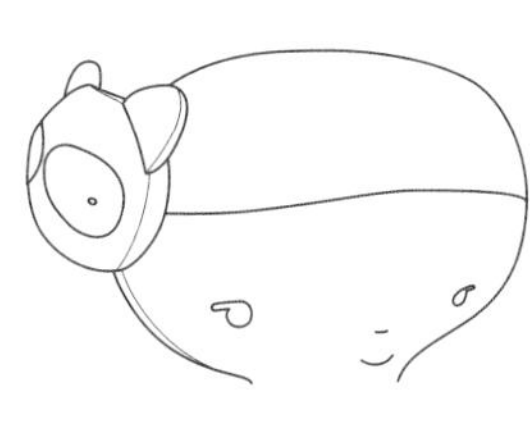

6 MAKE LEGS AND ATTACH TO BODY

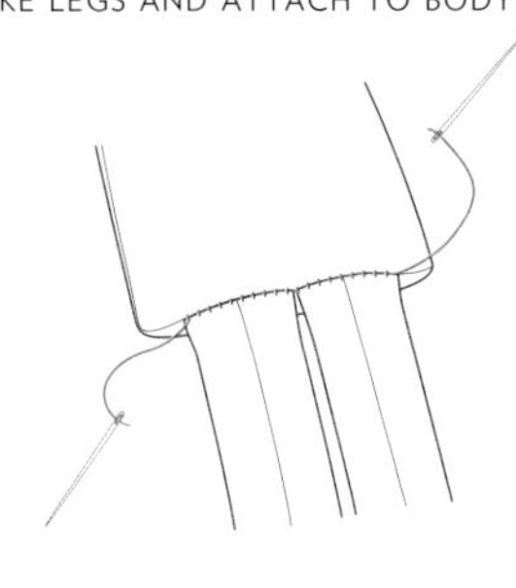

7 SEW SHOULDERS OF PAJAMA TOP

ENCLOSE SLEEVE EDGE WITH BIAS TAPE

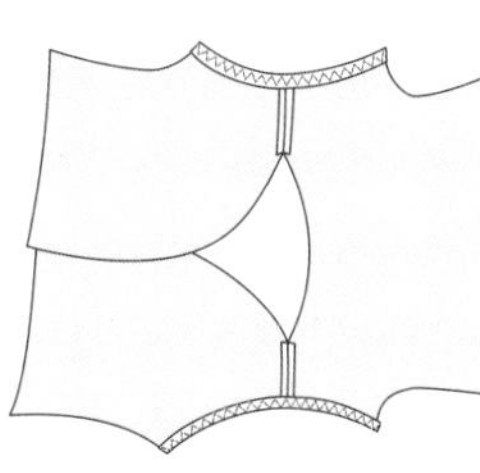

SEW FRONT AND BACK TOGETHER

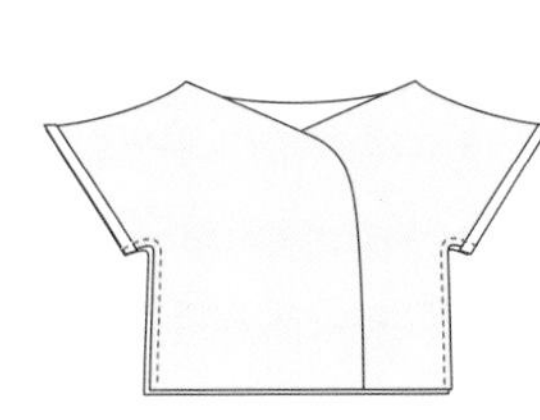

ENCLOSE NECK, FRONT, AND BOTTOM EDGES WITH BIAS TAPE

ATTACH BIAS TAPE TIES

8 ENCLOSE PANTS CUFFS WITH BIAS TAPE

SEW FRONT AND BACK SEAMS

SEW INSEAM

CREATE CASING AND ATTACH ELASTIC

9 MAKE SHOES

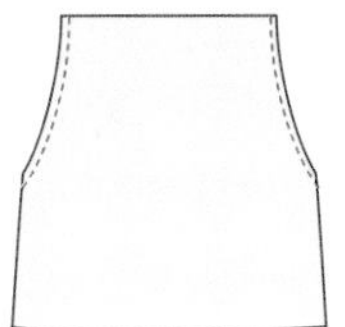

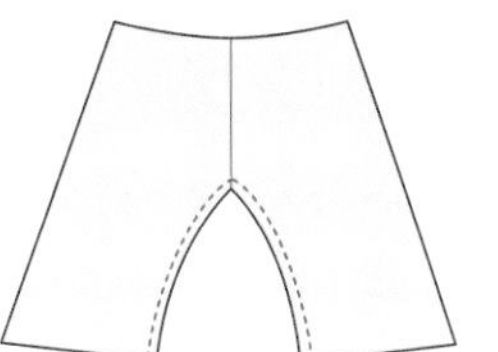

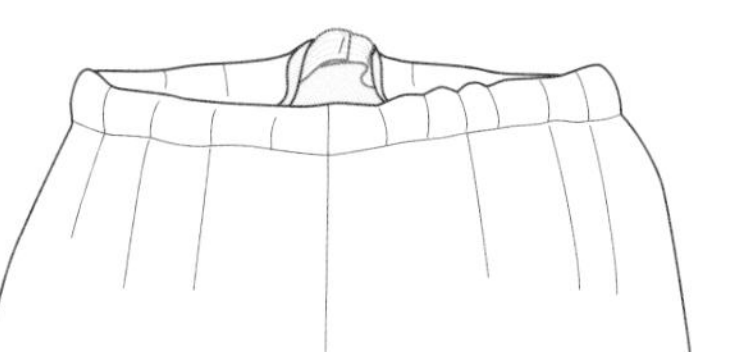

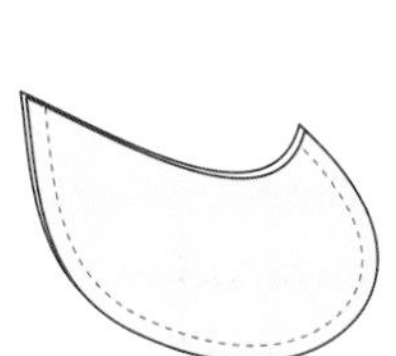

GREETINGS
from
ALBUQUERQUE
Gray Mountain
Cameron
Forest Lake
Many Farms
Newcomb
Farmington
Keams Canyon
Window Rock
Winslow

Wee Town Trolley

Clang, clang, clang went the trolley! I apologize in advance—there is no way to sew up this fellow without hearing Judy Garland singing in your head. I was flipping through the pages of a catalog of antique tin toys and this trolley seemed to be smiling at me, so I had to make him up in felt. I love the challenge of reimagining cold, hard metal things like robots and trolleys in soft, warm felt.

FINISHED SIZE
10″ x 4″ x 4″

PATTERN PIECES (see page 143)
Body Front and Back (A); Roof Front and Back (B); Window (C); Back Door (D); Side Door (E); Eye (F)

MATERIALS

14″ x 14″ (1⁄2 yd. or fat quarter) wool felt for trolley body
7″ x 10″ scrap of wool felt for roof
4″ x 8″ scrap of wool felt for windows
5″ x 6″ scrap of wool felt for doors
Scraps of wool felt for eyes
Sport- or DK-weight yarn for bolts
Embroidery floss in colors matching felt
Eight 1¼″–1½″ buttons for wheels
Chenille needle
Stuffing

STITCHES USED (see pages 125–128)
Running stitch, whipstitch, backstitch, French Knot.

NOTE
In cutting dimensions, the rectangle's width is always given first, followed by its height.

1. **Cut Out Pattern Pieces**
Cut out all the pattern pieces from the designated fabric, cutting the number of pieces called for on each pattern piece and transferring the face template to one of the cut Body Front and Back (A) pieces. Also cut a 14″ x 10″ rectangle of felt for the trolley body and a 4½″ x 10″ rectangle of felt for the top roof. For more information on cutting out patterns and transferring the face template, see pages 123–124.

2. **Sew Front and Back**
Place one Roof Front and Back (B) on each Body Front and Back (A), aligning the top edges. Hand-sew the roof's bottom edge to each body piece with a running stitch and six strands of floss (see diagram). Referring to the Basics sections on transferring and marking faces (see page 124) and using the same diagram as a guide, hand-sew the Eyes (F) in place on the body front with three strands of floss and a whipstitch and embroider the mouth with six strands of floss and a backstitch. Make dots on the eyes with French knots and six strands of floss. For the body back, center and align the bottom edge of the Back Door (D) ⅜″ from the bottom edge of the trolley back and hand-sew the door in place with a running stitch and six strands of floss (see diagram).

3. **Sew Roof on Trolley Body**
Center the 4½″ x 10″ top roof piece on the 14″ x 10″ trolley body, aligning the edges, as shown in diagram. Hand-sew the top roof in place along the long edges with a running stitch and six strands of floss.

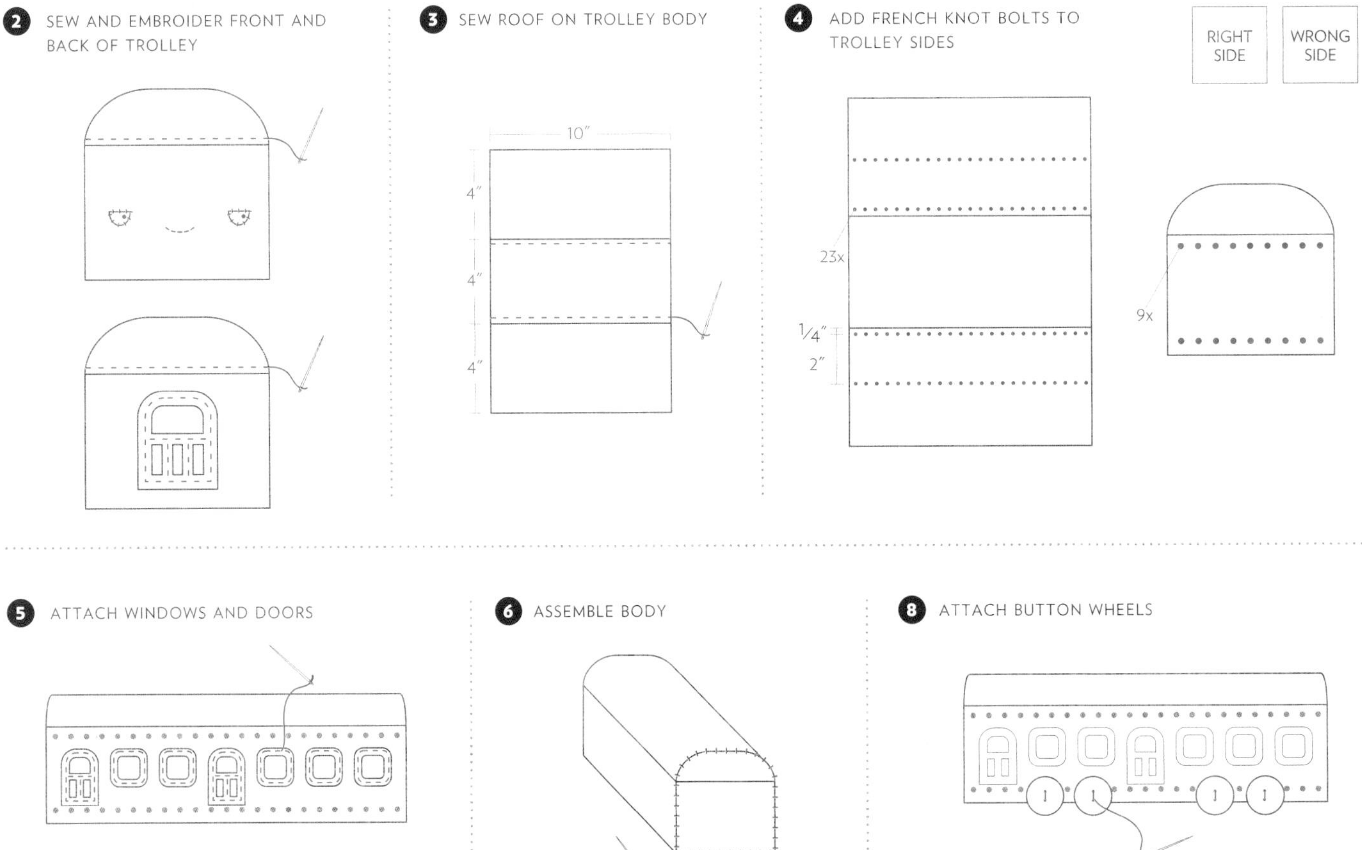

4. Add Bolts

Starting with a 15″ length of yarn, tie a knot at one end, and thread a chenille needle with the yarn. Hand-sew French knot "bolts" on the trolley body, carrying the yarn behind the felt without knotting it to each next knot placement. Embroider a row of 23 evenly spaced bolts on the side of the trolley body ¼″ from the edge of the top roof and then a second row 2″ below the first row (see diagram). Repeat these two lines of French knot bolts on the other side of the trolley body. Next embroider a row of nine French knot bolts on the body front and back pieces, placing the bolts as you did for trolley's sides (see diagram).

5. Attach Windows and Doors

Place the two Side Door (E) pieces and five Window (C) pieces on the trolley sides, using the diagram as a guide. Hand-sew the doors and windows in place with a running stitch and six strands of floss.

6. Assemble Body

With right sides facing out, bend the body/roof piece to curve around the body front piece, carefully matching up the roofs' edges, and pin the pieces in place (the ends of the body/roof piece will overlap under the trolley). Hand-sew the two pieces together with a whipstitch and six strands of matching floss, first sewing the body front's roof to the top's roof and then sewing the sides and bottom together, overlapping the ends on the bottom of the trolley (see diagram). Repeat for the body back piece.

7. Sew Up Bottom and Stuff

On the bottom of the trolley, hand-sew the overlapped edges together with a whipstitch and six strands of floss, leaving a 4″ opening for stuffing. Stuff the body firmly (see page 121) but without straining the whipstitches and hand-sew the opening closed.

8. Attach Button Wheels

Sew four buttons on the bottom edge of each trolley side, using the diagram as a placement guide and six strands of floss. If the trolley is for a child under the age of three, omit the button wheels.

OFF ON REJ

Sleepover Pals

What's better than one little bed bug? Why three, of course! Make the full trio, tuck them into their own customized sleeping bag, tie them up with a swell ribbon, and have a bundle of cute that'll knock everyone's socks off. Just don't let on that you cheated by using prequilted fabric, making the sleeping bag the easiest part.

FINISHED SIZE

Doll: 8″ tall; Blanket: 27″ x 12″

PATTERN PIECES (see page 144)

Body (A); Dress (B); Hair Front (C); Hair Back (D); Arm and Bun (E)

MATERIALS

For each doll

10″ x 12″ (1⁄4 yd. or fat quarter) solid-color cotton or flannel for body
8″ x 10″ (1⁄4 yd. or fat quarter) wool, wool felt or fleece for hair
6″ x 12″ (1⁄4 yd. or fat quarter) cotton print for dress
61⁄2″ length of lace or trim
Matching and coordinating thread
Embroidery floss for facial features
Stuffing

For sleeping bag

27″ x 20″ (3⁄4 yd.) quilted fabric
27″ x 20″ (3⁄4 yd.) cotton print for lining
40″ length of 1″-wide ribbon
matching and coordinating thread

STITCHES USED (see pages 125–128)

Edgestitch, backstitch, tacking stitch, gathering stitch, ladder stitch.

NOTES

In cutting dimensions, the rectangle's width is always given first, followed by its height.

Unless otherwise noted, all seam allowances are 1⁄4″ and built into the patterns.

Repeat steps 2-6 below for all three dolls.

1. Cut Out Pattern Pieces

Cut out all the pattern pieces from the designated fabrics, cutting the number of pieces called for on each pattern piece and transferring the face template to the cut Body (A). Also cut a 27″ x 20″ rectangle of both quilted fabric and lining fabric for the sleeping bag. For more on cutting out patterns and transferring the face template and pattern markings, see pages 123–124.

2. Attach Dress to Body

Press the top edge of the front and back Dress (B) 1⁄4″ to the wrong side. Pin the front and back dress pieces to the front and back Body (A), aligning the bottom edges. Edgestitch the top edge of each dress piece (see diagram).

3. Attach Hair to Body

Pin the Hair Front (C) to the front body, aligning the top edges, and edgestitch the hair's bottom edge with matching thread. Repeat to attach the Hair Back (D) to the back body (see diagram).

4. Add Facial Features

Referring to the Basics section on transferring faces to fabric (see page 124), embroider facial features on the doll using a backstitch and six strands of embroidery floss.

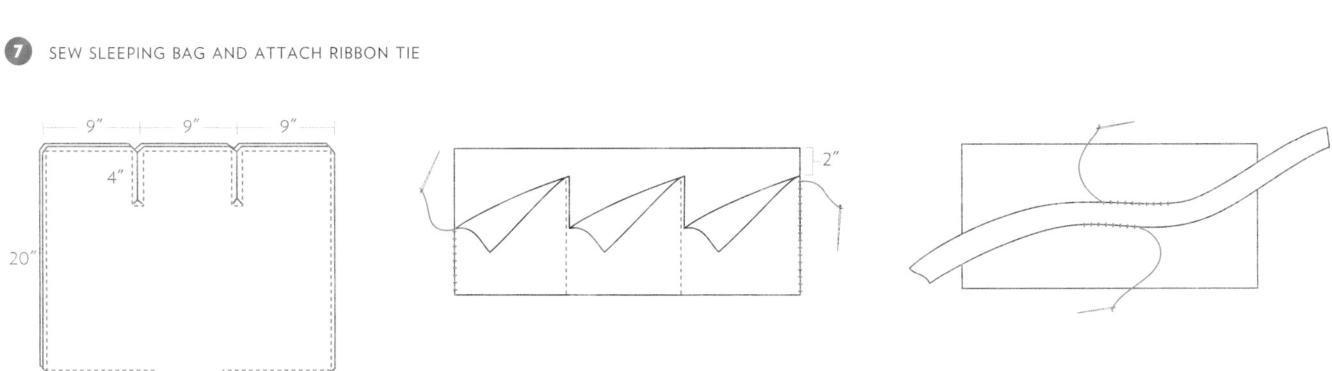

5. Sew and Stuff Body

With right sides together, sew the front and back Body (A) together, leaving a 3″ gap at the bottom. Turn the body right side out through the opening and stuff it (see page 121) so that it's full but still somewhat flat. Wrap the trim around the neckline, and hand-sew it to the back of the neck with a few tacking stitches.

6. Sew and Stuff Arms and Buns

For each Arm and Bun (E), fold the fabric or felt in half with right sides together, matching up the short ends, and sew the short sides together. For strength, thread a needle with two lengths of thread (which means that you'll be sewing with four strands of thread) and hand-sew a gathering stitch around the top edge. Pull the thread taut (see diagram) and tie it off with a sturdy knot. Turn each piece right side out and stuff it.

Hand-sew a gathering stitch around the bottom edge. Pull the gathers taut, tucking in the edges, and tie off with another sturdy knot (see diagram). Sew the fabric arms and felt buns to each body with a ladder stitch, following the placement in the diagram and repeating the stitches until the pieces are secure.

7. Sew Sleeping Bag and Attach Ribbon Tie

With right sides together, align and pin together the quilted fabric and cotton lining. On one long side, mark two 4″-long slits perpendicular to the top edge, with the first mark 9″ from one side and the second mark 9″ from the first (see diagram). Sew the two layers of fabric together around the edges and along the marked slits, leaving a 5″ opening along the bottom edge for turning (see diagram). Cut through the fabric along the marked slits and clip the corners (see page 125). Turn the bag right side out, and press it flat, tucking in the opening's edges. Use a ladder stitch to sew the opening closed.

Lay the bag flat with the lining facing up, fold up the bottom edge to 2″ below the top edge, and pin the fabric in place. Create three slots in the sleeping bag by sewing down the edges of each slot through all layers of fabric: Machine-sew the two center sections, and ladder-stitch the outer edges (see diagram); or edgestitch them to make them sturdier. Hand-sew the ribbon along the center back of the sleeping bag (see diagram) to be used as a tie. Turn the loose edges down and the sleeping bag is all set for its pals.

green yellow
Crayola
Crayola

Eddie

Shaggy mop and a cute striped top—what's your little boy made of? Make a bosom buddy for your boy by repurposing one of his favorite shirts or even a onesie. For fun, match skin and eye color to your guy's and pick a funky faux fur for his hair. Look for a long-pile curly or shaggy fur for a hairdo with some body.

FINISHED SIZE

12″ tall

PATTERN PIECES (see pages 145–146)

Body (A); Hair Front (B); Hair Back (C); Leg (D); Shoe (E); Shirt (F); Pants (G)

MATERIALS

10″ x 26″ (1⁄3 yd.) solid-color flannel or cotton for body
8″ x 16″ (1⁄4 yd.) corduroy for pants
6″ x 8″ scrap of fake fur for hair
6″ x 8″ scrap of wool felt for shoes
Felt scraps for eyes
Kids or baby T-shirt
Matching and coordinating thread
Embroidery floss
7″ length of 3⁄8″-wide elastic
Stuffing

STITCHES USED (see pages 125–128)

Zigzag stitch, whipstitch, backstitch, edgestitch, ladder stitch, topstitch.

NOTE

Unless otherwise noted, all seam allowances are 1⁄4″ and built into the patterns.

1. Cut Out Pattern Pieces

Cut out all the pattern pieces from the designated fabrics, cutting the number of pieces called for on each pattern piece (note the special directions in Step 8 for cutting the Shirt (F) from a T-shirt) and transferring the face template to the cut Body (A). For more information on cutting out patterns and transferring the face template, see page 123–124.

2. Sew Hair

With right sides facing up and the top edges aligned, pin the Hair Front (B) and Hair Back (C) to the front and back Body (A) pieces. Using a narrow zigzag stitch, sew the hair to the front and back head along the unfinished bottom edges (see diagram; note that trimming the fur beforehand at the edges to be sewn reduces its bulk and makes stitching much easier).

3. Embroider Facial Features

Referring to the Basics section on transferring faces to fabric (see page 124) and using the diagram as a guide, hand-sew the eyes in place with a whipstitch and two strands of floss. Embroider a mouth and nose with a backstitch and three strands of floss.

4. Sew Body

With right sides together, sew the front and back of the Body (A) together, leaving the bottom edge open for turning and stuffing (see diagram). Clip the body's curves (see page 125) and turn the body right side out. Press the body's bottom edge 1⁄4″ to the wrong side. Stuff the body (see page 121) so that it's full but still somewhat flat. Leave the bottom open for inserting the legs.

RIGHT SIDE

WRONG SIDE

2 SEW HAIR TO BODY

3 EMBROIDER FACIAL FEATURES

4 SEW TOGETHER FRONT AND BACK OF BODY

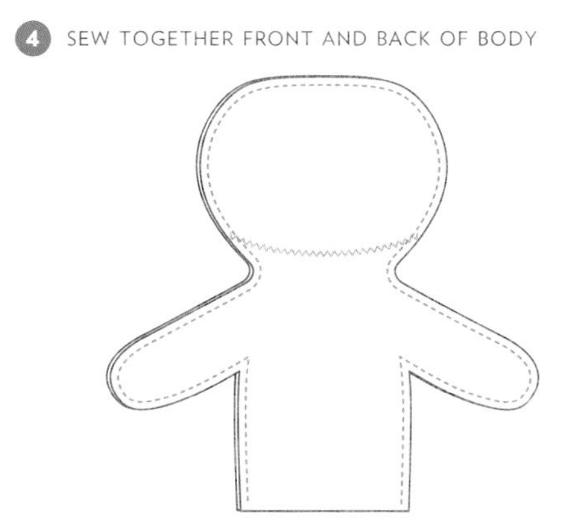

5 SEW LEGS

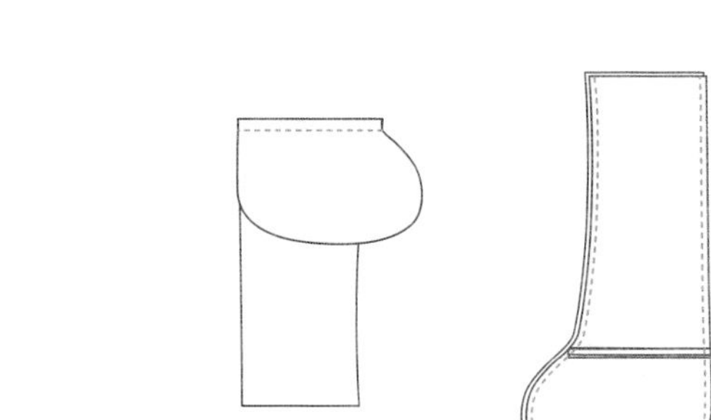

6 ATTACH LEGS TO BODY

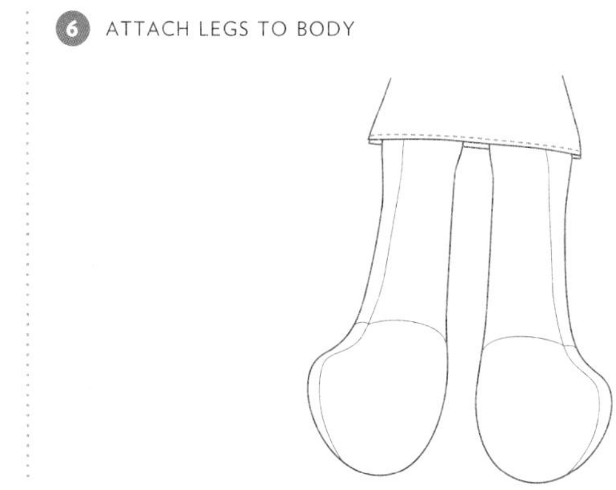

7 SEW FAUX CUFFS ON PANTS

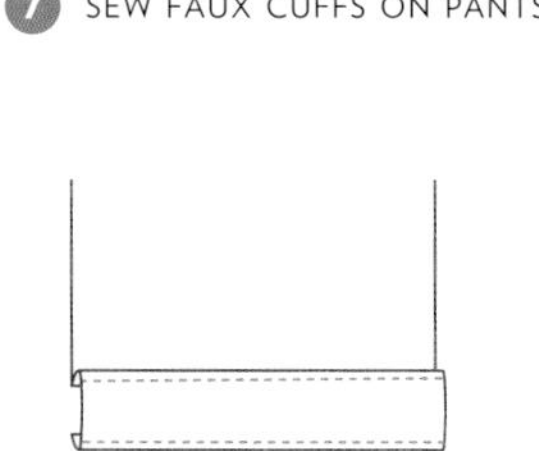

SEW FRONT AND BACK SEAMS

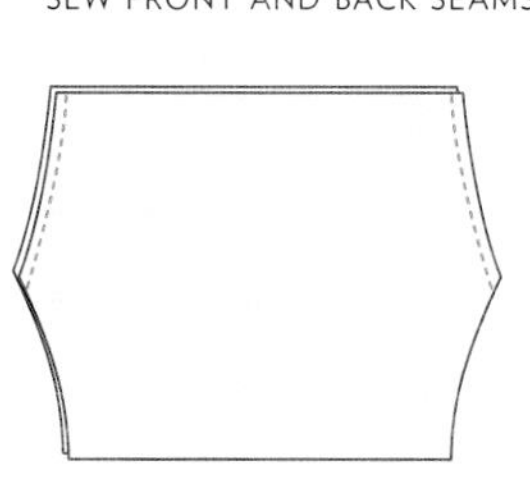

SEW INSEAM

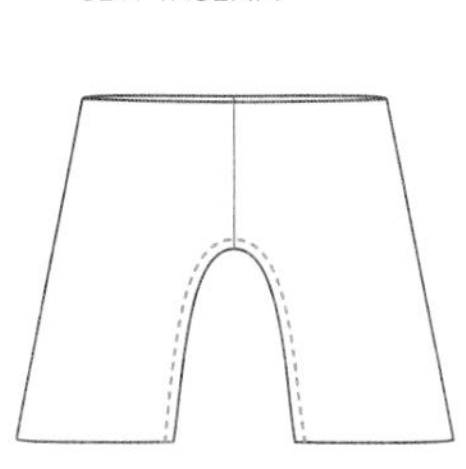

CREATE CASING AND ATTACH ELASTIC

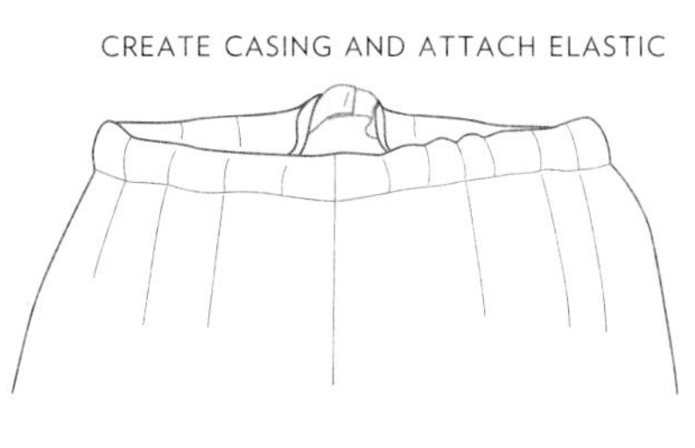

8 CUT OUT AND SEW SHIRT

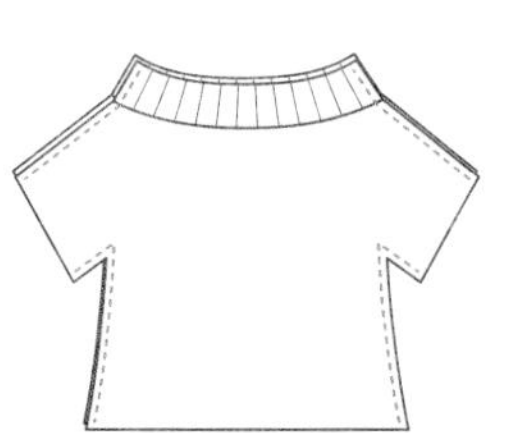

5. Sew Legs

With right sides together, sew one Shoe (E) piece to each Leg (D) piece (see diagram) and press the seam allowances together toward the feet. With right sides together, pin one leg/shoe front and back together, matching up the seams at the feet. Sew the leg together, leaving the top edge open for turning and stuffing (see diagram). Repeat for the other leg.

Turn the legs right side out and stuff them so that the stuffing is firm in the feet and thins toward the top of the legs. Fold the open tops of each leg so that what was the side seam now faces front and edgestitch the raw top of each leg shut.

6. Attach Legs

Position the tops of the legs inside the bottom of the body and pin the legs in place, catching both the front and back body. Edgestitch the body's bottom edge, being sure to catch the legs and the front and back body (see diagram). You can hand-sew the legs in place with a ladder stitch if you want the edge to look more finished, but since this seam will be covered up by Eddie's pants, it's not necessary.

7. Sew Pants

To make the faux cuffs on the pants, first press the bottom edge of each Pants (G) piece 1/4" to the wrong side and edgestitch the pressed fold. Next press another 1/4" fold 1/2" above the bottom edge and edgestitch that fold as well (see diagram). With right sides together, sew the pants' front and back seams (see diagram). Next open out the pants, keeping the right sides together and aligning the edges and seams, and sew the pants' inseam (see diagram). Clip the curve under the legs, turn the pants right side out, and press them flat.

To create a casing for the elastic waistband, press the pants' top edge 1" to the wrong side and topstitch the casing 3/4" from the fold, leaving a 1/2" opening at the back waist for inserting the elastic. Using a small safety pin or bodkin attached to one end of the elastic, thread the elastic through the casing, and sew the elastic's ends together (see diagram). Topstitch the opening closed.

8. Cut Out and Sew Shirt

Turn the T-shirt wrong side out, and lay it flat with the front- and back-neck ribbing aligned. If the front-neck ribbing is much lower than the back-neck ribbing, cut the shirt open at the shoulder seams, and match up the front- and back-neck ribbing. Be aware, if you're using a larger size shirt with a striped pattern, that the back and front stripes may not match up. Pin the Shirt (F) pattern to the T-shirt, matching up the pattern piece's neckline edge with the T-shirt's neckline ribbing (see diagram). Cut out the pattern piece through both the front and back of the shirt.

With right sides together, sew the two shirt pieces together along the tops of the arms. Press the shirt's bottom edge and the bottom edge of each arm 1/4" to the wrong side and finish these edges with an edgestitch or a zigzag stitch if your machine is fussy about knits, which most are. With right sides together, sew the shirt together under the arms along the sides. Clip the corners under the arms and turn the shirt right side out. Press the shirt flat and put it on Eddie.

Menu
café

Tag-a-Long Doll

Who doesn't want their own sidekick? Sassy and fun, Tag-a-Long comes with you anywhere, even on the run. Slide her into the apron and host a pretend tea party or picnic. Or, for more active pursuits, take her on a bike ride or out to the lemonade stand. Tag-a-Long will never have a hair out of place with her perky pigtails made from wool felt. The apron makes up quicky and fits kids of all ages. If you don't want to make the apron, you can sew the stowaway pocket onto a bag or a backpack.

FINISHED SIZE

13″ tall

PATTERN PIECES (see pages 147–148)

Body (A); Hair Front (B); Hair Back (C); Pigtail (D); Arm (E); Leg (F); Collar (G); Eye (H)

MATERIALS

For doll

14″ x 14″ (1/2 yd. or fat quarter) wool felt for body
8″ x 14″ (1/4 yd. or fat quarter) wool felt for hair
7″ x 16″ (1/4 yd. or fat quarter) cotton print for legs
8″ x 14″ (1/4 yd. or fat quarter) cotton print for dress
Felt scraps for eyes
Embroidery floss
1 1/2″ x 9″ scrap of wool felt for collar
Matching and coordinating thread
Stuffing

For apron

17″ x 17″ (1/2 yd. or fat quarter) cotton print for apron
17″ x 7″ (1/4 yd. or fat quarter) cotton print for apron pocket
Matching and coordinating thread

STITCHES USED (see pages 125–128)

Edgestitch, whipstitch, backstitch, tacking stitch, ladder stitch, topstitch, gathering stitch.

NOTES

In cutting dimensions, the rectangle's width is always given first, followed by its height.

Unless otherwise noted, all seam allowances are 1/4″ and built into the patterns.

TAG-A-LONG DOLL

1. **Cut Out Pattern Pieces**

Cut out all the pattern pieces from the designated fabrics, cutting the number of pieces called for on each pattern piece and transferring the face template to the cut Body (A) and all pattern markings to the cut pieces. For more information on cutting out patterns and transferring the face template and pattern markings, see pages 123–124. In addition, cut the following:

From dress fabric, two 8″ x 7″ rectangles.

From apron fabric, one 17″ x 12″ rectangle for apron and two 17″ x 2 1/2″ strips for apron ties.

From apron pocket fabric, one 17″ x 5 1/2″ rectangle for pocket and two 4″ x 1 1/4″ strips for shoulder straps.

RIGHT SIDE | WRONG SIDE

TAG-A-LONG

2 SEW HAIR AND EMBROIDER FACE

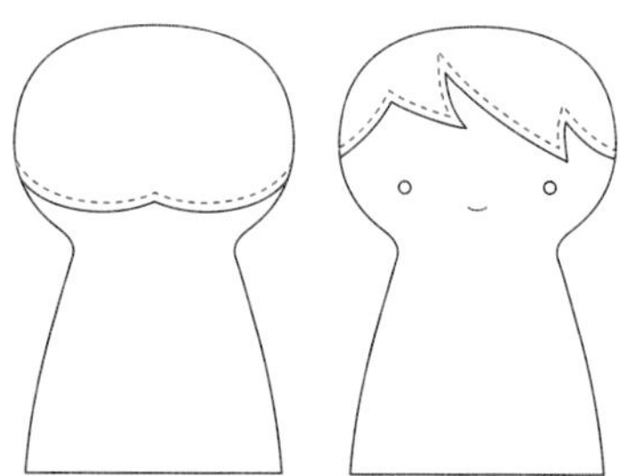

3 SEW PIGTAILS

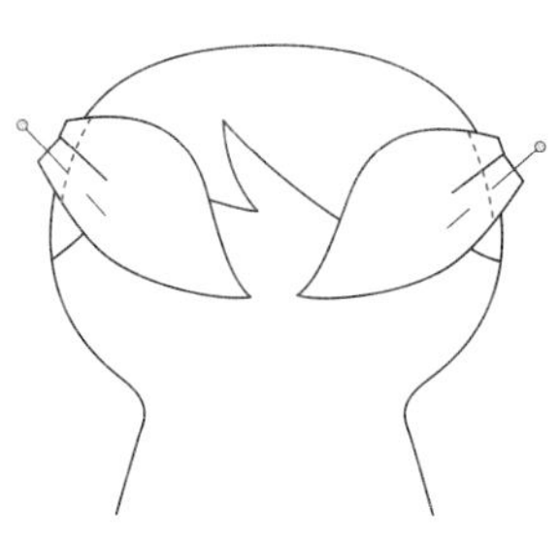

4 SEW TOGETHER BODY FRONT AND BACK

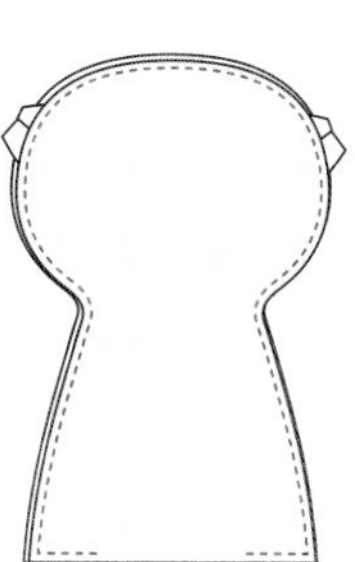

5 MAKE ARMS AND ATTACH TO BODY

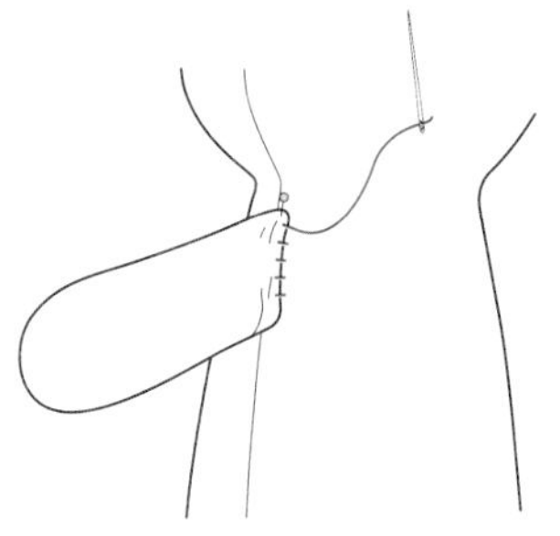

6 MAKE LEGS AND ATTACH TO BODY

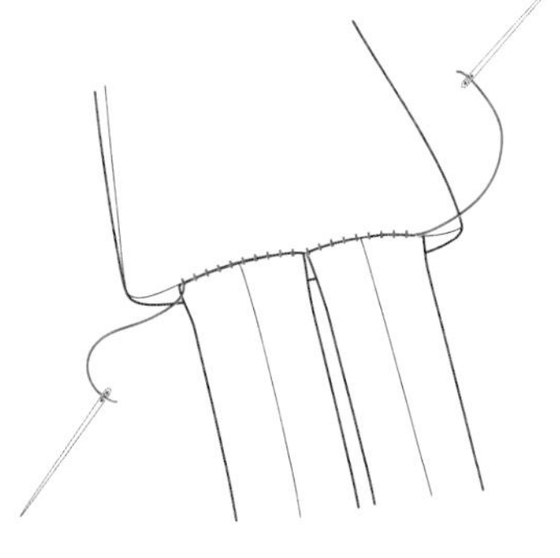

7 MAKE DRESS AND ATTACH TO BODY

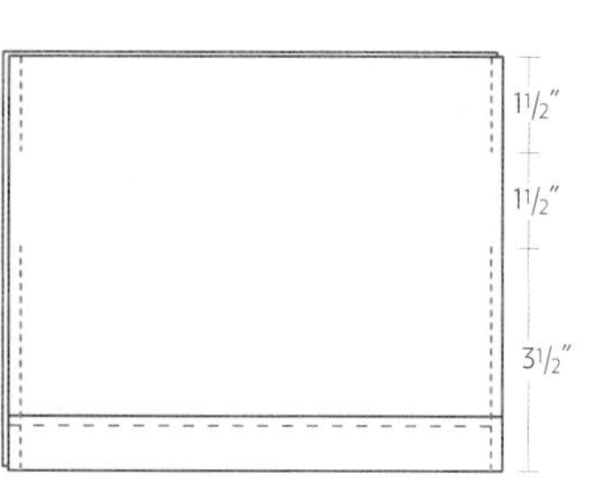

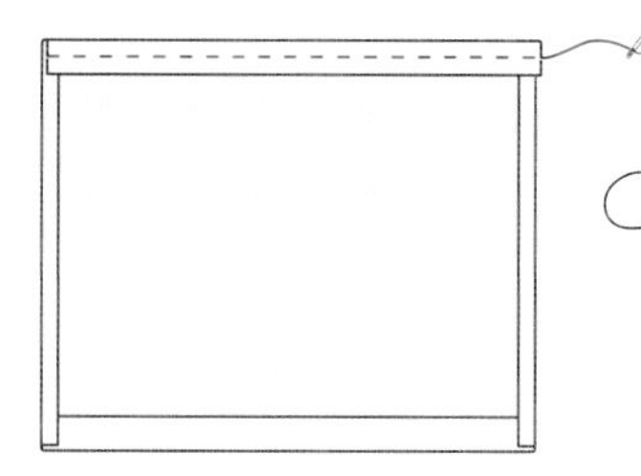

8 ATTACH COLLAR

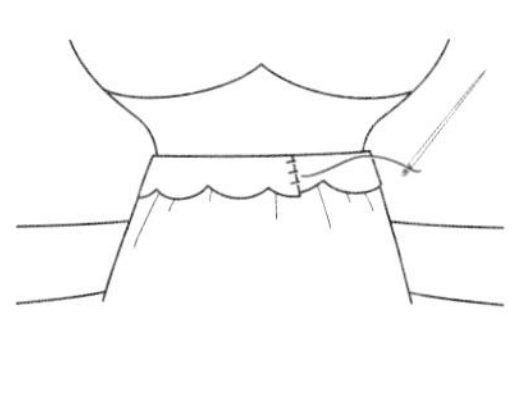

2. Sew Hair and Embroider Face

With right sides facing up and the top edges aligned, pin the Hair Front (B) and Hair Back (C) to the front and back Body (A) pieces. Using matching thread, edgestitch the hair front and back along the bottom edge (see diagram). Referring to the Basics section on transferring faces to fabric (see page 124) and using the same diagram as a guide, hand-sew the eyes in place with whipstitch and two strands of floss. Embroider the mouth with backstitch and four strands of floss.

3. Sew Pigtails

Make a 1/4" fold where marked in the center of each Pigtail (D), and hand-sew the fold in place with a few tacking stitches. With the body front right side up, pin one pigtail on each side of the head, using the diagram as a placement guide, and edgestitch the pigtails in place.

4. Sew Body

With right sides together and the edges aligned, sew the body front and back together, leaving a 3" opening at the bottom for turning and stuffing (see diagram). Clip the corners and curves at the neck, and turn the body right side out. Inspect your pigtail loops to make sure they're caught in the seams, and restitch the seams if not. Stuff the body firmly and hand-sew the opening closed with a ladder stitch, tucking in the opening's edges as you sew.

5. Make and Attach Arms

With right sides together and the edges aligned, sew two Arm (E) pieces together, leaving the top, slanted edge open. Turn the arm right side out and stuff it firmly. Turn the top edge 1/4" to the wrong side and hand-sew the arm shut with a whipstitch. Repeat for the other arm. Then pin the stuffed arms to the body, using the diagram as a placement guide, and ladder stitch them in place, repeating the stitches until the arms are secure.

6. Make and Attach Legs

With right sides together and the edges aligned, sew two Leg (F) pieces together, leaving the top edge open. Turn the leg right side out, and stuff it firmly. Fold the open tops of each leg so that what was the side seam now faces front, turn the top edge 1/4" to the wrong side, and hand-sew the leg shut with a whipstitch. Repeat for the other leg. Then pin the stuffed legs to the body, centering them on the body and, using the diagram as a placement guide, ladder stitch them in place, repeating the stitches until the legs are secure.

7. Make and Attach Dress

Press the bottom edge of the two dress pieces 1/2" to the wrong side and topstitch 1/4" from each pressed fold. With right sides together, sew the front and back dress together along the side edges, leaving 1 1/2" opening on each side for the arms, as shown in the diagram. Press the side seam allowances open. Press the dress's top edge 1/2" to wrong side and hand-sew a gathering stitch around the neckline 1/4" from the pressed fold (see diagram).

Pull the dress on over the doll's head and pull the arms through the armholes. Pull the neckline gathers taut around the doll's neck and tie off the thread with a knot. Using a ladder stitch, hand-sew the dress's bottom edges together for about 1" from each side seam towards the leg, as shown in the diagram (this will keep her dress from flipping up when she's put in the apron pocket).

8. Attach Collar

Fold the long straight edge of the Collar (G) 1/2" to the wrong side. Wrap the collar around the neck, overlapping its edges in back. Hand-sew the collar in place at the back with a few tacking stitches (see diagram).

APRON

RIGHT SIDE | WRONG SIDE

1 MAKE APRON TIES

¼″ ¾″ ½″

3 BEGIN APRON POCKET

8″

4 ATTACH POCKET TO APRON

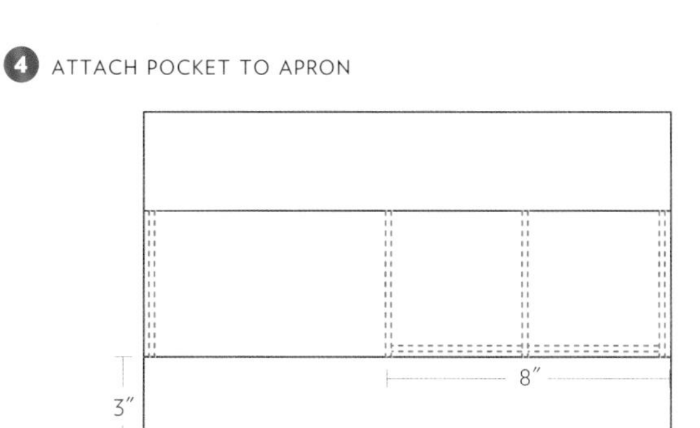

5 ATTACH STRAPS AND TIES

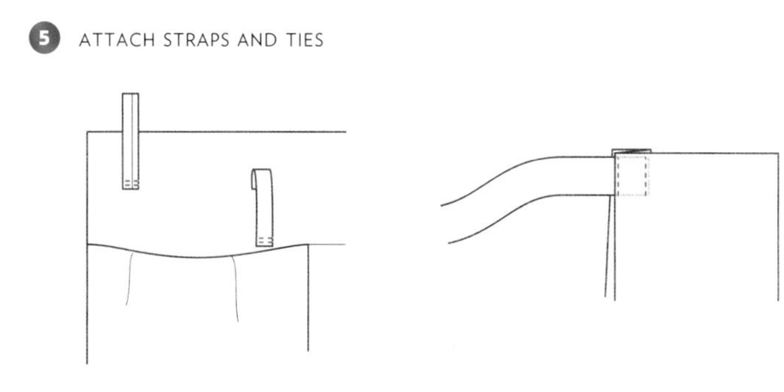

APRON

1. Make Apron Ties and Shoulder Straps

For the apron ties, begin with one of the 17″ x 2½″ strips and press its long top edge ¼″ to the wrong side. Next press the strip's long bottom edge ½″ to the wrong side. Then fold the top edge down ¾″ over the bottom edge and edgestitch the top edge in place (see diagram). Finish one of the strap's short ends by folding it ¼″ to the wrong side and edgestitching it. Repeat for the other strap.

For the shoulder straps, begin with one of the 4″ x 1¼″ strips and press both its long top and bottom edges ¼″ to the wrong side. Then fold the strip in half along its length, aligning its folded edges, and stitch down the middle of the strap.

2. Begin Apron

Press each edge of the 17″ x 12″ apron fabric ½″ to the wrong side and topstitch ¼″ from each pressed edge.

3. Begin Apron Pocket

Press each edge of the 17″ x 5½″ piece of apron pocket fabric ½″ to the wrong side. Edgestitch the pocket's top edge and then topstitch it ¼″ from the edge. Repeat this stitching along the bottom edge for 8″, starting at the left side (see diagram).

4. Attach Pocket to Apron

Lay the apron right side up and place the pocket right side up on top of it, with the side edges aligned and the pocket's bottom edge 3″ above the apron's bottom edge (see diagram). Pin the pocket in place and attach it using the same pattern of edge- and topstitching as above, sewing along the sides and across the bottom edge for 8″ starting on the right side. Then create two pockets on the right half, as shown in the same diagram, stitching vertically, first at about 4″ and then about 8″ in from the right edge. You're leaving the pocket's left top and bottom edges open to slide the doll in.

5. Attach Straps and Ties

Slide the doll into the pocket, and use pins to mark on the apron's right side where the shoulder straps for the doll should go. For each strap, first sew the bottom edge in place with double topstitching. Then fold the strap down into place, and attach the other edge with double topstitching (see diagram).

For the apron ties, first make a 1″ fold on each side edge of apron's waist. Tuck a tie, right side up, into each fold and edgestitch it in place at the apron's edge; then topstitch it about ¾″ in from that edge (see diagram).

I Heart You

My love of folk art inspired this doll. She is wonderfully stiff and has a great antique feeling about her. I admit that in my world the line between plaything and decoration is fuzzy, but I think even the most sophisticated interior decorators would have to agree that this doll makes a lovely addition to a bookshelf or mantle. Pick heavier weight cottons like denim or canvas in subdued country colors or go with saturated folk colors, whichever matches your mood.

FINISHED SIZE

12″ tall

PATTERN PIECES (see page 149)

Doll (A); Face (B); Skirt (C)

MATERIALS

11″ x 20″ (1⁄3 yd. or fat quarter) midweight cotton print for body
6″ x 20″ (1⁄4 yd. or fat quarter) midweight cotton print for head
9″ x 14″ (1⁄4 yd. or fat quarter) cotton print for skirt and bib
5″ x 6″ scrap of linen for face
Matching and coordinating thread
Embroidery floss
Stuffing

STITCHES USED (see pages 125–128)

Ladder stitch, backstitch, edgestitch.

NOTES

In cutting dimensions, the rectangle's width is always given first, followed by its height.

Unless otherwise noted, all seam allowances are 1⁄4″ and built into the patterns.

1. Begin Cutting Out Pattern Pieces

Cut out the Skirt (C) from the designated fabric, cutting the number of pieces called for on the pattern piece. You'll cut the other pattern pieces from fabric as explained in steps 2 and 4, but for now just cut out a full paper pattern piece for the Doll (A), transferring the marking for the neck line. In addition, cut two 2½″ x 2″ strips of skirt fabric for the bib. For more information on cutting out patterns and transferring pattern markings, see pages 122–123.

2. Prepare Fabric and Trace Doll Shape

With right sides together and the edges aligned, sew the head fabric to the body fabric and press the seam allowances open, as shown in the diagram. Fold the sewn fabric in half widthwise, with right sides together and the ends of the seam aligned. Lay the full paper Doll (A) pattern you made in Step 1 on the folded fabric with the marked neck line aligned with the fabric's seam (see diagram). Pin the pattern in place and trace around it.

3. Sew and Stuff Doll

Sew the front and back doll together along the traced line, leaving a 3″ opening on one side for turning and stuffing. Cut out the doll with a 1⁄4″ seam allowance (see diagram). Clip the curves under the arms, at the neck, and between the legs. Turn the doll right side out, and stuff it firmly (see page 121). Hand-sew the opening closed with a ladder stitch, tucking in the opening's edges as you sew.

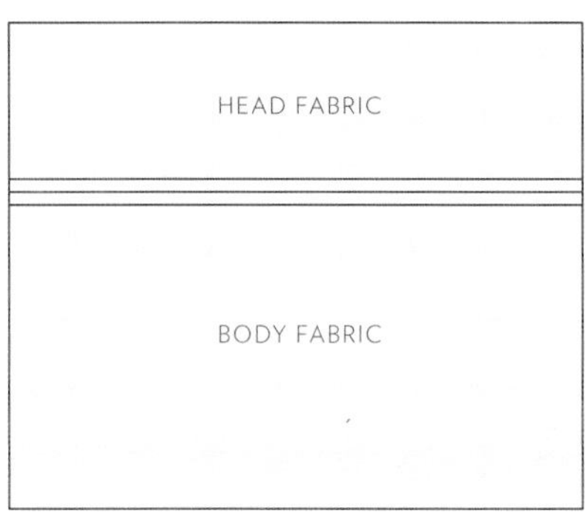

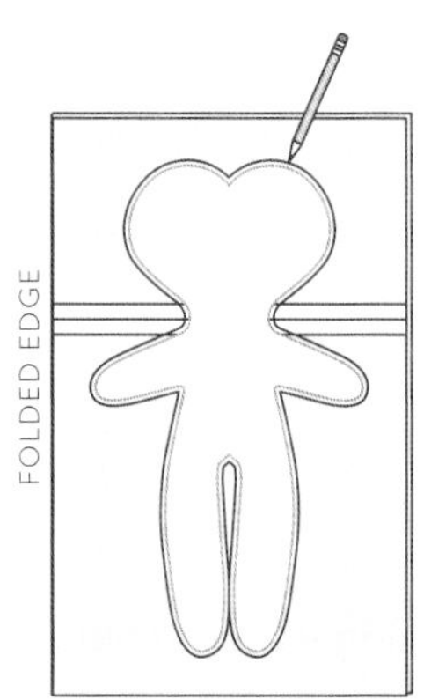

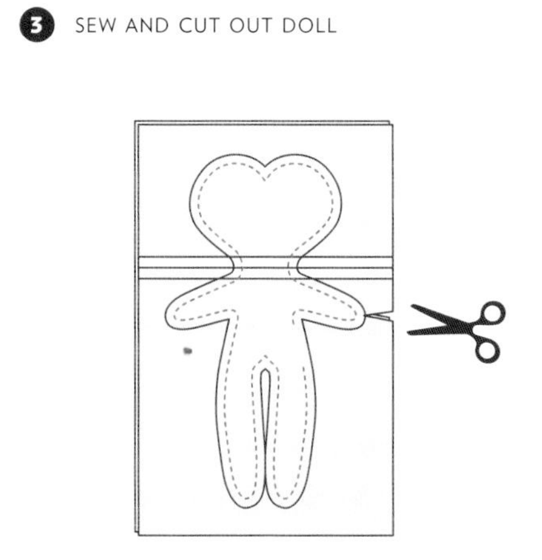

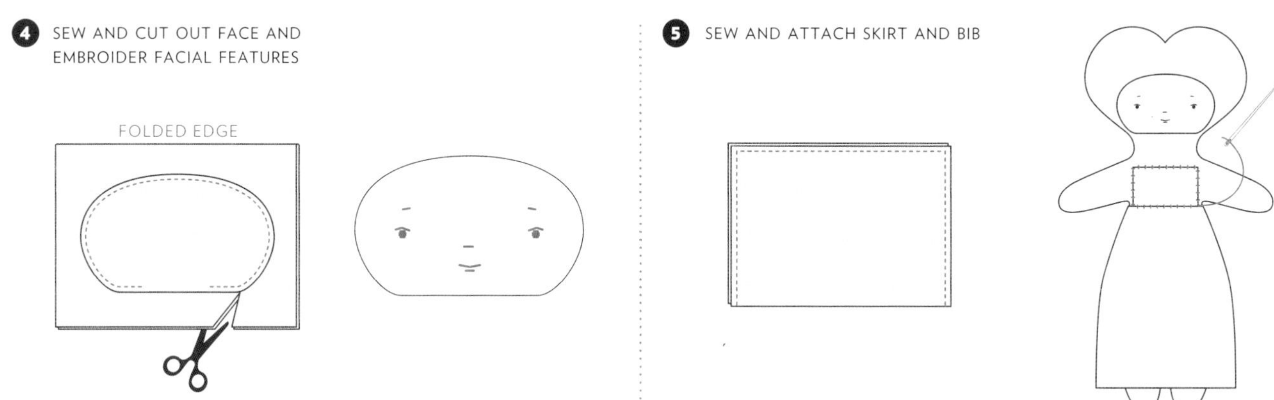

4. Sew and Attach Face

With right sides together, fold the 5″ x 6″ piece of fabric for the face in half, matching up the short ends to get a 5″ x 3″ piece. Trace the Face (B) on the fabric and sew along the traced line, leaving a 1″ opening for turning (see diagram). Cut out the face with a ¼″ seam allowance. Notch the curves (see page 125), turn it right side out, and press it flat.

Referring to the Basics section on transferring faces to fabric (see page 124), transfer the face template to the sewn-and-turned face. Using the diagram as a guide, embroider the facial features with six strands of floss and a backstitch. Tie off the knots from the embroidery on the back. Hand-sew the face to the head with a ladder stitch, stitching the opening closed as you sew.

5. Sew and Attach Skirt and Bib

With right sides together, sew the two bib pieces you cut in Step 1 along three sides (see diagram). Clip the bib's corners, turn it right side out, and press it flat. With right sides together, sew the Skirt (C) pieces along the sides and press the seams open. Press the skirt's top edge ¼″ to the wrong side. Press the skirt's bottom edge ¼″ to the wrong side and edgestitch the hem.

Pin the bib to the doll's chest. Pull the skirt up over the legs so that it overlaps the bib's bottom edge by ¼″ and pin the skirt in place at the waist. Using a ladder stitch, hand-sew the bib to the body along the top and sides and stitch the skirt to the body around the waist (see diagram).

Wes, the Baby Giraffe

Boys and girls alike always seem to love giraffes—it must be the long, grabbable neck. My Wes was inspired by an adorable giraffe appliqué on a vintage baby romper. I love how he holds his nose high in the air like he's sniffing out adventure—or maybe he's just trying to stretch tall in order to look older. When picking fabric, let your mind wander. Wes looks great made up in dots or other bright geometric patterns.

FINISHED SIZE

10″ tall

PATTERN PIECES (see pages 150-151)

Body Side (A); Underbelly (B); Gusset Front (C); Gusset Back (D); Ear (E); Eye (F)

MATERIALS

½ yd. of midweight cotton print for body

Felt scraps for eyes

Matching and coordinating thread

About 5 yds. of worsted-weight yarn

Chenille needle

Stuffing

STITCHES USED (see pages 125–128)

Whipstitch, ladder stitch, tacking stitch.

NOTE

Unless otherwise noted, all seam allowances are ¼″ and built into the patterns.

1. Cut Out Pattern Pieces

Cut out all the pattern pieces from the designated fabrics, cutting the number of pieces called for on each pattern piece and transferring all pattern markings to the cut pieces. For more information on cutting out patterns and transferring pattern markings, see pages 122–123.

2. Sew Underbelly

With right sides together, sew the Underbelly (B) pieces together along the top edge, leaving a 1½″ opening for stuffing (see diagram). Press the seam allowances open.

3. Sew Front Gusset to Underbelly

With right sides together, sew the Front Gusset (C) to the underbelly's marked front edge by pulling this curved front edge into a straight line and matching it up with the gusset's straight edge (see diagram).

4. Sew Back Gusset to Underbelly

With right sides together, sew the Back Gusset (D) to the underbelly's back edge by pulling the curved back edge into a straight line and matching it up with the gusset's straight edge (see diagram). With the front and back gussets sewn to each end of the underbelly, you've created one long gusset.

5. Sew Sides to Gusset

With right sides together, pin one Body Side (A) to the gusset, matching up the legs first to the underbelly legs and then pinning the gusset out and around the body. Sew the side body in place, starting at the marked dot at the tip of the front gusset, sewing down and around the legs, up the back, around the neck, and over the head to the marked dot at the back gusset's nose (see diagram). (Note that, when sewing such a long gusset, expect that everything won't seem to match up perfectly; if you keep the width of the seam allowance consistent, things will work out evenly, if not perfectly.) Repeat with the other body side. Finally, with right sides together, sew the body's two sides together from the marked dot at the tip of the nose to the top of the front gusset. Clip the corners (see page 125) under all four feet, clip the curve under the neck, clip the point off the nose, and turn the piece right side out through the opening.

6. Stuff Body

Using a stuffing fork, knitting needle, or the eraser end of a pencil to push stuffing into the opening, stuff the body firmly from the nose down to the toes. Hand-sew the opening closed with a whipstitch, tucking in the opening's edges as you sew.

7. Sew and Attach Ears

With right sides together, sew two Ear (E) pieces together, leaving a 1⁄2″ opening on one side (see diagram). Clip the points, trim the seam allowances to 1⁄8″, and turn the ear right side out. Hand-sew the opening shut with a ladder stitch, tucking in the opening's edges as you sew. Pin the ear to the head, following the diagram for placement, and hand-sew the ear in place with a few tacking stitches, repeating the stitches until the ear is secure. Repeat for the other ear.

8. Attach Eyes, Horns, Tail, and Nose

Hand-sew each Eye (F) in place with a whipstitch and three strands of floss, using the diagram as a placement guide and hiding the knots under the felt pieces (see page 128).

For horns, cut six 4″-long pieces of yarn, and tie the yarn together in a knot at one end. Braid the yarn, and tie off the other end with another knot about 2 1⁄2″ from the first. Clip the yarn ends close to the knots. Fold up the ends of the knotted braid as shown

in diagram; and, using thread matching your yarn color, hand-sew through the corners to hold the ends upright. Then attach the center section to the head with a tacking stitch, repeating the stitches until the braid is secure.

For the tail, fold three 8″-long pieces of yarn in half and tie off the strands in the middle with a separate 6″-long piece of yarn. Braid the six strands and tie them off near the bottom. Using the diagram as a placement guide, attach the braid to the giraffe's bottom by sewing one 3″-long end of the yarn you tied around the strands into the bottom and back out in a small tacking stitch. Tie this end with the other yarn end, and knot the yarn securely. Bury the yarn tails inside the stuffed body (see page 128).

For the nose, tie a double knot in the center of a 3″-long piece of yarn. Thread a chenille needle with one tail of yarn, and sew a knot to the tip of the nose. Knot off the yarn and bury the yarn tails inside the stuffed body.

RIGHT SIDE | WRONG SIDE

2 SEW UNDERBELLY

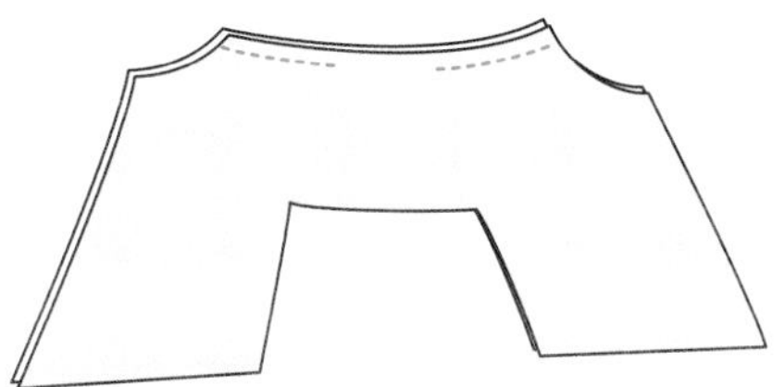

3 SEW FRONT GUSSET TO UNDERBELLY

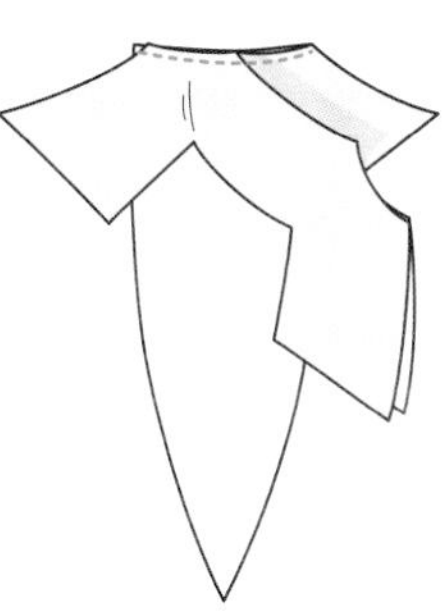

4 SEW BACK GUSSET TO UNDERBELLY

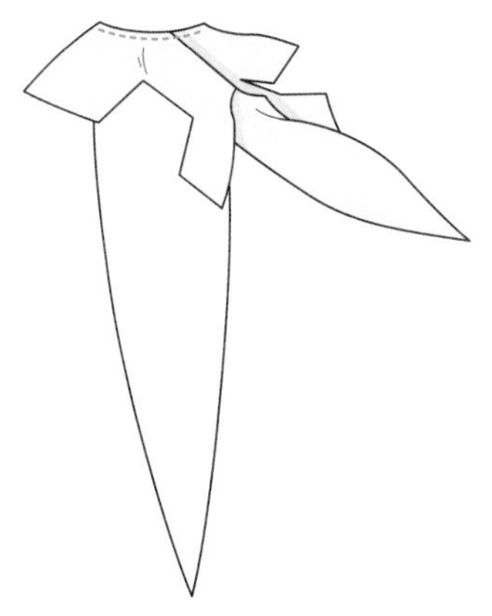

5 SEW SIDES TO GUSSET

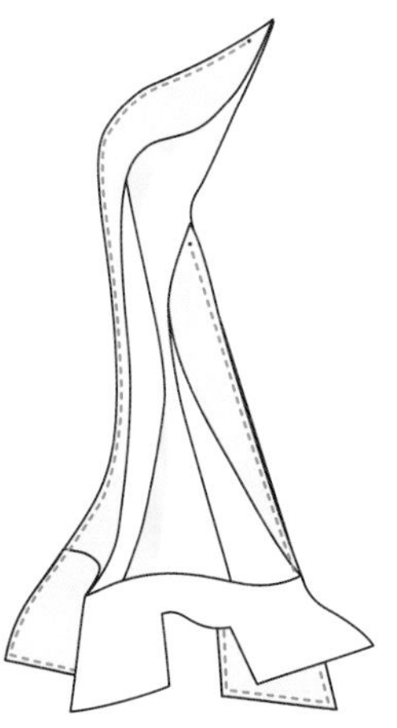

7 SEW EARS

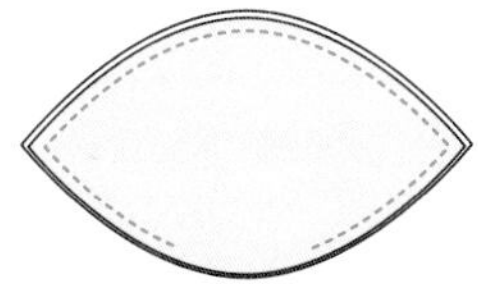

8 ATTACH EYES, HORNS, TAIL, AND NOSE TO BODY

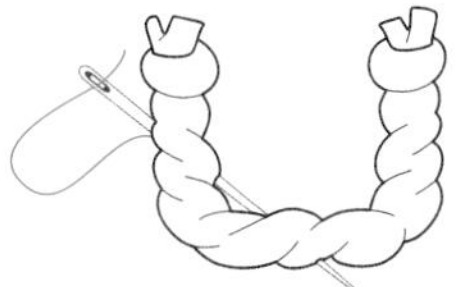

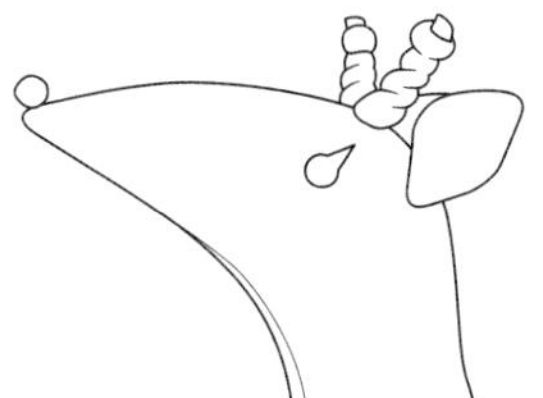

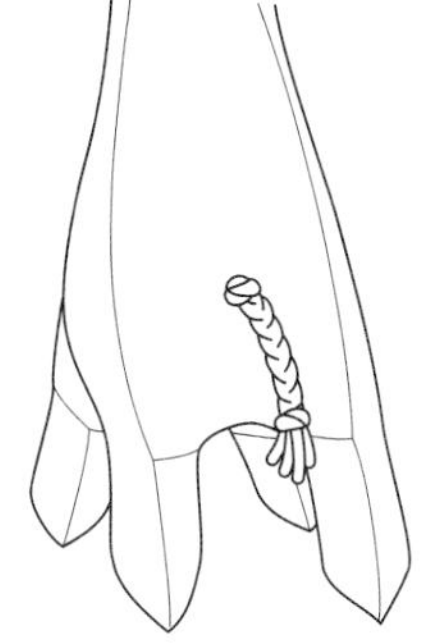

Katie Kitty

My family and I have a fierce love for the illustrations of children's book author Richard Scarry. In fact, one of the main reasons I started making toys was to see if I could create animals in outfits as cute as the ones his animal wear. Katie Kitty was one of my first attempts and I think she's a "real gone cat!" Smart and stylish in her mod party dress and matching shoes, she's ready to go out on the town. And with a social calendar like hers, she'll need a whole closetful of dresses. The basic dress pattern included here is easily customizable; add collars or bows, puffed sleeves, or pockets. And don't forget the shoes—everyone always goes gaga over shoes.

FINISHED SIZE

13″ tall

PATTERN PIECES (see pages 152-154)

Head Side (A); Head Gusset (B); Ear (C); Body (D); Arm (E); Leg (F); Tail (G); Dress Front (H); Dress Back (I); Sleeve (J); Shoe Front (K); Shoe Back (L); Eye (M); Nose (N)

MATERIALS

20″ x 36″ (2⁄3 yd.) wool, wool felt, flannel, or fleece for body
8″ x 5″ scrap of wool, wool felt, flannel, or fleece for gusset
12″ x 20″ (1⁄3 yd. or fat quarter) cotton or light- to midweight fabric for dress
5″ x 6″ scrap of wool felt for shoes
Small scraps of wool felt for eyes and nose
Matching and coordinating thread
Embroidery floss for facial features
20″ length of 1⁄2″-wide ribbon for dress detail and shoe ribbons
Two 1⁄2″ buttons or 1⁄2″ wool felt circles for eyes
Six small buttons for dress detail
Snap closure or Velcro
Stuffing

STITCHES USED (see pages 125–128)

Ladder stitch, whipstitch, backstitch, edgestitch, tacking stitch.

NOTE

Unless otherwise noted, all seam allowances are 1⁄4″ and built into the patterns.

1. Cut Out Pattern Pieces

Cut out all the pattern pieces from the designated fabrics, cutting the number of pieces called for on each pattern piece and transferring all pattern markings to the cut pieces (note that you'll transfer the face template to your toy in Step 8 after stuffing it). For more information on cutting out patterns and transferring pattern markings, see pages 122–123.

2. Sew and Stuff Head

With right sides together, start by aligning the marked front points on one Head Side (A) and the Head Gusset (B); then pin and sew the two pieces together (see diagram). Next pin and sew the other head side to the gusset. Then sew the two head sides together at the back neck. Finally sew the head sides together along the front edge (see diagram). Turn the head right side out and stuff it firmly through the bottom opening (see page 121).

3. Sew and Attach Ears

With right sides together, sew two Ear (C) pieces together, leaving the long side open (see diagram). Clip the points (see page 125), trim the seam allowances to 1⁄8″, and turn the ear right side out. Turn the bottom edges of the ear 1⁄4″ to the wrong side and pin the ear to the top of the stuffed head. Hand-sew the ear in place with a ladder stitch (see diagram), repeating the stitches until the ear is secure. Repeat for the second ear.

4. Make and Attach Body

With right sides together, sew the Body (D) pieces together around three sides, leaving the top edge open for turning and stuffing. Clip the corners (see diagram) on the body, turn the body right side out, and stuff it firmly. Turn the body's open top edge 1⁄4″ to the wrong side, turn the head's bottom open edge 1⁄4″ to the wrong side, and pin the stuffed head to the top of the body. Hand-sew the head in place with a ladder stitch, repeating the stitches until the head is secure (see diagram).

5. Make and Attach Arms

With right sides together, sew two Arm (E) pieces together, leaving the top angled edge open for turning and stuffing. Trim the seam allowances to 1⁄8″, turn the arm right side out, and stuff it firmly. Turn the arm's open top edge 1⁄4″ to the wrong side and, using the diagram as a guide, pin the arm to the body. Ladder stitch the arm in place, repeating the stitches until the arm is secure. Repeat for the other arm.

6. Make and Attach Legs

With right sides together, sew two Leg (F) pieces together, leaving the top edge open for turning and stuffing. Trim the seam allowances to 1⁄8″, turn the leg right side out, and stuff it firmly. Turn the leg's open top edge 1⁄4″ to the wrong side and, using the diagram as a guide, pin the leg to the body. Ladder stitch the leg in place, repeating the stitches until the leg is secure. Repeat for the other leg.

7. Make and Attach Tail

With right sides together, sew two Tail (G) pieces together, leaving the top edge open for turning and stuffing. Trim the seam allowances to 1⁄8″, turn the tail right side out, and stuff it firmly. Turn the tail's open top edge 1⁄4″ to the wrong side and, using diagram as a guide, pin the tail to the body. Ladder stitch the tail in place, repeating the stitches until the tail is secure.

8. Create Face

Using the marking method in the Basics section on transferring faces to fabric (see page 124), the face template, and the diagram as a placement guide, hand-sew each almond-shaped felt Eye (M) in place with a whipstitch and two strands of floss, hiding the knots under the felt pieces (see page 128). If you're using buttons on the eyes, sew them securely atop the felt eyes. If this toy is intended for a child under the age of three, use wool felt circles instead of buttons, whipstitching each circle on a felt eye with two strands of floss.

Using two strands of floss, whipstitch the Nose (N) in place. Using a backstitch and two strands of floss, embroider the mouth.

9. Sew Dress

Cut an 8″-long piece of ribbon and edgestitch the ribbon down the center front of the dress. With right sides together, sew the Dress Front (H) to each Dress Back (I) at the shoulders, and press the seam allowances open. Press the neckline 1⁄4″ to the wrong side, and edgestitch it. On each Sleeve (J), press the straight bottom edge 1⁄4″ to the wrong side and edgestitch it. With right sides together, pin the sleeves to the dress and sew them in place (see diagram), notching the curves.

With right sides together, sew the dress front and backs together under each arm and down each side (see diagram). Clip under the arms and press the side seams open. Turn the dress right side out. Press the bottom hem and center-back edges 1⁄4″ to the wrong side and edgestitch these pressed folds. To finish, hand-sew the buttons on the ribbon, spacing them evenly (leave off buttons for a child under three). Sew a snap closure (or Velcro for a child under three) at the back neck.

10. Make and Attach Shoes

With right sides together, sew each Shoe Front (K) to a Shoe Back (L) with a 1⁄8″ seam.

Turn the shoes right side out. Cut two 6″-long pieces of ribbon and clip notches at both ends for decoration and to prevent fraying. Then, using the diagram as a guide, fold and hand-sew a ribbon bow to each shoe with a few tacking stitches. Put the shoes on Kitty's feet and hand-sew them in place with tacking stitches at the sides.

RIGHT SIDE | WRONG SIDE

2 SEW HEAD SIDES TO HEAD GUSSET

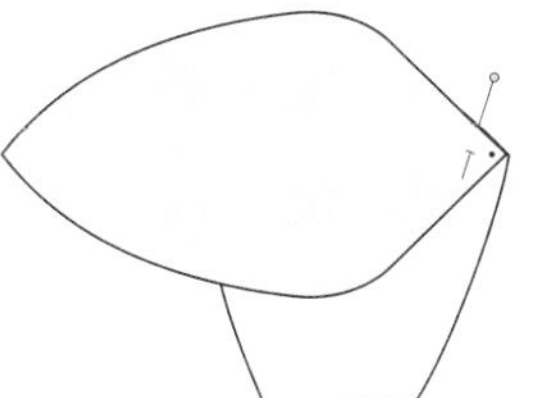

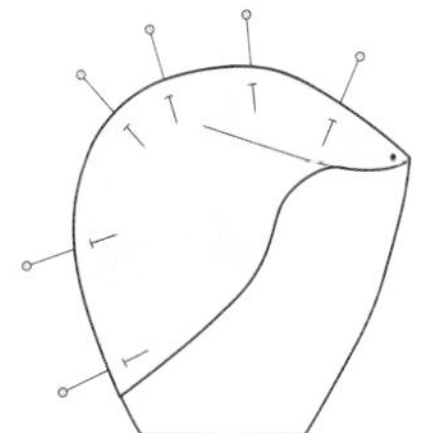

3 SEW EARS AND ATTACH TO HEAD

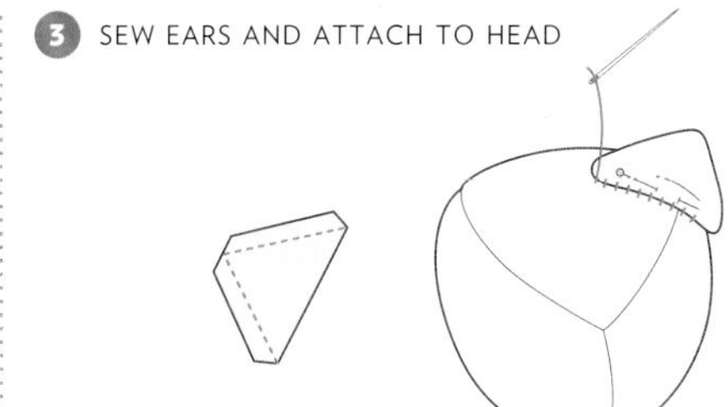

4 MAKE BODY AND ATTACH HEAD

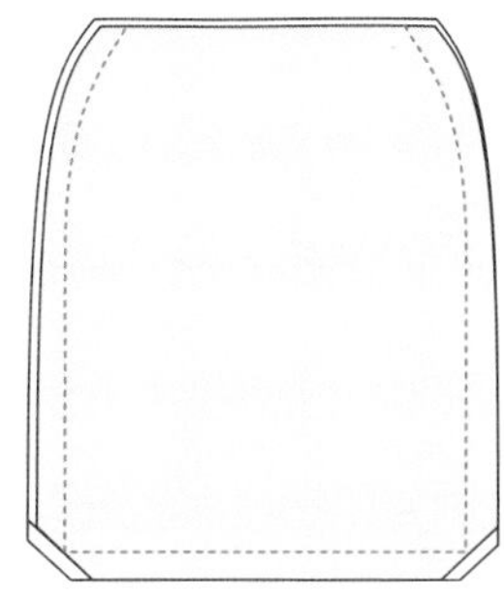

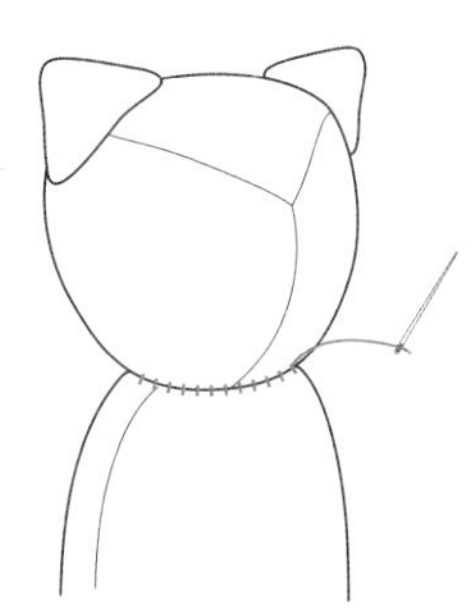

5 - 7 ATTACH ARMS, LEGS, AND TAIL TO BODY

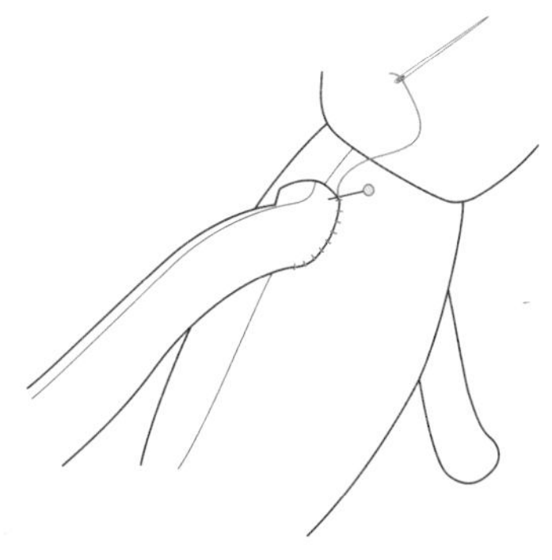

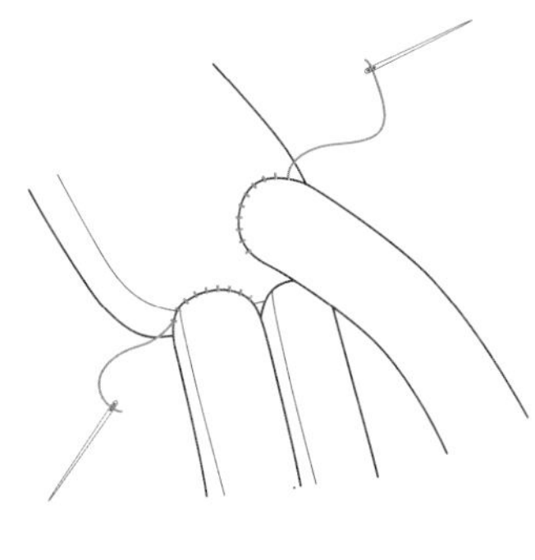

8 CREATE FACE

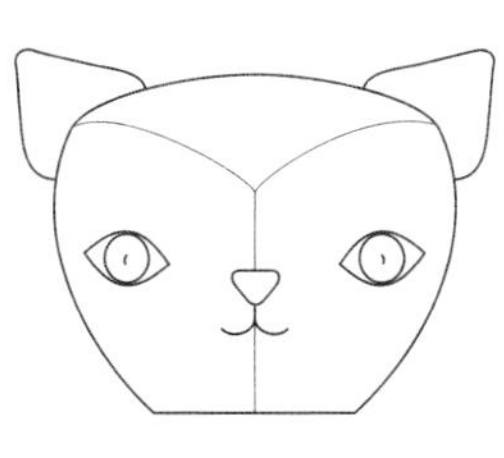

9 SEW DRESS

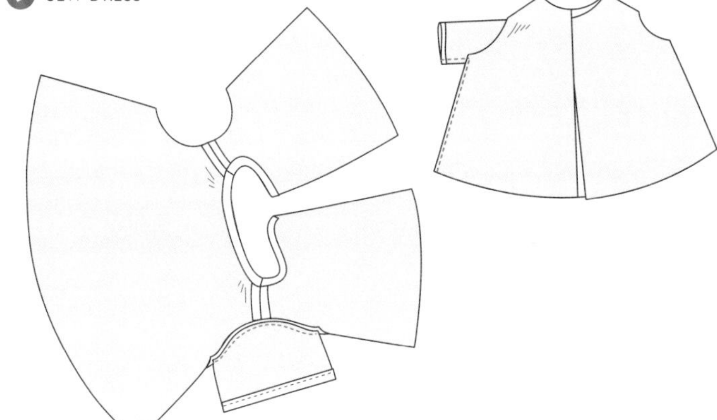

10 ATTACH RIBBON TO SHOES

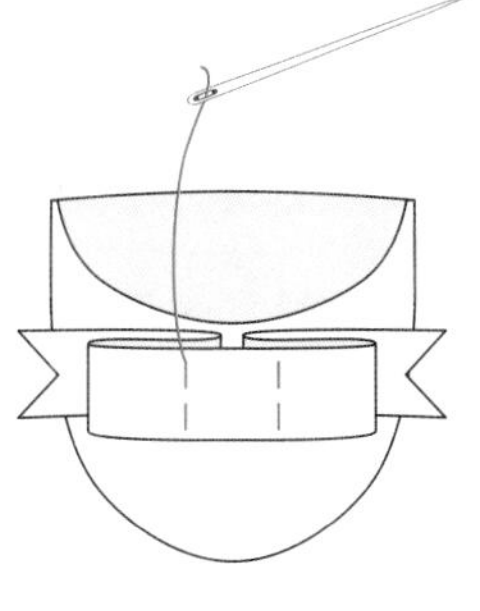

Melvin and Marian

Sometimes I want to make something a little bit fussy and not entirely kid-friendly, something that's all for me. That's how I ended up with Melvin and Marian, the bear librarians, who sit on my shelves and guard my books. They are a charming little pair with a dignified air—more decoration than plaything. Their body pieces and clothing are quickly sewn on the machine with assembly and finishing details worked by hand later.

FINISHED SIZE

9″ tall

PATTERN PIECES (see pages 155–157)

Head Side (A); Head Gusset (B); Body (C); Bottom (D); Arm (E); Leg (F); Ear (G); Nose (H); Eye (I); Dress Front (J); Dress Back (K); Sleeve (L); Dress Collar (M); Pants (N); Shirt Front (O); Shirt Back (P); Shirt Collar (Q); Tie (R)

MATERIALS

14″ x 18″ (1⁄4 yd. or fat quarter) wool or wool felt for each bear
12″ x 18″ (1⁄4 yd. or fat quarter) cotton print for dress
10″ x 14″ (1⁄4 yd. or fat quarter) cotton print for shirt
8″ x 12″ (1⁄4 yd. or fat quarter) of cotton print for pants
Scraps of cotton print for tie, shirt, collar and dress collar
Felt scraps for eyes and nose
Matching and coordinating thread
Embroidery floss
Stuffing

STITCHES USED (see pages 125-128)

Ladder stitch, backstitch, whipstitch, gathering stitch, edgestitch, tacking stitch.

NOTE

Unless otherwise noted, all seam allowances are 1⁄4″ and built into the patterns.

BEARS

1. Cut Out Pattern Pieces

Cut out all the pattern pieces for the bears and their garments, except for the Dress Collar (M), Shirt Collar (Q), and Tie (R), from the designated fabrics, cutting the number of pieces called for on each pattern piece (you'll cut the dress collar and shirt collar as explained in Step 5 of the directions for making the dress, and the tie as explained in Step 6 of the directions for making the shirt). For more information on cutting out patterns, see page 123.

2. Construct Head

With right sides together and the edges aligned, start at the bottom edge to pin and then sew one Head Side (A) to the Head Gusset (B) (see diagram). Likewise pin and sew the other head side to the gusset. Trim the seam allowances to 1⁄8″, turn the head right side out, and stuff it firmly (see page 121).

3. Construct Body

Sew the two Body (C) pieces together along each side, leaving the top and bottom edges open. With right sides together, pin the Bottom (D) to the body, starting by matching up the side seams with the center points on the bottom's sides. (Note that positioning a flat bottom onto a two-dimensional body can be tricky and may take some adjusting—which is why you're pinning it in place before sewing—but it will fit.) After pinning the bottom in place, sew the two together (see diagram), turn the body right side out, and stuff it firmly.

2 SEW HEAD SIDES TO HEAD GUSSET

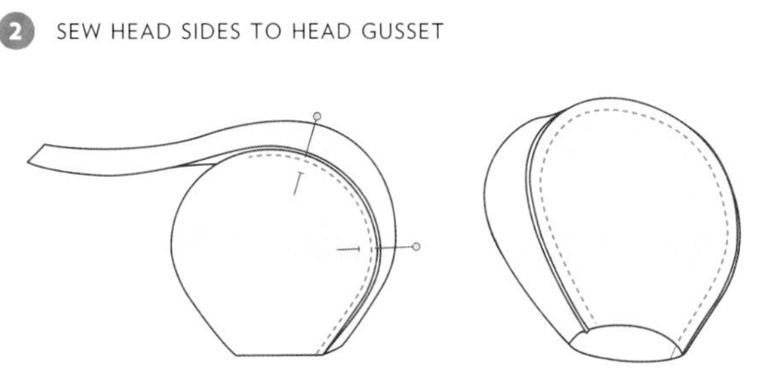

3 SEW BODY PIECES TO BODY BOTTOM

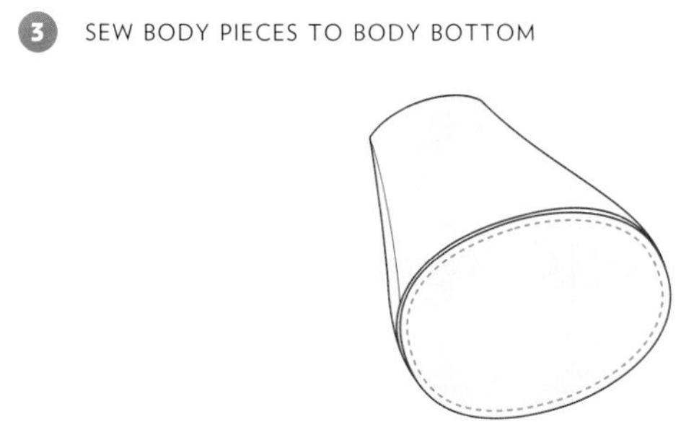

6 AND 7 ATTACH EARS AND EMBROIDER FACIAL FEATURES

8 SEW HEAD, ARMS, AND LEGS TO BODY

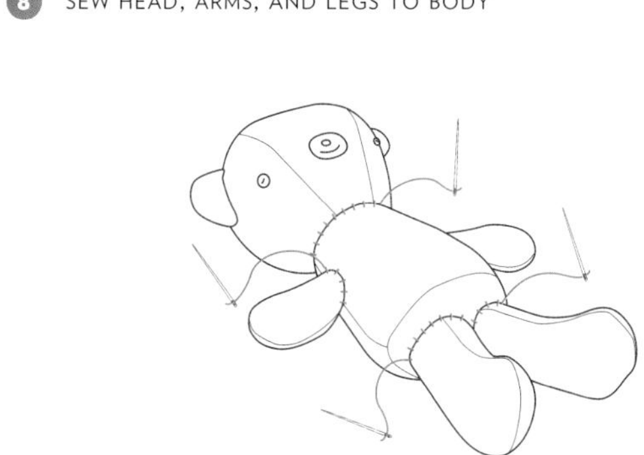

4. Construct Arms

With right sides together, sew two Arm (E) pieces together, leaving the slanted top open for stuffing. Trim the seam allowances to 1⁄8″, turn the arm right side out, and stuff it firmly. Repeat for the other arm.

5. Construct Legs

With right sides together, sew two Leg (F) pieces together, leaving the straight top edge open for stuffing. Trim the seam allowances to 1⁄8″, turn the leg right side out, and stuff it firmly. Repeat for the other leg.

6. Sew and Attach Ears

With right sides together, sew two Ear (G) pieces together, leaving the straight bottom edge open. Notch the outer curves (see page 125), and turn the ear right side out. Fold the bottom edge 1⁄4″ to the wrong side and pin the ear to the stuffed head, using the diagram as a placement guide. Hand-sew the ear in place with a ladder stitch, repeating the stitches until the ear is secure. Repeat the process for the second ear.

7. Embroider Facial Features

Using the marking method in the Basics section on transferring faces to fabric (see page 124), the face template, and the diagram as a placement guide, embroider a nose and mouth on the felt Nose (H) using a backstitch and four strands of floss. Then embroider a single stitch on each felt Eye (I) with four strands of contrasting floss. Hand-sew the felt eyes and nose/mouth piece in place with a whipstitch and three strands of floss, hiding the knots (see page 128) under the felt pieces.

8. Putting It All Together

Using the diagram as a placement guide, pin the head, arms, and legs to the body and hand-sew each piece in place with thread and a ladder stitch, repeating the stitches until each piece is securely attached.

DRESS

RIGHT SIDE | WRONG SIDE

1 SEW SHOULDER SEAMS

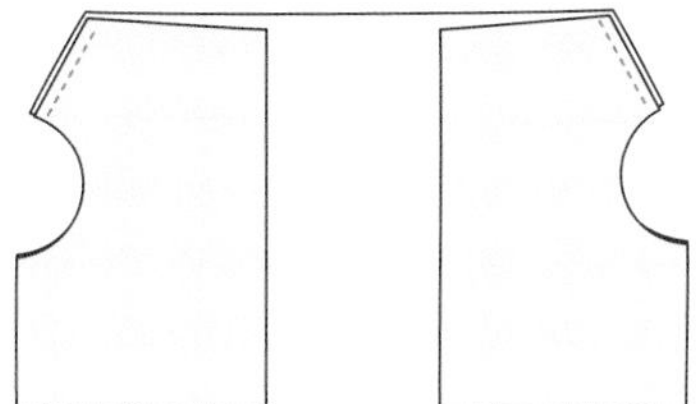

2 GATHER FRONT'S TOP EDGE

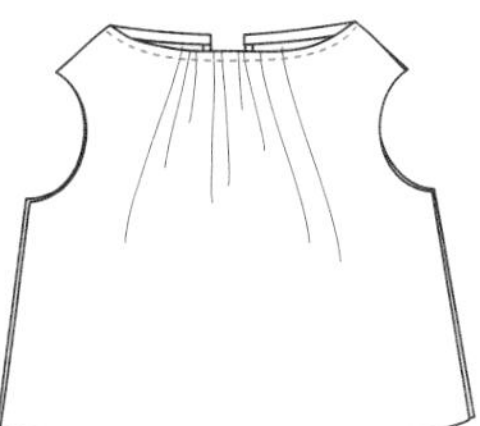

3 HEM AND ATTACH SLEEVES

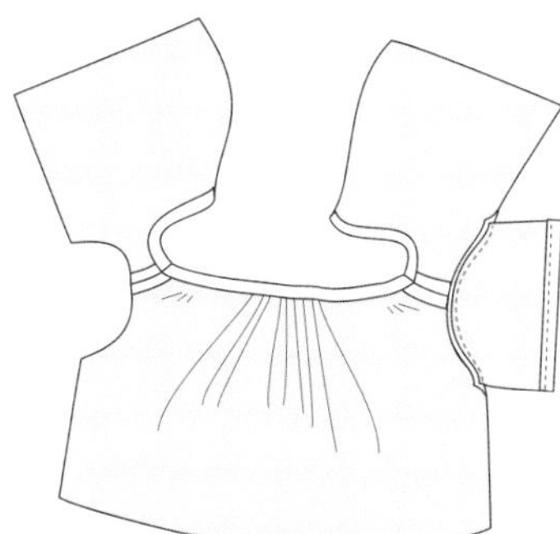

4 SEW SIDE SEAMS AND HEM EDGES

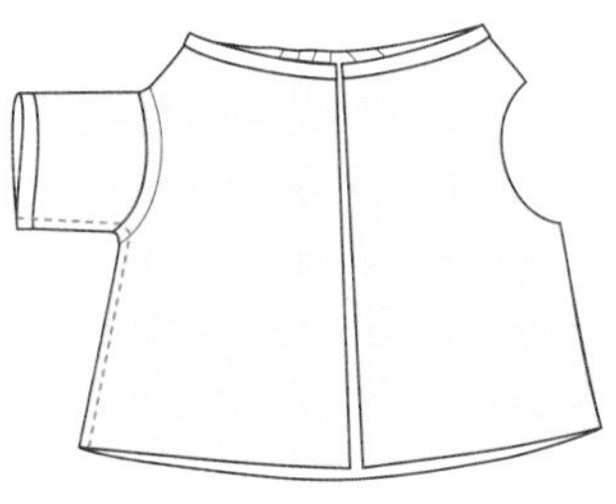

DRESS

1. Sew Shoulders Seams

With right sides together, sew the Dress Front (J) to the Dress Back (K) pieces at the shoulders (see diagram). Press the seam allowances open.

2. Gather Front's Top Edge

Sew a gathering stitch across the top center 4″ of the dress front. Pull the gathers so the top edge of the dress front measures 3¾″. Fold the top gathered edge of the dress ¼″ to the wrong side and edgestitch the folded edge in place (see diagram).

3. Hem and Attach Sleeves

Press the bottom straight edge of each Sleeve (L) ¼″ to the wrong side and edgestitch the pressed edge. With right sides together, pin the sleeves to the dress' armholes, and sew them in place (see diagram). Notch the curve and press the seam allowances together towards the sleeve.

4. Sew Side Seams and Hem Edges

With right sides together, sew the dress front and backs together under the arms and down the sides (see diagram). Clip under the arms (see page 125), and press the side seam allowances open. Turn the dress right side out. Press the bottom hem and center-back edges ¼″ to the wrong side and edgestitch the pressed edges in place.

5. Sew and Attach Collar

Place the two pieces of the collar fabric right sides together and center and trace the Dress Collar (M) pattern on the fabric. Sew around the traced line, leaving the long, straight, top edge open. Cut around the sewn collar, leaving a ⅛″ seam allowance along the stitching and a ¼″ seam allowance along the top edge. Turn the collar right side out and press it. Fold the open top edge ¼″ to the wrong side, and press the folded edge flat. Hand-sew the collar to the dress with a ladder stitch, or edgestitch it in place. Overlap the dress's center-back edges and sew them in place to the body with a few tacking stitches.

RIGHT SIDE | WRONG SIDE

PANTS

SHIRT

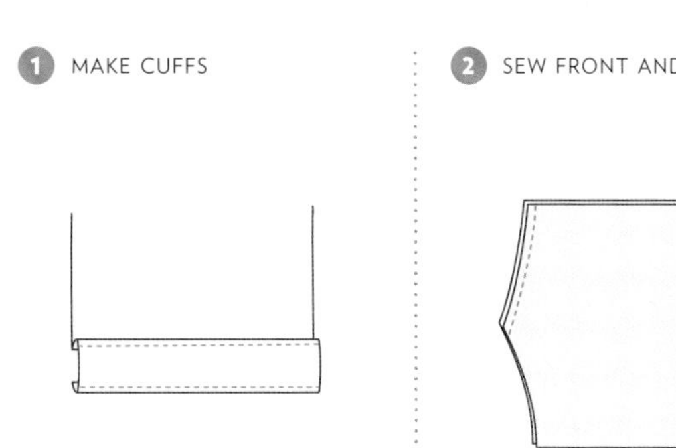

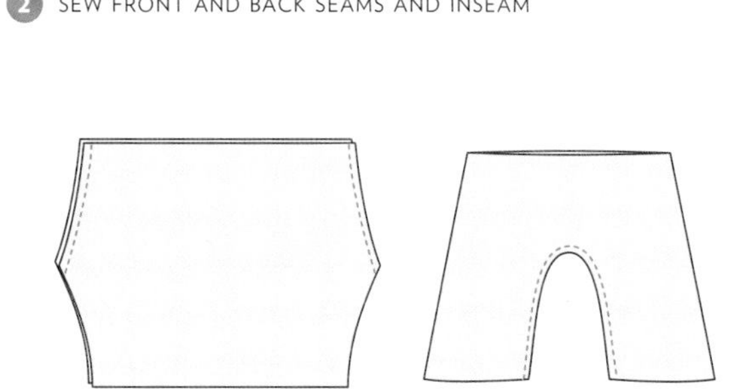

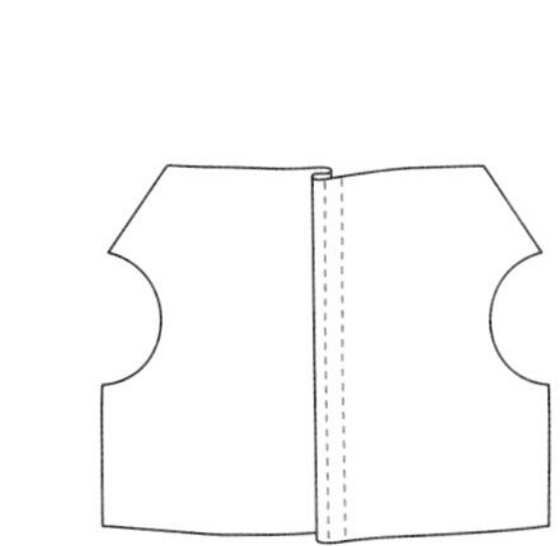

PANTS

1. Make Cuffs

To make the faux cuffs on the pants, first press the bottom edge of each Pants (N) piece 1⁄4″ to the wrong side and edgestitch the pressed fold. Next press another 1⁄4″ fold 1⁄2″ above the bottom edge and edgestitch that fold as well (see diagram).

2. Construct Pants

With right sides together, sew the pants' front and back seams (see diagram). Next open out the pants, keeping the right sides together and aligning the edges and seams, and sew the pants' inseam (see diagram). Clip the curve under the legs, turn the pants right side out, and press them flat.

3. Finish Pants

Fold and press the top edge of the pants 1⁄4″ to the wrong side and sew a gathering stitch along the top of the fold. Put the pants on the bear, pull the gathers taut to the belly, and tie the thread off with a knot.

SHIRT

1. Sew Center-Front Fold

Fold and press a 1⁄4″ tuck at the center of the Shirt Front (O), and edgestitch the pressed tuck. Topstitch another line parallel to the edgestitched tuck 1⁄4″ to the right of it to make a front "placket" for the shirt (see diagram).

2. Sew Shirt Front to Backs

With right sides together, sew the shirt front to the two Shirt Back (P) pieces at the shoulders (see Step 1 of Dress). Press the seam allowances open.

3. Make and Attach Sleeves

Make cuffs for the sleeves as you did for the pants (see Step 1 of Pants). With right sides together, pin the sleeves to the shirt's armholes and sew them in place (see Step 3 of Dress).

4. Sew Side Seams and Hem Edges

With right sides together, sew the shirt front to the shirt backs under the arms and down the sides (see Step 4 of Dress). Clip under the arms and press the side seam allowances open. Turn the shirt right side out. Press the bottom hem and center-back edges 1⁄4″ to the wrong side and edgestitch the pressed edges in place.

5. Sew and Attach Collar

Working with the Shirt Collar (Q) pattern, sew and attach the shirt collar to the bear following the directions for the dress collar (see Step 5 of Dress).

6. Sew and Attach Tie

Place two pieces of the tie fabric right sides together and center and trace the Tie (R) pattern on the fabric. Sew around the traced line, leaving a 1″ gap along one long side. Cut around the sewn tie, leaving a 1⁄8″ seam allowance. Clip the corners and turn the tie right side out. Press the tie flat, tucking in the opening's edges to the wrong side, and edgestitch around the tie's edges. Hand-sew the tie to the shirt's neck with a few tacking stitches.

Bjorn Bjornson

I'm not always a fan of traditional-looking teddy bears, but I do love the classic button-joint style. So for Bjorn I tried to match that construction style with a more modern aesthetic. I think he turned out just perfect—at least perfect for the kooky bear collector in my life (hi, Mom!). With a long doll needle, button joints are a snap and make the arms and legs wonderfully poseable. If making Bjorn for a child under three, skip the buttons; instead, sew the arms and legs in place.

FINISHED SIZE

12″ tall

PATTERN PIECES (see pages 158-159)

Head (A); Head Gusset (B); Body Front (C); Body Back (D); Ear (E); Arm (F); Leg (G); Foot (H); Nose (I); Tail (J)

MATERIALS

½ yd. of fake fur for body and head
Scrap of wool felt for nose
Two ¼″ buttons or scraps of wool felt for eyes
Four ⅞″ buttons for joints
Matching and coordinating thread
Embroidery floss for facial features and sewing button joints
Doll needle
Stuffing

STITCHES USED (see pages 125–128)

Ladder stitch, whipstitch, backstitch.

NOTE

Unless otherwise noted, all seam allowances are ¼″ and built into the patterns.

1. Cut Out Pattern Pieces

Cut out all the pattern pieces from the designated fabrics, cutting the number of pieces called for on each pattern piece and transferring all pattern markings to the cut pieces (note that you'll transfer the face template to your toy in Step 9 after stuffing it). For more information on cutting out patterns and transferring pattern markings, see pages 122–123.

2. Sew Head

Sew the darts on the top of each Head (A) piece with right sides together (see diagram). Then, with right sides together, sew the two head pieces together along the front edge under the nose and down the chin (see diagram).

Next pin the Head Gusset (B) to one of the Head (A) pieces with right sides together, starting by aligning the dot at the center of the gusset's nose end with the head's center-front seam line (see diagram). Pin the gusset out from the center-front point, turning the head to match the gusset. Starting at the center-front point, sew the gusset to the head (see diagram). Then pin and sew the other head piece to the other side of the gusset in the same way. Turn the head right side out and stuff it firmly (see page 121).

3. Sew and Attach Ears

With right sides together and the edges aligned, sew two of the Ear (E) pieces together, leaving the bottom edge open (see diagram). Trim the seam allowances to 1⁄8″ and turn the ear right side out. Turn the ear's open bottom edge 1⁄4″ to the wrong side, and pin the ear to the top of the stuffed head. Hand-sew the ear in place with a ladder stitch (see diagram), repeating the stitches until the ear is secure. Repeat for the second ear.

4. Sew Body

With right sides together and the edges aligned, sew one Body Front (C) to one Body Back (D) (see diagram). Repeat with the other body front and back pieces. Then, with right sides together and the edges aligned, sew these two body front/back pieces together (see diagram), leaving the flat neck edge open. Turn the body right side out through the opening and stuff it firmly.

5. Sew Head to Body

Turn the open neck edges on the body and on the head 1⁄4″ to the wrong side. Pin the stuffed head to the top of the body and hand-sew the head in place with a ladder stitch, repeating the stitches until the head is secure (see diagram).

6. Sew Legs

With right sides together and the edges aligned, sew two Leg (G) pieces together, leaving the flat bottom edge open (see diagram). Open up the sides of the leg, and pin one Foot (H) in place. Sew the foot to the leg, leaving a 1″ opening for turning and stuffing (see diagram). Clip the leg's curves (see page 125), turn the leg right side out, and stuff it firmly. Hand-sew the opening closed with a ladder stitch, tucking in the opening's edges as you sew. Repeat for the second leg.

7. Sew Arms

With right sides together and the edges aligned, sew two Arm (F) pieces together, leaving a 1″ gap for turning and stuffing (see diagram). Turn the arm right side out and stuff it firmly. Hand-sew the opening closed with a ladder stitch, tucking in the opening's edges as you sew. Repeat for the other arm.

8. Assemble Body

Using six strands of floss, a doll needle, and buttons for button joints, hand-sew the stuffed arms and legs to the body, as follows: Double-thread a doll needle with a 40″ length of floss. Leaving a 6″ floss tail outside the body, insert the needle through the left button, left leg, body, right leg, and right button (see diagram). Then re-insert the needle into the right button's other hole, back through the right leg, body, and left leg, and exit through the empty hole on the left button. Repeat this circuit again; then pull the floss taut and tie off the end and the 6″ tail in a big knot. Sew the floss-tail ends back through the button and bury the tails in the body (see page 128). Repeat for the arms.

Alternatively, if the bear is intended for a child under the age of three, instead of using buttons, hand-sew the arms and legs in place with a ladder stitch, repeating the stitches until each limb is securely attached. Note that, unlike with the button joints, attaching the arms and legs this way prevents them from moving.

9. Finishing

Using the marking method in the Basics section on transferring faces to fabric (see page 124), the face template, and the diagram as a placement guide, hand-sew the facial features with three strands of embroidery floss as follows: Pin and hand-sew the Nose (I) in place with a whipstitch and use a backstitch to embroider a mouth. Hand-sew the button eyes (or felt-circle eyes if this is for a child under the age of three) in place with three strands of floss.

With right sides together and the edges aligned, sew together the two Tail (J) pieces, leaving the straight bottom edge unsewn. Trim the seam allowances to 1⁄8″. Turn the tail right side out and turn the tail's open bottom edge 1⁄4″ to the wrong side. Pin the tail to the bottom of the bear. Hand-sew the tail in place with a ladder stitch (see diagram), repeating the stitches until the tail is secure.

RIGHT SIDE

WRONG SIDE

2 SEW DARTS ON HEAD

SEW HEAD PIECES ALONG FRONT EDGE

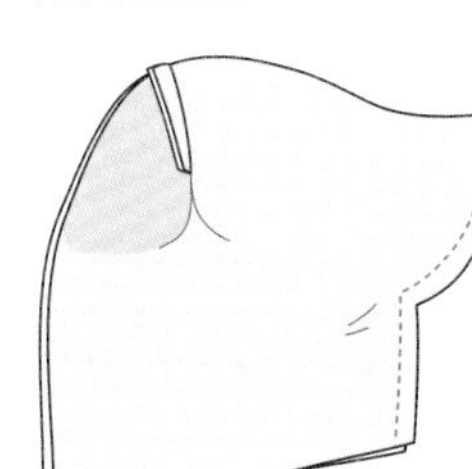

SEW GUSSET TO ONE HEAD PIECE

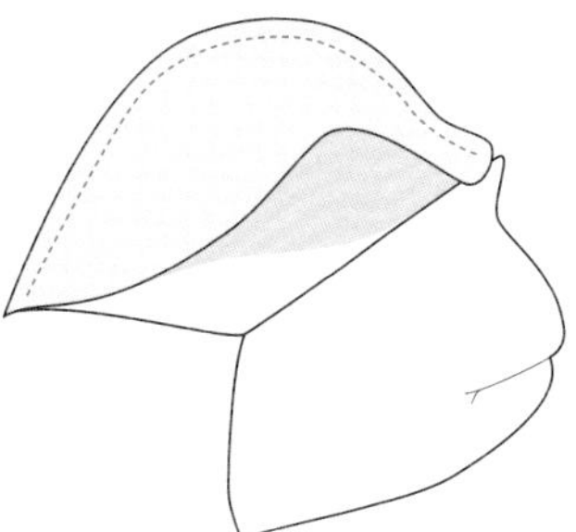

SEW GUSSET TO OTHER HEAD PIECE

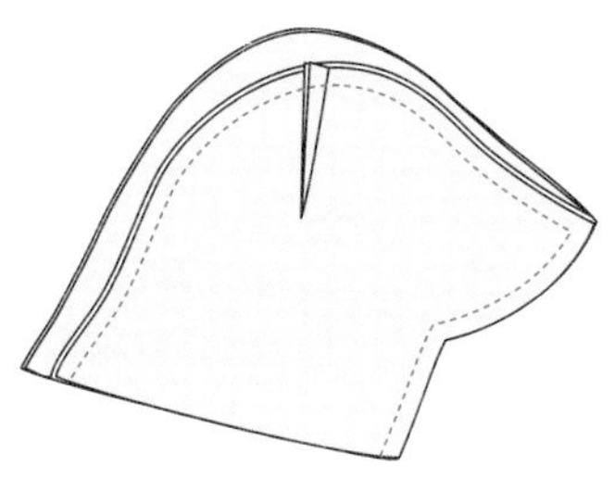

3 SEW AND ATTACH EARS

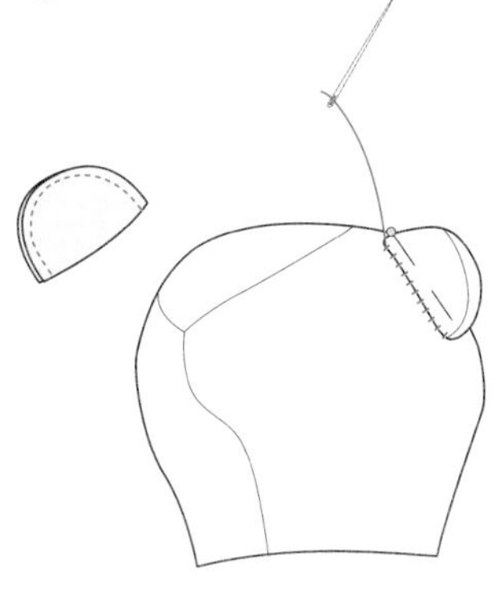

4 SEW BODY FRONT TO BODY BACK

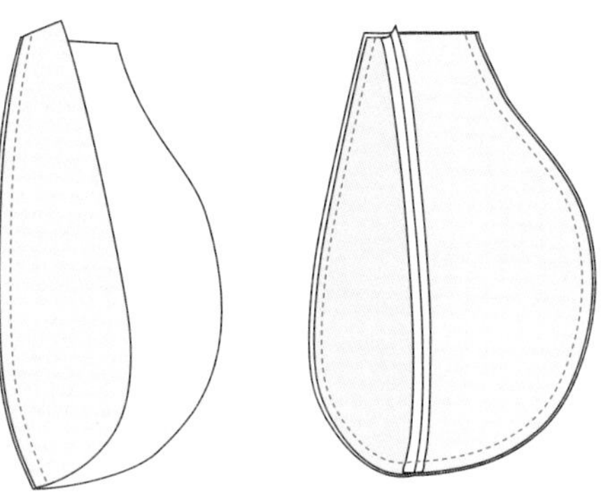

5 SEW HEAD TO BODY

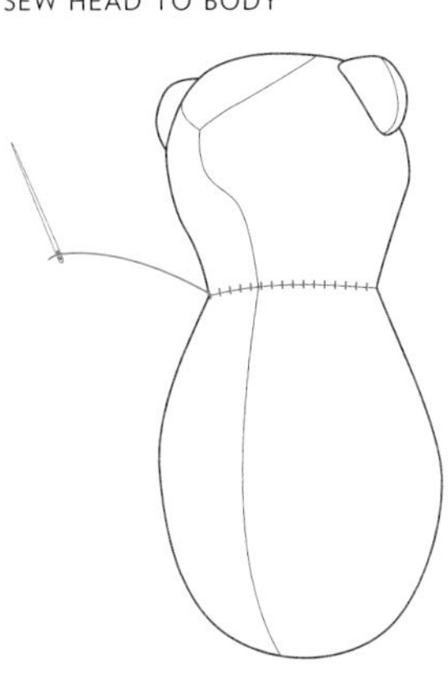

6 SEW LEGS AND FEET

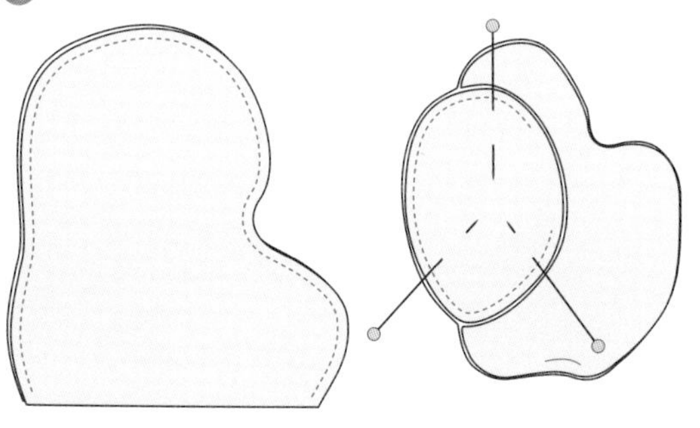

7 SEW ARMS

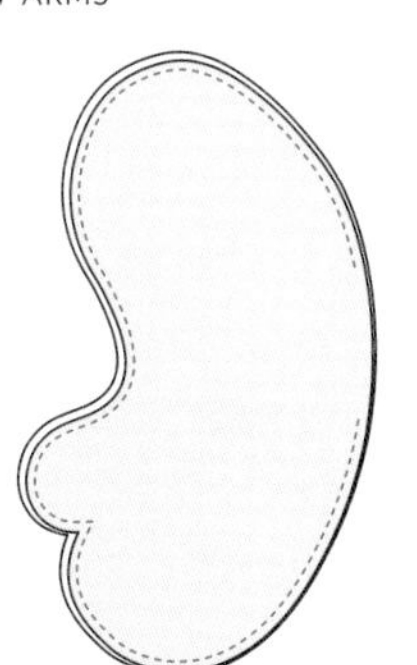

8 ATTACH LIMBS TO BODY

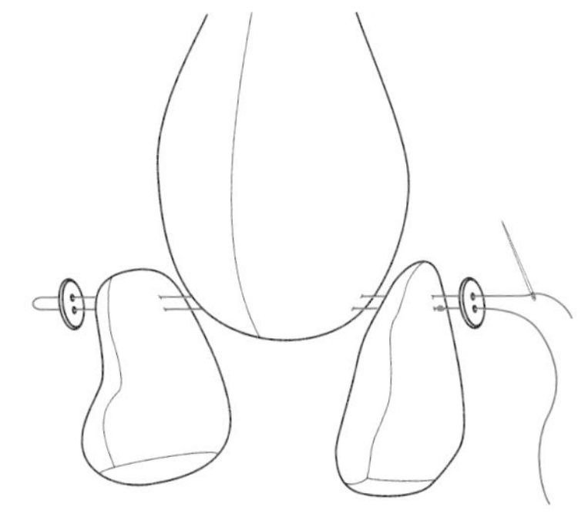

9 STITCH FACE AND ATTACH TAIL TO BODY

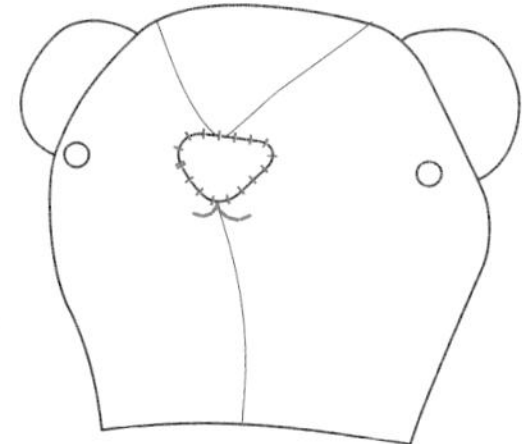

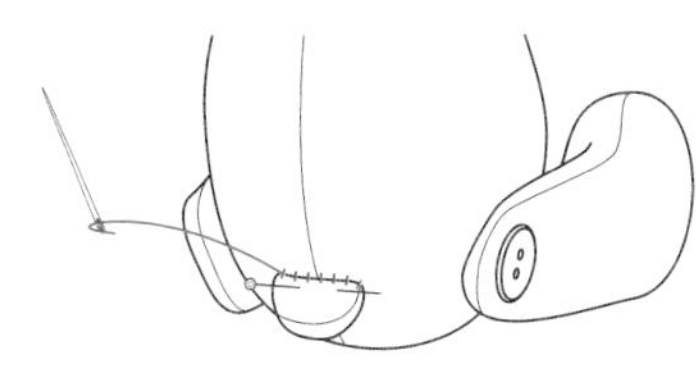

Little Miss Storybook

Once upon a time I sat staring into my supply closet trying to think of a new and exciting way to create doll hair. When I closed in on a spool of gold grosgrain ribbon, I immediately thought of Goldilocks. The cape for my new girl, shown on page 93, was inspired by Little Red Riding Hood. The result is a new heroine with all sorts of storytelling potential.

FINISHED SIZE

15″ tall

PATTERN PIECES (see pages 160–162)

Body (A); Dress (B); Cheek (C); Eye (D); Bottom (E); Arm (F); Leg (G); Foot (H); Three Bears Appliqué (I); Little Red Riding Hood Appliqué (J); Cape (K); Hood (L)

MATERIALS

16″ x 16″ (1/4 yd. or fat quarter) solid-color cotton or cotton flannel for body
14″ x 16″ (1/4 yd. or fat quarter) cotton print for dress
6″ x 10″ scrap of cotton print for legs
8″ x 8″ scrap of cotton print for feet
16″ x 24″ (1/2 yd.) cotton print for cape
7″ x 8″ scrap of cotton print for apron
4″ x 6″ scrap of wool felt for trees
2″ x 4″ scrap of wool felt for wolf
4″ x 6″ scrap of wool felt for bears
Scraps of wool felt for eyes and cheeks
1 spool of 5/8″-wide grosgrain ribbon for hair
26″ length of 1/2″-wide ribbon for apron
9″ length of different 1/2″-wide ribbon or trim for neckline
Package of 1/4″-wide bias tape for cape's trim
Button for cape
Matching and coordinating thread
Embroidery floss
Stuffing

STITCHES USED (see pages 125–128)

Edgestitch, whipstitch, backstitch, ladder stitch, gathering stitch, tacking stitch, zigzag stitch.

NOTES

In cutting dimensions, the rectangle's width is always given first, followed by its height.

Unless otherwise noted, all seam allowances are 1/4″ and built into the patterns.

1. Cut Out Pattern Pieces

Cut out all the pattern pieces from the designated fabrics, cutting the number of pieces called for on each pattern piece and transferring the face template to the cut Body (A) and all the pattern markings to the cut pieces. Also cut two 7″ x 2 1/2″ pieces of dress fabric for the sleeves. For more information on cutting out patterns and transferring pattern markings, see pages 122–123.

2. Sew Body/Dress

Press the top edge of each Dress (B) piece 1/4″ to the wrong side. Lay one Body (A) piece right side up, and place one dress piece right side up on top of it, aligning the bottom and side edges. Edgestitch the dress's top folded edge to the body (see diagram). Repeat with the other dress and body pieces.

3. Sew Ribbon Hair

With the body pieces side by side and right side up, create the hair on the front and back of the head starting at the bottom and working up, cutting the ribbon to the approximate lengths needed as you work. Follow the placement diagram for positioning and pinning the ribbon on the front and back heads, overlapping each ribbon by 1⁄4″ as you work up to the top. Use matching thread to edgestitch each ribbon's bottom edge to the head. After attaching all the ribbons, flip the front and back body pieces over, and trim the ribbon ends flush with the head (see diagram).

4. Create Facial Features

Referring to the Basics section on transferring faces to fabric (see page 124) and using the diagram as a placement guide, hand-sew the eyes and cheeks in place with a whipstitch and two strands of floss. Using six strands of floss and a backstitch, embroider the eyelashes, nose, and mouth.

5. Make Pigtails

The pigtails are made by folding ribbon into "fans." Here's how: Start by cutting a 24″ length of ribbon. Fold the ribbon into four 3″-long loops. Holding the loops together at the bottom, fan the loops out until they're about 3″ wide across the top. Sew the fan loops in place by stitching across the bottom as close to the edge as possible, catching all four loops (see diagram). Repeat the process to make a second fan.

With the front body right side up, pin one fan on each side of the head, using the diagram as a placement guide. Sew the fans in place 1⁄8″ from the head's edge, making sure to position the new stitching lines beyond the old stitching lines to prevent them from showing on the finished doll.

6. Construct Body

With right sides together and the top edges of the dress front and back aligned, sew the front and back body together. Clip the curves (see page 125) at the neck and turn the body right side out. Inspect your ponytail loops to make sure they're caught in the seams and the stitching doesn't show.

With right sides together, pin the Bottom (E) to the dress, matching up the transferred marked dot on the bottom to the center of dress front's hem edge (see diagram). Starting at the hem's center-front point, sew the bottom to the body, turning the body as you stitch around the curved edge and sewing about 1″ past the side seam. Backstitch, cut your thread, and go back to the center point. Stitch from the center point in the opposite direction, again sewing about 1″ past the other side seam and backstitching. Stuff the body firmly (see page 121) and then hand-sew the opening closed with a ladder stitch, tucking in the opening's edges as you sew.

7. Make and Attach Arms

With right sides together and the edges aligned, sew two Arm (F) pieces together, leaving the top edge open. Clip the seam between the thumb and fingers, turn the arm right side out, and stuff it firmly. Tuck in the open top edge 1⁄4″ to the wrong side and hand-sew the arm shut with a whipstitch. Repeat for the other arm. Then pin the stuffed arms to the body, using the diagram as a placement guide, and ladder stitch them in place, repeating the stitches until each arm is securely attached.

8. Make and Attach Sleeves

Fold one of the two 7″ x 2½″ pieces of dress fabric you cut for the sleeves with right sides together, sew the short ends together, and press the seam allowances open. Fold and press the sleeve's top and bottom edges 1⁄4″ to the wrong side. Hand-sew a gathering stitch around the folded top edge.

Place the sleeve over one of the arms and pull the gathers taut, so they are snug to the top of the arm. Pin the top of the sleeve in place, and knot off the gathering thread. Ladder stitch the sleeve's top edge to the body (see diagram). Hand-sew a gathering stitch around the sleeve's bottom edge. Pull the gathers taut against the arm (see diagram), and knot off the thread. Repeat this step for the other sleeve. To finish off the dress, wrap the 9″-long piece of ribbon or trim around the neckline, and sew it in place at the back neck with a few tacking stitches.

9. Make and Attach Legs

With right sides together and the adjoining edges aligned, sew the straight edge of one Foot (H) to one Leg (G) and press the seam allowances toward the foot. Repeat with a second foot and leg. Then, with right sides together, sew the pair of joined foot/leg pieces together, leaving the top edge open. Turn the leg right side out and stuff it firmly. Fold open each leg so that what was the side seam now faces front, tuck in the leg's open top edge 1⁄4″ to the wrong side, and hand-sew the leg shut with a whipstitch. Repeat the entire process for the other leg. Then pin the legs to the bottom, centering them front to back and side to side and ladder stitch them in place, repeating the stitches until each leg is securely attached (see diagram).

RIGHT SIDE | WRONG SIDE

2 SEW TOGETHER BODY AND DRESS

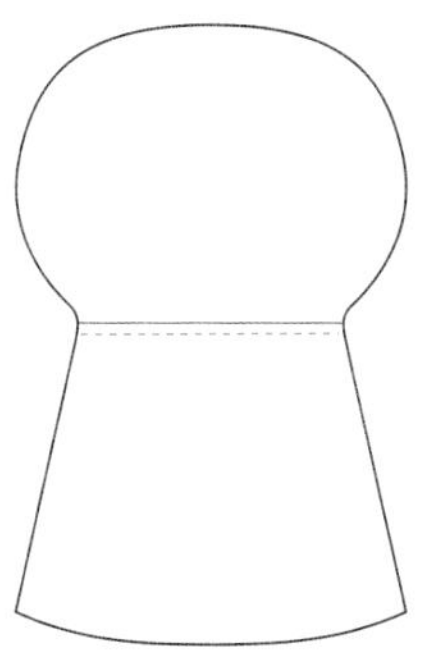

3 SEW RIBBON HAIR ONTO BODY

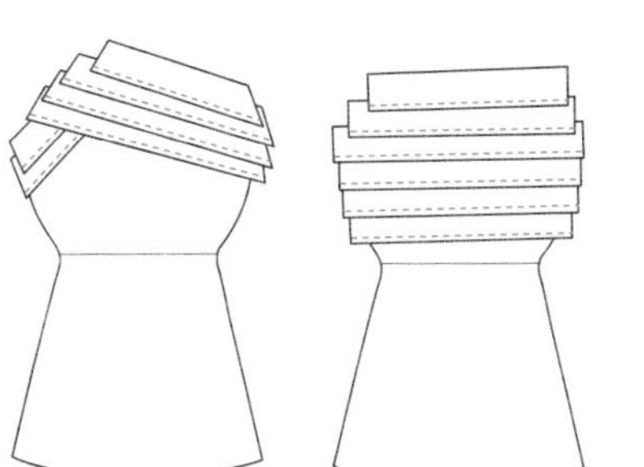

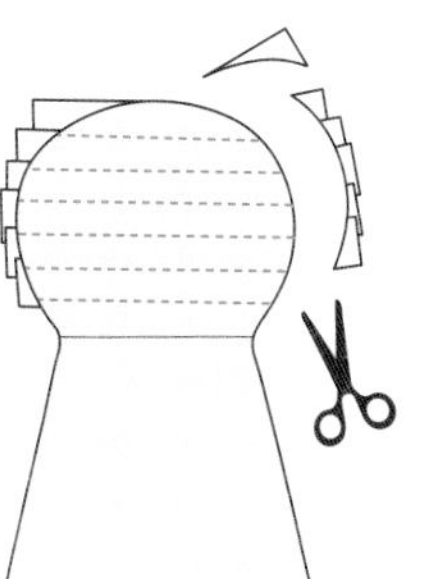

4 CREATE FACIAL FEATURES

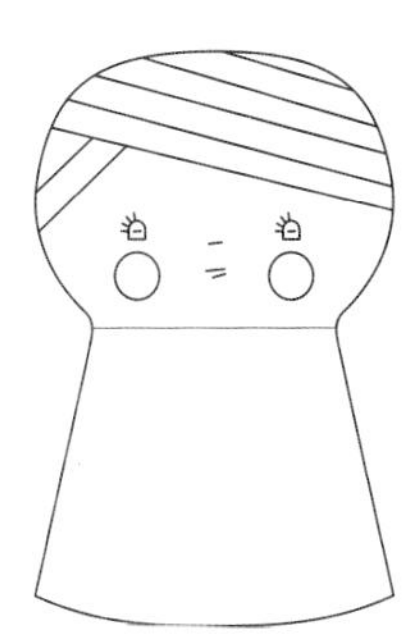

5 MAKE PIGTAILS

6 SEW BOTTOM TO BODY

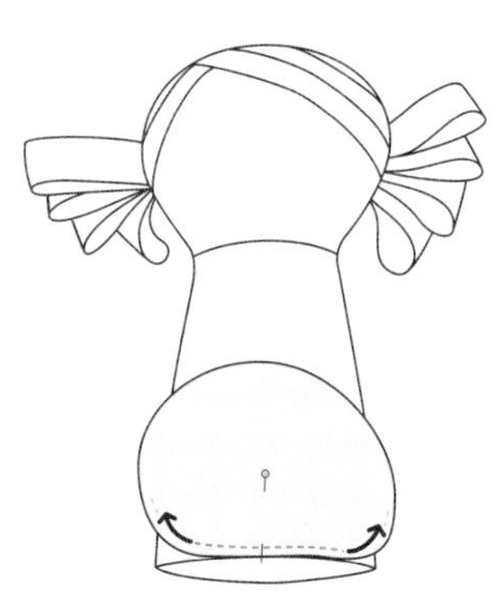

7 MAKE ARMS AND ATTACH TO BODY

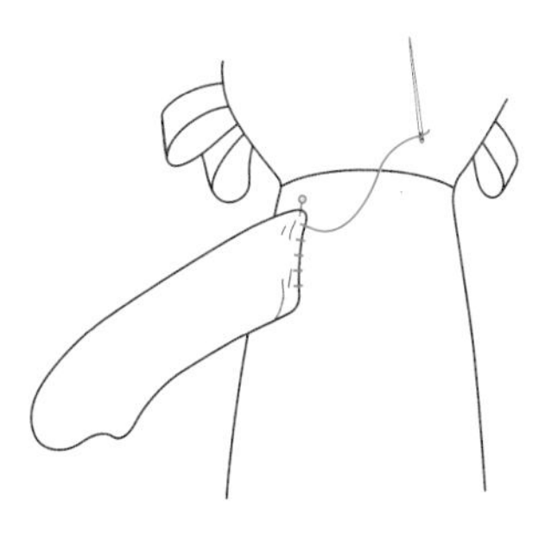

8 MAKE SLEEVES AND ATTACH TO DRESS

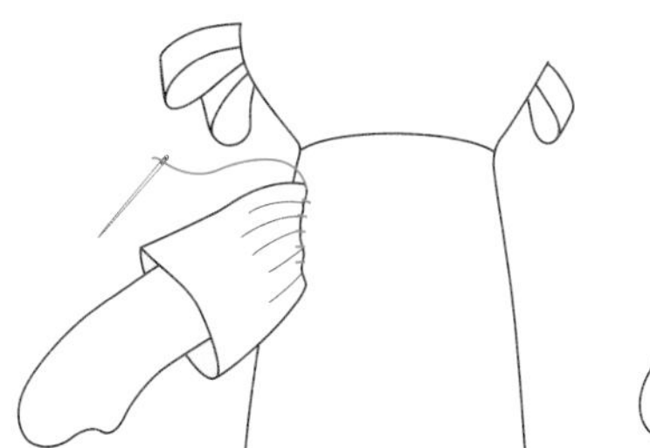

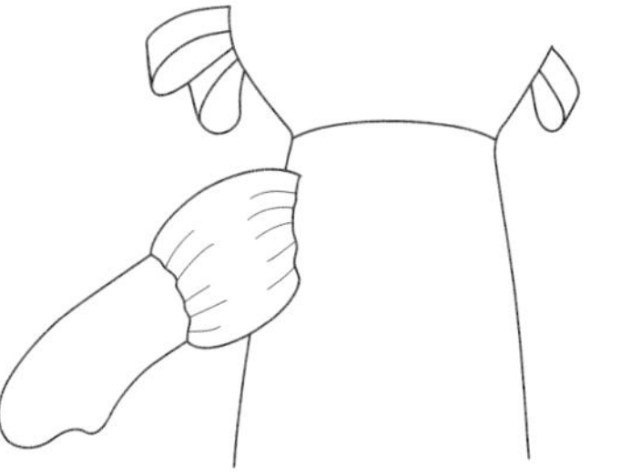

9 MAKE LEGS AND ATTACH TO BODY

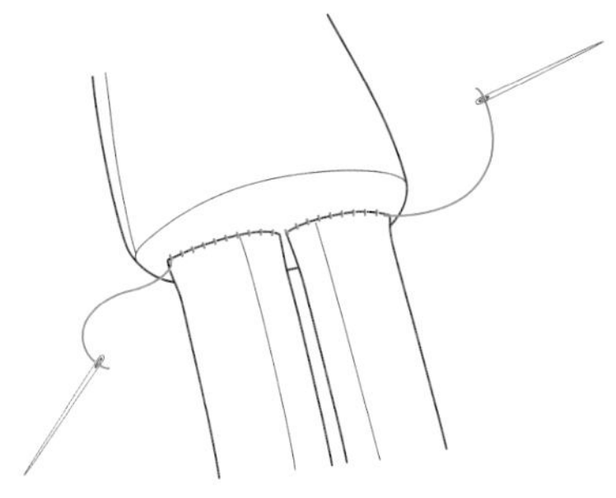

RIGHT SIDE

WRONG SIDE

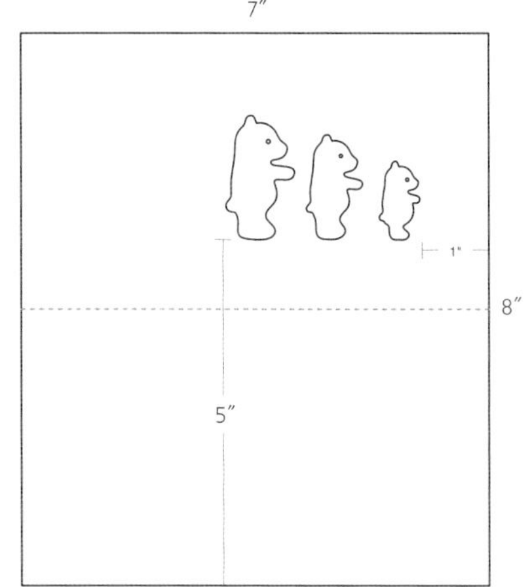

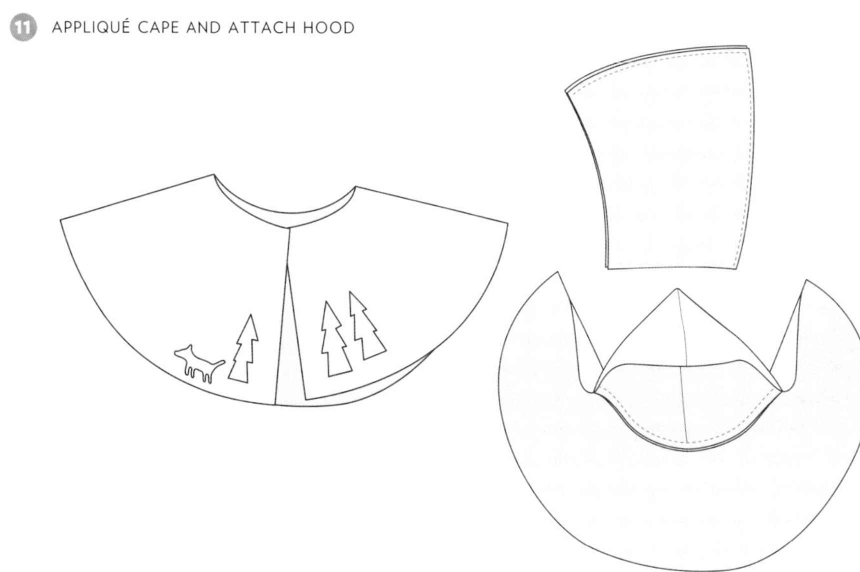

10. Appliqué and Sew Apron

Pin the Three Bears Appliqué (I) pieces to the 7″ x 8″ apron fabric, using the diagram as placement guide. Hand-sew the bears in place with a whipstitch and three strands of floss.

With right sides together, fold the apron fabric in half widthwise and sew the sides together. Turn the apron right side out, tuck in the top edge 1⁄4″ to the wrong side, and press the apron flat. Sew a gathering stitch across the top edge and pull the gathers so that the top measures 4″ across. Center and sew the 26″ length of ribbon across the apron's top edge and tie the ends around the waist.

11. Appliqué and Sew Cape

Pin the Little Red Riding Hood Appliqué (J) pieces to the Cape (K), using the diagram as a placement guide. Hand-sew the appliqués in place with a whipstitch and three strands of floss.

With right sides together and the edges aligned, sew the Hood (L) pieces together along the top and back (see diagram) and clip the top corner. With right sides together, pin the hood's bottom edge to the cape's neck edge and sew the two together (see diagram). Enclose the outside edge of the cape and hood with 1⁄4″ bias tape, sewing the tape in place with a zigzag stitch and starting at the back of the cape. Sew a button on one side at neck and make a loop from the bias tape—large enough for little fingers to easily maneuver—and machine-sew it in place on the other side of the neck.

Doxie Necklace

Just like a real-life dachshund, Doxie is small in size but big on attitude. Slightly puffed, tied off with a rickrack leash, and completely hand-sewn, this heartwarming accessory is just the right type of bling for the young girls in your life. Doxie can be finished in just one night; and, trust me, the handwork is very satisfying (and easier than fussing with those tiny corners on the machine). Be prepared though—as soon as the little girls in your life see Doxie's floppy ears and wagging tail—they'll all be begging for one of their own.

FINISHED SIZE

Doxie: 3½″ long

PATTERN PIECES (see page 162)

Body (A); Ear (B)

MATERIALS

6″ x 8″ scrap of cotton print for body
30″ length of ¼″-wide baby rickrack
Matching and coordinating thread
Embroidery floss
Stuffing

STITCHES USED (see pages 125–128)

Backstitch, ladder stitch, whipstitch, French knot, tacking stitch.

NOTE

Unless otherwise noted, all seam allowances are ¼″ and built into the patterns.

1. Sew Body and Ears

With right sides together, fold the 6″ x 8″ scrap of fabric in half, matching up the short sides to get a 6″ x 4″ piece. Trace the Body (A) and then trace the Ear (B) twice on the fabric (see diagram). Hand-sew along the traced lines with a small backstitch, leaving the top edges on the ears open and also leaving a ¾″ opening on the body's bottom edge for turning and stuffing (see diagram). Trim the seam allowance to ⅛″ and clip the curves (see page 125). Turn the ears right side out and finger-press the open top edges ⅛″ to the wrong side.

2. Stuff Body

Carefully turn Doxie right side out, using a pin to help fully turn out the small parts. Stuff the body (see page 121) lightly and evenly, using a stuffing fork or small knitting needle to gently push stuffing into the legs and tail. Be careful not to push through the hand-sewn seams as you stuff and also not to overstuff the body—aim for slightly puffy. Hand-sew the opening closed with a ladder stitch, tucking in the opening's edges as you sew.

RIGHT SIDE

WRONG SIDE

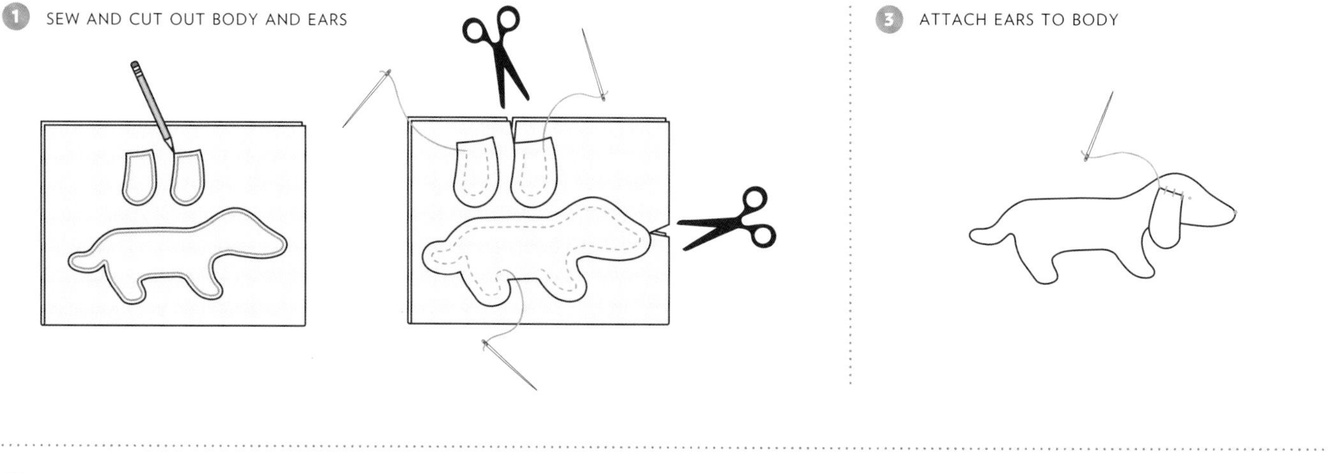

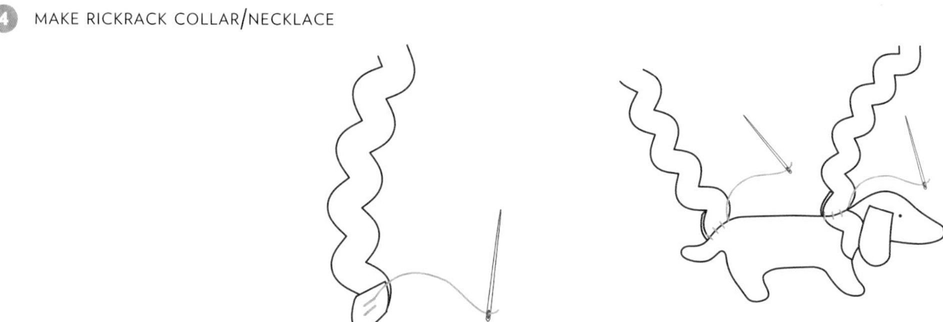

3. Attach Ears

Pin the ears to the body, using the diagram as a placement guide, and hand-sew the ears in place with a whipstitch.

4. Finishing

Using the diagram as a placement guide, hand-sew French-knot eyes on each side of Doxie's head and a French-knot nose, burying the thread tails (see page 128). Wrap a piece of rickrack around the neck for a collar and hand-sew it in place with a tacking stitch. Cut the remaining rickrack into two equal lengths, finger-press under $1/4''$ at the end of each length, and hand-sew each folded end in place with a few tacking stitches (see diagram). Then hand-sew one folded edge of rickrack to Doxie's collar and the other to Doxie's rear, using the diagram as a placement guide.

Patchwork Penny

Matchy-matchy is a "do," not a "don't," when it comes to pairing up this bubbly moppet with her very own customized quilt. With her soft yarn braids and kickin' it go-go boots, bright-eyed Penny is a mix of homespun charm and willful adventure—Holly Hobbie meets Gidget. And for a girl like that, a quilt will come in very handy—you never know when she'll want to set up an impromptu picnic or need a makeshift tent. Keep Penny's quilt modern and striking by choosing a solid background that really lets the prints shine. The little girl in your life will surely love to help you pick out the fabrics.

FINISHED SIZE

Doll: 18″ tall; Quilt: 14″ x 24″

PATTERN PIECES (see page 163)

Head (A); Body/Dress (B); Arm (C); Leg (D); Boot (E); Eye (F)

MATERIALS

10″ x 25″ (1/4 yd.) cotton or flannel for body
8″ x 16″ (1/4 yd. or fat quarter) velvet or velour for boots
26″ x 18″ (1/2 yd.) solid-color cotton for dress/quilt background
Ten 10″ x 2″ strips in different cotton prints for patchwork
24″ x 14″ (1/2 yd.) cotton print for quilt backing
24″ x 14″ (1/2 yd.) quilt batting
1 package of 7/8″-wide single-fold bias tape or 80″ of handmade 1/2″-wide binding
Scraps of wool felt for eyes
Matching and coordinating thread
Embroidery floss
1 skein Lamb's Pride Worsted yarn
Tracing paper
Stuffing

STITCHES USED (see pages 125–128)

Ladder stitch, edgestitch, whipstitch, backstitch, tacking stitch.

NOTES

In cutting dimensions, unless otherwise noted, the rectangle's width is always given first, followed by its height.

Unless otherwise noted, all seam allowances are 1/4″ and built into the patterns.

1. Cut Out Pattern Pieces

Cut out all the pattern pieces from the designated fabrics, cutting the number of pieces called for on each pattern piece and transferring the face template to the cut Head (A). In addition, cut from the quilt background fabric a 6″ x 15″ rectangle and a 12″ x 15″ rectangle. For more information on cutting out patterns and transferring pattern markings, see pages 122–123.

2. Make Patchwork Fabric

Arrange the ten 10″ x 2″ strips for the patchwork in an order you like. Align and sew the strips together along their long edges, and press the seam allowances open. Cut the patchwork lengthwise, as shown in the diagram, into a 6 1/2″ section for the quilt and a 3 1/2″ section for the dress front.

3. Piece Quilt Top

With right sides together and the edges aligned, sew the 6″ x 15″ and 12″ x 15″ pieces of solid-color cotton to each side of the 6 1/2″ patchwork rectangle (see diagram).

4. Make Quilt Sandwich and Quilt

Assemble your quilt sandwich by layering the quilt backing fabric right side down, the batting, and finally the quilt top, right side up. Pin the three layers together with safety pins (eight or fewer should do the trick) to prevent them from shifting during quilting (see diagram).

Prepare to free-motion quilt your sandwich by dropping the feed dogs on your sewing machine and replacing your regular presser foot with a darning foot if you have one (if not, any foot with a wide opening will work well). Starting at an edge of the quilt sandwich and holding the fabric steady with your hands on either side of the needle, guide the fabric under the needle in a stippling, or curving, pattern across the quilt top, trying to avoid stitching over any of your stippling lines. Cover the quilt top in this swirling design, trying to end by running your stitching off an edge (see diagram). If you get stuck in the middle with nowhere to go, just backstitch, cut your thread, and start again at the edge. Don't worry about the quilting being perfect. When you're finished, it will look dimpled and terrific.

5. Sew on Quilt Binding

Unfold one edge of the bias tape so that it's flat and, beginning in the middle of one of the quilt's sides, align and pin the bias tape's unfolded edge along the quilt's edge (see diagram). Machine-sew the binding to the quilt ¼″ from the edge, stopping ¼″ before you reach the corner. Cut your thread and take the quilt out of the machine. Turn the quilt; fold the bias tape into a mitered corner, as shown; and, starting ¼″ in from the corner, start sewing the tape to the new side. Continue as above for each of the remaining sides, sewing back to the starting point for attaching the tape, and leave 1″ extra tape loose at the end for finishing.

Now the flip quilt over, fold the binding over the edge of the quilt sandwich, and hand-sew the bias tape's folded edge to the back of the quilt with a ladder stitch. Miter the corners as you sew. To miter a corner, stop sewing the binding or trim ¼″ from the corner. Take the project out from under the needle and fold down first one side of the trim or binding diagonally at the corner, then the second side diagonally over the first and pin the folded mitered corner in place. Put the project back under the needle, and begin sewing where you left off, taking a stitch or two towards the corner and then stopping, with the needle down (and removing the pin at the corner), raising the presser foot, and pivoting the work to position it to sew the new side. Lower the presser foot, sew down the new side to the next corner, and repeat the process above. At the end of the tape, fold under ½″ of the 1″ loose, leftover tape. Ladder stitch the folded end in place over the tape's beginning end.

6. Attach Patchwork Strip to Dress

Press both long edges on the 3½″ patchwork strip ½″ to the wrong side. Pin the patchwork strip right side up on the front of the Body/Dress (B), positioning the strip so that the patchwork section you like best shows on the dress. Edgestitch the strip in place on both long sides. Trim the patchwork along the top and bottom edges of the dress (see diagram).

7. Attach Head and Embroider Facial Features

With right sides together, align the bottom of the Head (A) with the top edge of the body/dress front, sew the two pieces together, and press the seam allowances together towards the head (see diagram). Repeat for the back head and body/dress back.

Referring to the Basics section on transferring faces to fabric (see page 124) and using the diagram as a placement guide, hand-sew the Eye (F) pieces in place with two strands of floss and a whipstitch. Using the same diagram as a guide, three strands of floss, and a backstitch, embroider eyelashes, eyebrows, a nose, and dashes through the center of the eyes. Embroider a mouth with six strands of floss and a backstitch.

8. Sew and Attach Arms

With right sides together and the edges aligned, sew two Arm (C) pieces together, leaving the top angled edge open for turning and stuffing. Turn the arm right side out, and stuff it (see page 121) so that the stuffing is firm in the hand, thins toward the top of the arm, and has no stuffing at the top, which will make it easier to sew the arm to the body. Edgestitch the arm's open top edge shut. Repeat for the other arm.

Pin the stuffed arms to the right side of the front of the body/dress 1¼″ beneath the neck, using the diagram as a placement guide, with the top edge of each arm overlapping the body's edge by about ¼″. Edgestitch the arms to the body.

9. Sew Body

With right sides together and the edges aligned, sew the front and back of the body together, leaving a 4″ opening at the bottom for turning and stuffing (see diagram). Clip the corners and notch the curves at the neck (see page 125). Turn the body right side out and stuff it so that it's full but not firm. Hand-sew the opening closed with a ladder stitch.

RIGHT SIDE

WRONG SIDE

2. MAKE PATCHWORK FABRIC FOR DRESS FRONT AND QUILT TOP

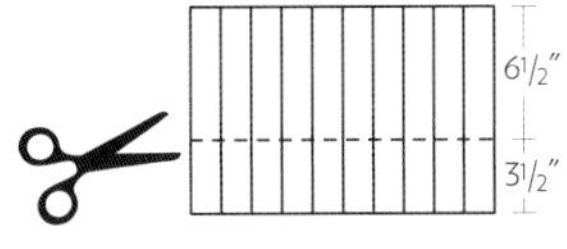

3. PIECE QUILT TOP

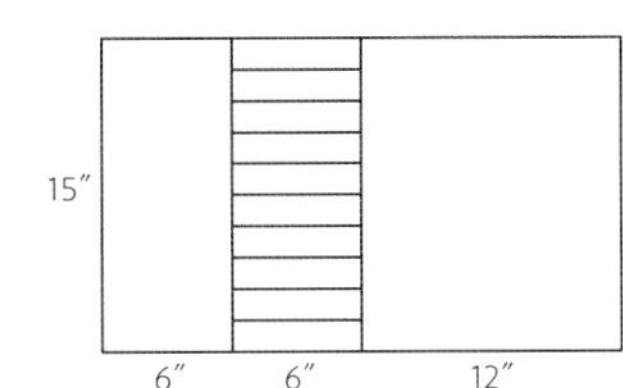

4. MAKE QUILT SANDWICH AND QUILT

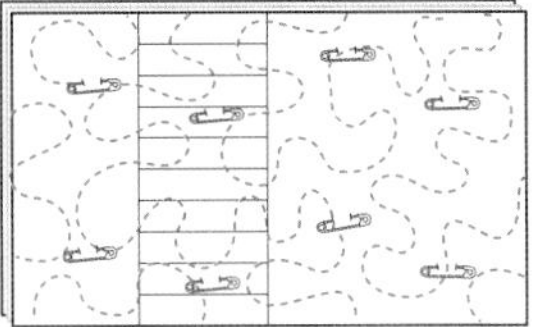

5. SEW ON QUILT BINDING

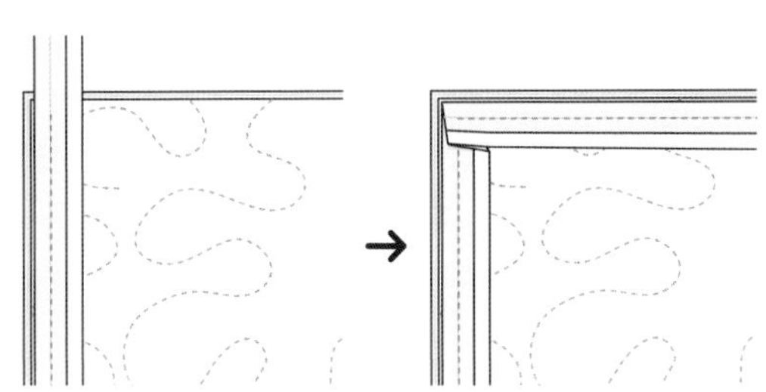

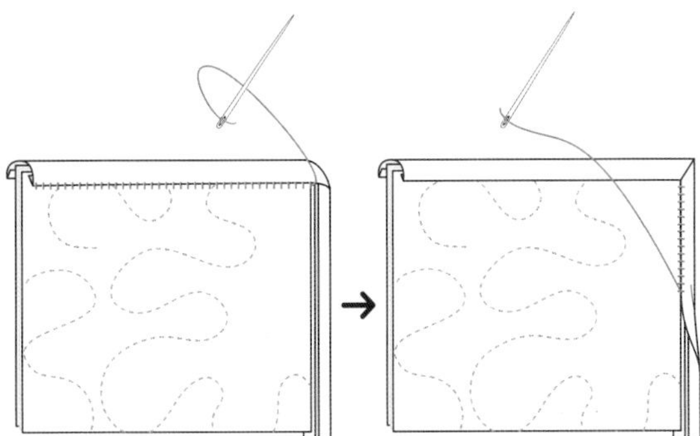

6. ATTACH PATCHWORK STRIP TO DRESS

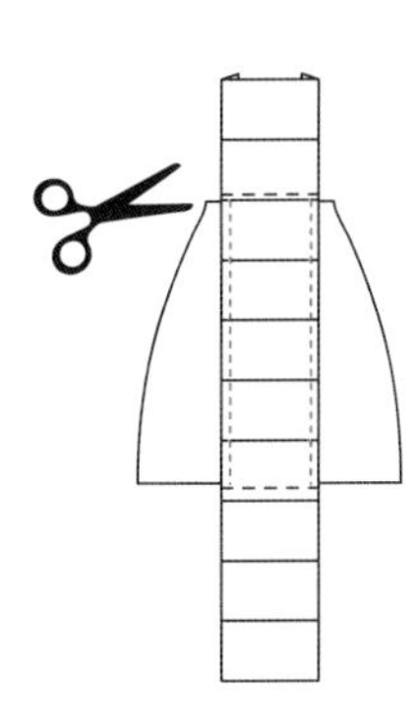

7. ATTACH HEAD TO DRESS AND EMBROIDER FACIAL FEATURES

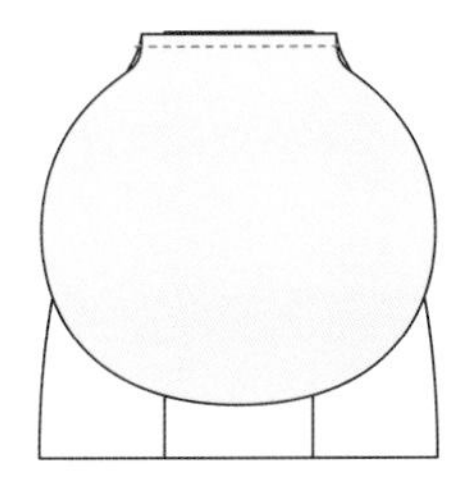

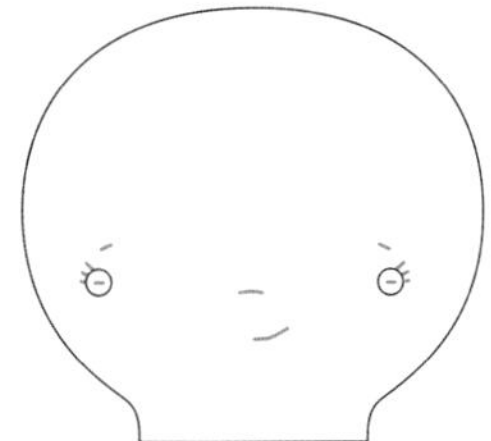

8. SEW AND ATTACH ARMS TO BODY/DRESS

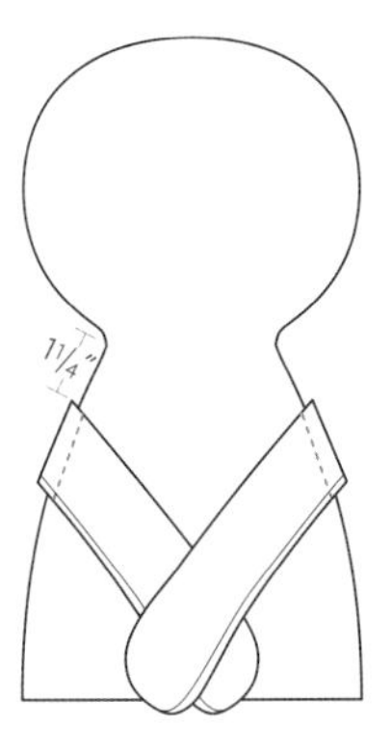

9. SEW FRONT AND BACK OF BODY TOGETHER

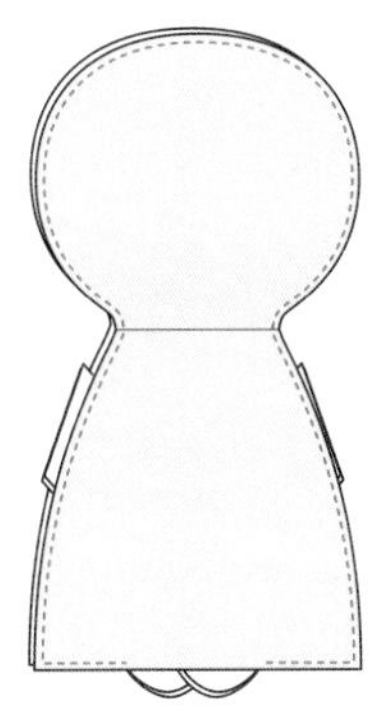

10 SEW LEGS AND ATTACH TO BODY

11 MAKE WIG FOR HAIR

RIGHT SIDE | WRONG SIDE

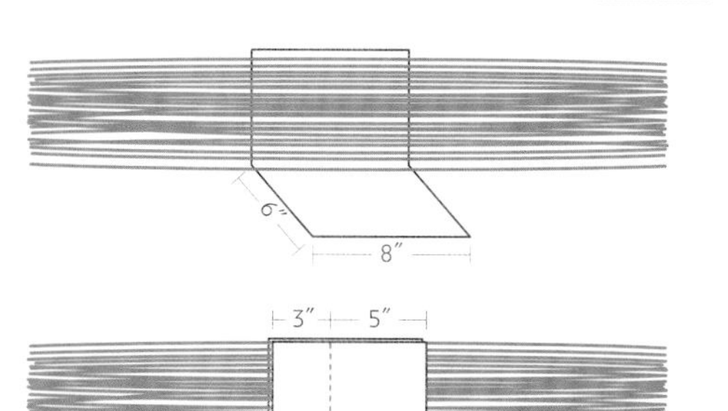

12 ATTACH HAIR TO HEAD AND BRAID

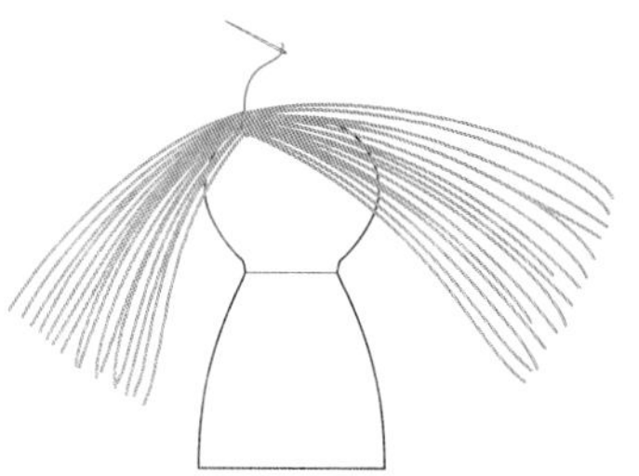

10. Sew Legs and Attach to Body

With right sides together and the edges aligned, sew one Leg (D) piece to each Boot (E) piece (see diagram) and press the seam allowances together toward the boots. With right sides together and the seams and edges aligned, pin one leg/boot front and back together and sew the pair together, leaving the top edge open for turning and stuffing. Repeat for other leg.

Turn the legs right side out and stuff them firmly in the feet and thin the stuffing toward the top of the leg. Fold open the top of each leg so that what was the side seam now faces front, fold the open top edge 1/4" to the wrong side and hand-sew the leg shut with a whipstitch. Pin the legs to the bottom of the body and hand-sew them in place with a ladder stitch, repeating the stitches until the legs are securely attached (see diagram).

11. Make Wig for Hair

Hold one end of the yarn in one hand, and wrap the yarn around your elbow and back through your hand 50 times (your arm length will determine your loop length, which will probably be from 30"-40", which is fine). After wrapping the 50 loops, cut through the ends of the loops to open them, lay the bundle flat, and set it aside. Repeat the wrapping process to make a second set of 50 loops, cut them open, and lay the bundle flat.

Fold a 12" x 8" piece of tracing paper in half lengthwise. Center both yarn bundles inside the 6" x 8" tracing-paper sleeve, making sure the yarn is as flat and evenly spread as possible (see diagram). Draw a line 5" from the paper's edge to indicate the hair's side part and machine-sew along this line, pressing the yarn flat as you sew to prevent it from catching or shifting during sewing (see diagram). Tear away the tracing paper from what's now your doll's hair.

12. Attach Hair to Head

Pin and then hand-sew the hair to the stuffed head along the side part using a matching thread color, repeating the stitches until the hair is securely attached (see diagram). Separate the hair on each side into three equal sections, and braid each side, pulling the hair down and forward a bit as you braid and making the braids as long as you like. Tie off each braid with a short length of yarn and trim its edges (see diagram). Secure the hair to the head along the side of the face by hand-sewing a few tacking stitches in a matching thread color. To further secure hair, tack stitch throughout the hair, spreading it as you do to make sure it is lies flat and has no gaps.

Bonneted Baby

The inspiration for this pillow-doll was an illustration of a Shaker girl in a book by two of my favorite children's book artists, Alice and Martin Provensen. I made her up in soft, warm wool in pastel pink, but she would look equally sweet in darker colors or even brights. She is stuffed softly, so babies can get ahold of her and give her a proper hug.

FINISHED SIZE

7″ tall

PATTERN PIECES (see page 164)

Body (A); Arm (B); Hand (C); Collar (D); Face (E); Hair (F); Bonnet Bottom (G); Bonnet Top (H)

MATERIALS

8″ x 10″ scrap of wool felt for dress
6″ x 6″ scrap of wool felt for body
2″ x 4″ scrap of wool felt for hair
9″ x 9″ scrap of wool felt for bonnet
10″ x 13″ (1⁄4 yd. or fat quarter) wool felt or flannel for backing
Matching and coordinating thread
Embroidery floss
Stuffing

STITCHES USED (see pages 125–128)

Edgestitch, backstitch, ladder stitch.

NOTE

Unless otherwise noted, all seam allowances are 1⁄4″ and built into the patterns.

1. Cut Out Pattern Pieces

Cut out all the pattern pieces for the designated fabrics, cutting the number of pieces called for on each pattern piece and transferring the face template to the cut Face (E). For more information on cutting out patterns and transferring the pattern markings, see pages 122–123.

2. Sew Hair and Features on Face

Place the Hair (F) on the Face (E), aligning the top edges. Edgestitch the hair's bottom curve to the head (see diagram). Referring to the Basics section on transferring faces to fabric (see page 124) and using the same diagram as a guide, embroider the eyes and mouth on the face with six strands of embroidery floss and a backstitch.

3. Prepare Body

Position and pin the two Collar (D) pieces and the two Arm (B) and Hand (C) pieces on the Body (A), following the diagram for placement and overlapping the pieces in this order: arms over hands and collar over arms. Edgestitch the hands, arms, and collar to the body. For more control as you edgestitch the tight curves on the hands, manually turn the wheel on your sewing machine.

RIGHT SIDE

WRONG SIDE

2 SEW HAIR TO FACE AND EMBROIDER FEATURES

3 SEW COLLARS, ARMS, AND HANDS TO BODY

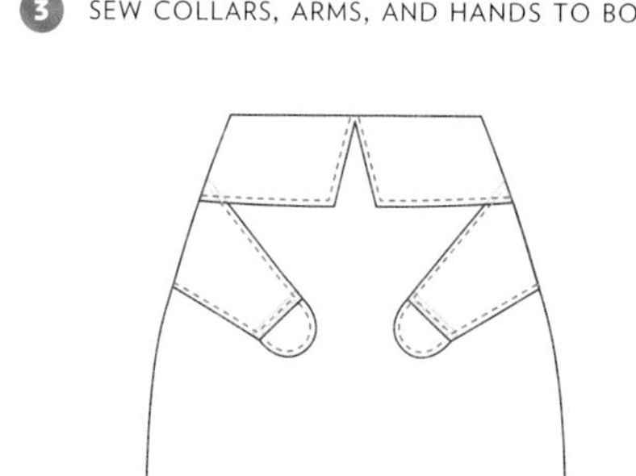

4 SEW BONNET

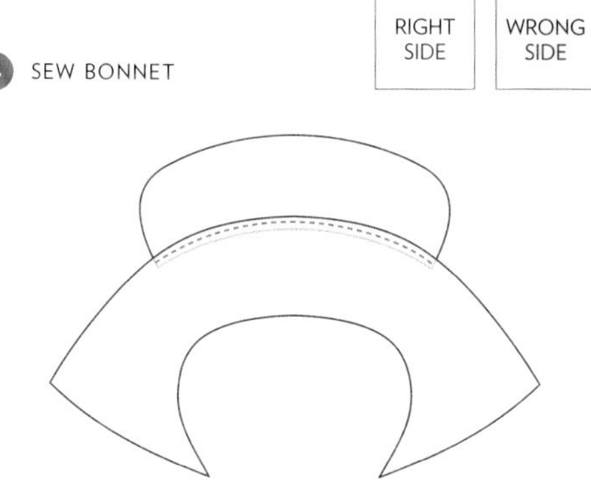

5 SEW HEAD TO BODY

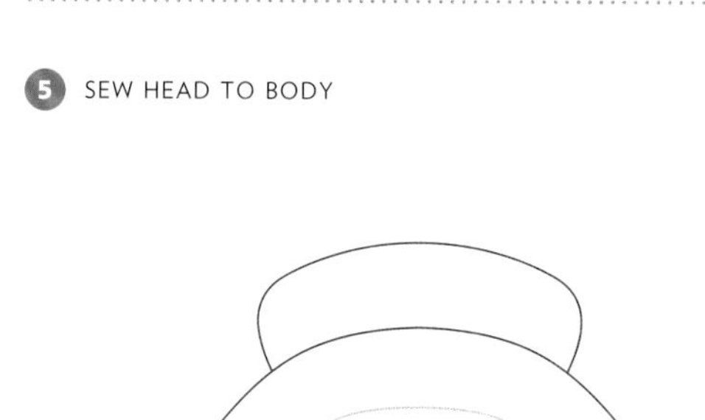

6 SEW DOLL AND BACKING TOGETHER

4. Sew Bonnet

Lay the Bonnet Bottom (G) over the Bonnet Top (H), with the bonnet bottom overlapping the bonnet top by about ½″ on the bottom edge. Edgestitch the overlapping edge in place (see diagram).

5. Putting It All Together

Pin the bonnet to the face, overlapping the top edge of the face by about ½″, and edgestitch the overlapped edge (see diagram). Pin the head to the body so that it overlaps the body by about ½″ and edgestitch the bottom edge of the face and bonnet (see diagram).

6. Sew Doll and Backing Together

Lay the backing fabric right side up and center the bonneted baby right side down on top of it. Sew the doll and backing fabric together, stitching around the doll's edges with a ¼″ seam and leaving a 3″ opening at the bottom for turning and stuffing (see diagram). Cut around the stitched doll, leaving ¼″ seam allowances. Clip the curves and corners (see page 125), turn the doll right side out, and finger-press the seams flat. Stuff (see page 121) the doll loosely so that's it's full but still soft and pliable enough for a baby to handle and hand-sew the opening closed with a ladder stitch, tucking in the opening's raw edges as you sew.

Haus Sweet Haus

This sweet cottage looks just as at home on a living room shelf as it does in the kids' room. Choose bias tape in solid colors to create more subdued half-timbering or go all out and use ribbon printed or woven with a pattern. For the side gusset, use a wide embroidered ribbon with a folk design. Vary house size and shape to make a whole village or use seasonal fabric to make charming holiday decorations.

FINISHED SIZE

11″ tall

MATERIALS

8″ x 8″ scrap of midweight cotton print for roof
2½″ x 4½″ scrap of midweight cotton print for door
8″ x 6″ scrap of midweight cotton print for house
8″ x 14″ (¼ yd. or fat quarter) midweight cotton print for backing
2 yds. of ½″-wide twill tape, trim, or ribbon
1 yd. of 1½″-wide ribbon
Matching and coordinating thread
Stuffing

STITCHES USED (see pages 125–128)

Zigzag stitch, edgestitch, ladder stitch.

NOTES

In cutting dimensions, the rectangle's width is always given first, followed by its height.

Unless otherwise noted, all seam allowances are ¼″ and built into the patterns.

1. Cut Roof

Cut the roof from the 8″ x 8″ roof fabric, as shown in the diagram.

2. Sew Door on House

Center the 2½″ x 4½″ door on the bottom edge of the 8″ x 6″ house, and edgestitch the door in place (see diagram).

3. Sew Trim on House

Using matching thread, a zigzag stitch, and the diagram as a guide, sew the trim on the house front in the numbered order shown so that the unfinished edges of the door are caught under the trim pieces.

4. Sew Trim on Roof

Using matching thread, a zigzag stitch, and the diagram as a guide, sew the trim on the roof front in the numbered order shown.

1. CUT ROOF

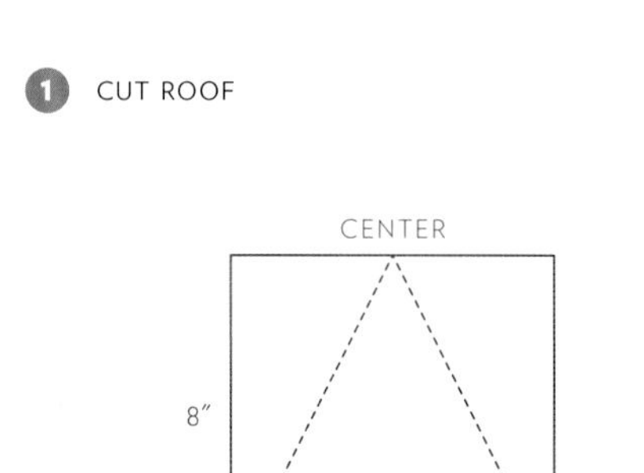

2. SEW DOOR ON HOUSE

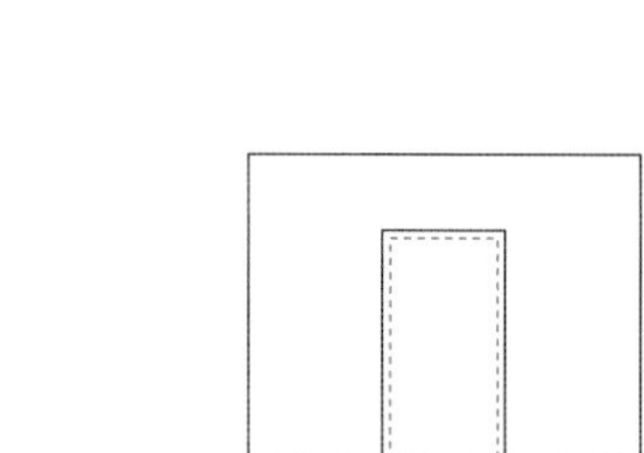

3. SEW TRIM ON HOUSE

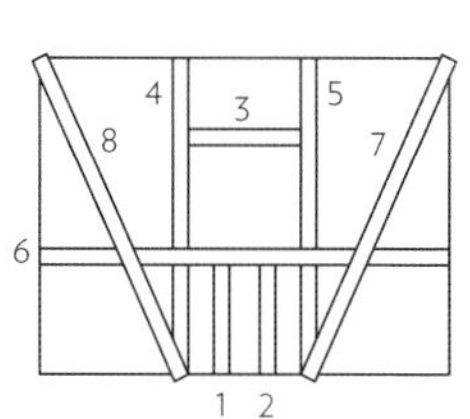

4. SEW TRIM ON ROOF

5. ASSEMBLE FRONT AND CUT BACKING

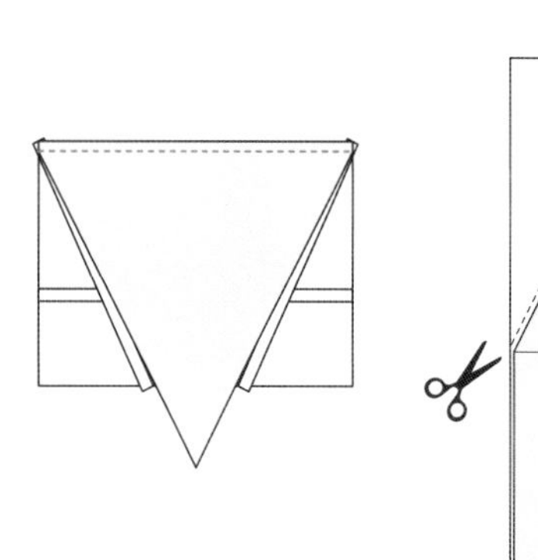

6. SEW RIBBON GUSSET TO FRONT

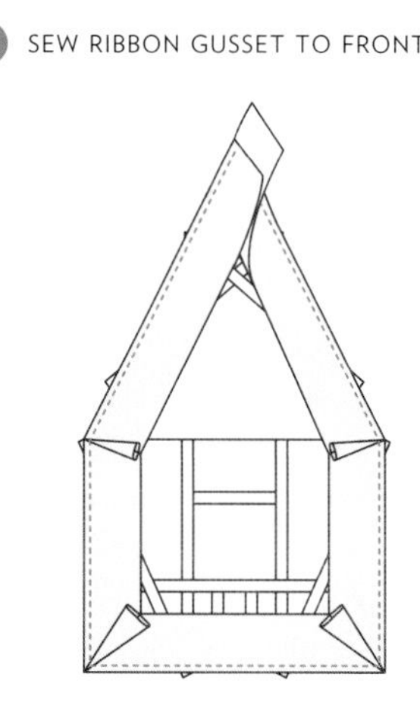

7. SEW RIBBON GUSSET TO BACKING

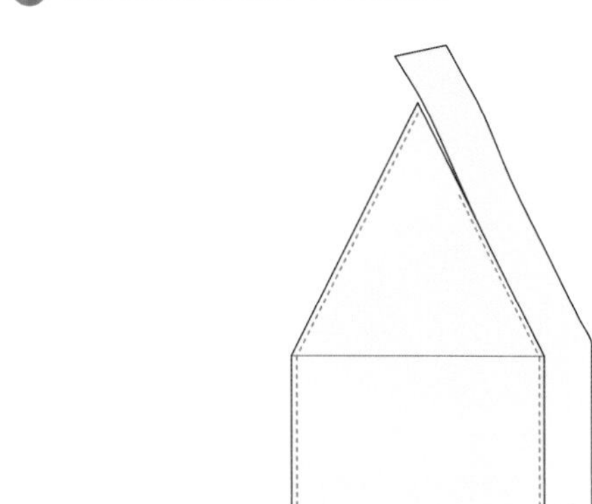

8. FOLD EXTRA RIBBON AND STITCH CLOSED

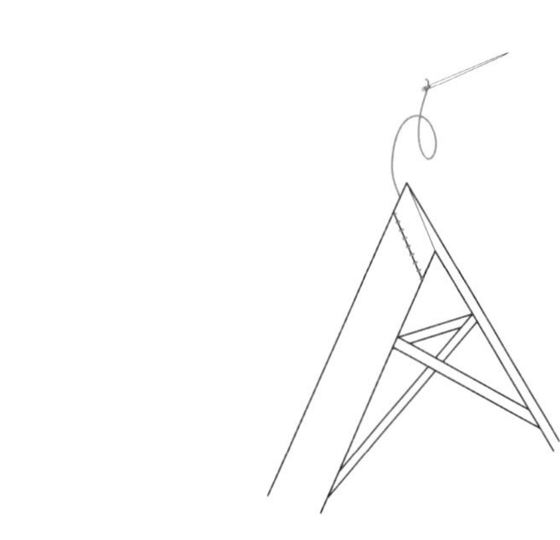

RIGHT SIDE

WRONG SIDE

5. Assemble Front and Cut Backing

With right sides together and the top of the house and bottom of the roof aligned, sew the house to the roof (see diagram) and press the seam allowances toward the house. Lay the house/roof right side down on the backing fabric and cut the backing fabric the same shape (see diagram).

6. Sew Ribbon Gusset to Front

With right sides together, align one edge of the ribbon with the roof's top point, and pin the ribbon's edge along the house's outside edge. Starting at the roof's top point, edgestitch the ribbon to the house along the outside edge (see diagram). Sew all way around the perimeter of the house and back up to the roof point, leaving 1″ of ribbon loose at the end.

7. Sew Ribbon Gusset to Backing

With right sides together, align the starting end of the ribbon's remaining edge with the backing's roof point (just as you did on the front side), and pin the ribbon in place around the backing's perimeter. As you pin the ribbon, be sure that the house front and backing remain aligned and don't shift. Edgestitch the ribbon in place, leaving a 3″ opening at the end for turning and stuffing (see diagram).

8. Stuff and Finish

Turn the house right side out and stuff it (see page 121) so that it's full but still rather flat; don't overstuff it. Hand-sew the opening closed with a ladder stitch, folding over the extra ribbon at the end and ladder stitching it down to the ribbon gusset (see diagram).

1½ cups he
1¼ cups
1 whole
6 lar
½ cu

Hansel and Gretel

When I discovered spoon puppets in a craft book from the 1970s, I wanted to make them right away. Such a fun idea! But they needed cool outfits. For Hansel and Gretel's bodies, I patchworked fabric outfits onto felt and then created interchangeable costumes that are poseable with pipe cleaner armature. After you stir up trouble with Hansel and Gretel, let your imagination run wild and create a whole cast of characters. These look wonderfully cute displayed in a cup or a vase and make great gifts for adults as well as kids.

FINISHED SIZE

12″ tall

PATTERN PIECES (see pages 165-166)

Hansel (A); Hansel's Hair Front (B); Hansel's Hair Back (C); Hansel's Hat (D); Hansel's Feather (E); Gretel (F); Gretel's Hair Front (G); Gretel's Hair Back (H)

MATERIALS

Two 12″-long wooden spoons
Four 7″ x 7″ scraps of wool felt for template and backing of outfits
Scraps of wool felt for hair and hat
Scraps of fabric for Hansel's and Gretel's outfits
10″ length of 1⁄4″-wide baby rickrack
Matching and coordinating thread
Two 9″-long pipe cleaners
Acrylic paint
Small paintbrush
Craft glue (optional)

STITCHES USED (see pages 125–128)

Edgestitch, tacking stitch.

NOTES

In cutting dimensions, the rectangle's width is always given first, followed by its height.

Unless otherwise noted, all seam allowances are 1⁄4″ and built into the patterns.

HANSEL

To make Hansel, you'll first create the front of the puppet by patchworking the fabrics onto the felt template of Hansel that you'll cut out. Next you'll make his hair and hat. Then you'll jump down to the finishing steps (at the end of Gretel's directions) to join Hansel's front and back, insert the pipe-cleaner arms, and finish assembling the puppet.

1. Cut Out Template and Sew Shoes

Cut the Hansel (A) template from wool felt, and cut a 4″ x 1½″ piece from one of your fabric scraps for the shoes. Using the diagram as a guide for placing the fabric and stitches, lay the fabric right side down and the template on top and machine-sew the template to the fabric (note that you're stitching on the back of the puppet), making sure that your bobbin thread is the stitch color you want to see on the fabric's right side. (You can choose to use a coordinating color of bobbin thread to make the entire puppet or change bobbin-thread colors to match each new fabric you add. Either way, your final puppet will look terrific!) Trim the fabric to the template's edge.

2. Sew Pants, Undershirt, and Shirt

Using your scraps, cut the following: 4″ x 2½″ pants fabric, two 1½″ x 1½″ pieces of undershirt fabric, and 4″ x 3½″ shirt fabric. Then, following the method described in Step 1 and using the diagrams for placing the fabric and stitches, machine-sew each fabric to the template, one at a time in the order given above. Trim each fabric to the template's edge.

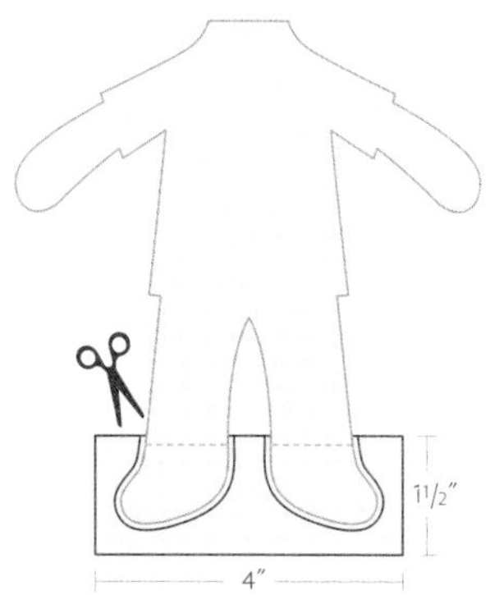

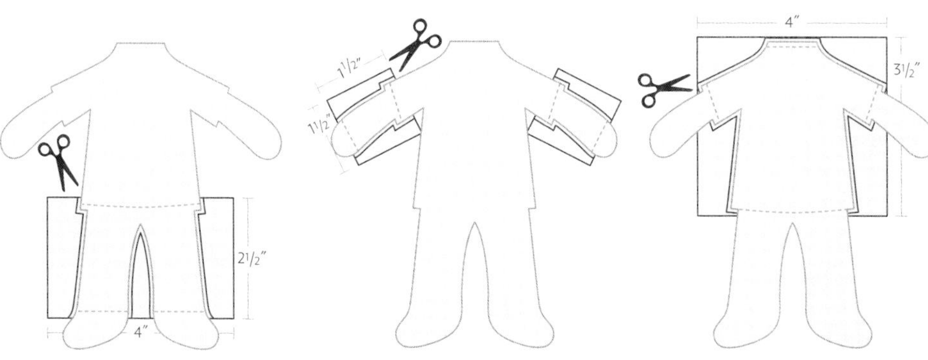

3 ADD RICKRACK LEDERHOSEN STRAPS TO SHIRT

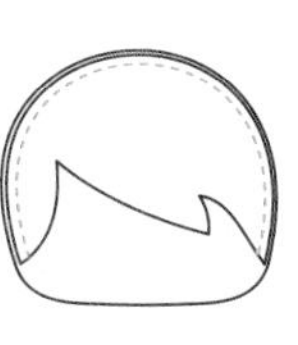

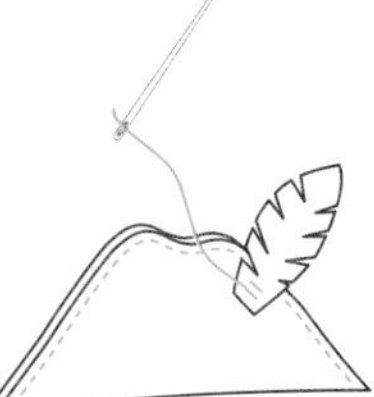

3. Add Rickrack Lederhosen Straps

Sew strips of ¼"-wide baby rickrack to the shirt for lederhosen straps, using the diagram as a placement guide and stitching down the center of the rickrack.

4. Sew Hair and Hat

Align the top edges of Hansel's Hair Front (B) and Hair Back (C), and edgestitch these top edges together with matching thread (see diagram). Sew a bit of rickrack along the bottom edge of one of Hansel's Hat (D) pieces. Align and edgestitch the two hat pieces together around the entire edge with matching thread. Hand-sew the Hansel's Feather (E) to the back of the hat with tacking stitches (see diagram).

Now jump ahead to the Finishing Instructions after the directions for assembling Gretel.

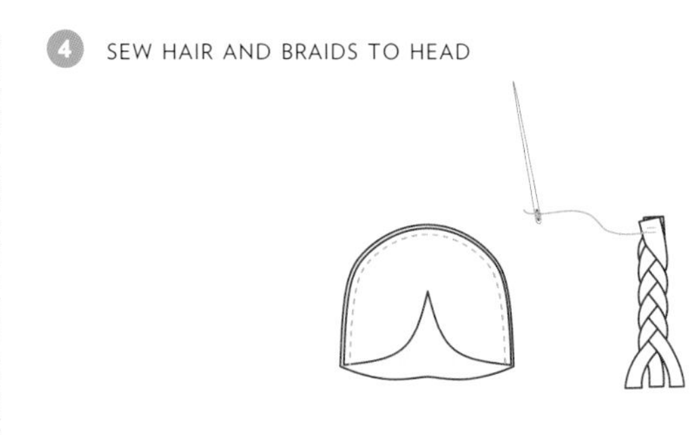

GRETEL

To make Gretel, you'll first create the front of the puppet by patchworking the fabrics onto the felt template of Gretel that you'll cut out. Next you'll make her hair. Then you'll join Gretel's front and back, insert the pipe cleaner arms, and finish assembling the puppet.

1. Cut Out Template and Sew Undershirt

Cut out the Gretel (F) template from wool felt. Cut two 1½″ x 1½″ pieces of undershirt fabric. Using the diagram as a guide for placing the fabric and stitches, lay the fabric right side down and the template on top and machine-sew the template to the fabric (note that you're stitching on the back of the puppet), making sure that your bobbin thread is the color you want the stitches to be on the fabric's right side. (You can use a coordinating color of bobbin thread to make the entire puppet or change bobbin-thread colors to match each new fabric you add.) Trim each fabric to the template's edge.

2. Sew Dress Top and Skirt

Cut fabric from your scraps to measure 3½″ x 1½″ for the dress top and 6½″ x 4½″ for the skirt. Then, following the method described in Step 1 and using the diagrams for placing the fabric and stitches, machine-sew each fabric to the template one at a time in the order given above. Trim each fabric to the template's edge.

3. Sew Apron and Rickrack Lederhosen Straps

Sew strips of ¼″-wide baby rickrack to the dress top for lederhosen straps, using the diagram as a placement guide and stitching down the center of the rickrack. Cut a 2″ x 4″ piece of apron fabric and edgestitch it to the skirt's top edge from the right side with your choice of coordinating or matching thread.

4. Sew Hair and Braids

Align the top edges of Gretel's Front Hair (G) and Back Hair (H), and edgestitch these top edges together with matching thread (see diagram). Cut six ⅛″ x 2½″ strips of wool felt for braids. Hand-sew the ends of three strips together with a tacking stitch or two, braid, and then tack stitch the ends together. Fold the braid in

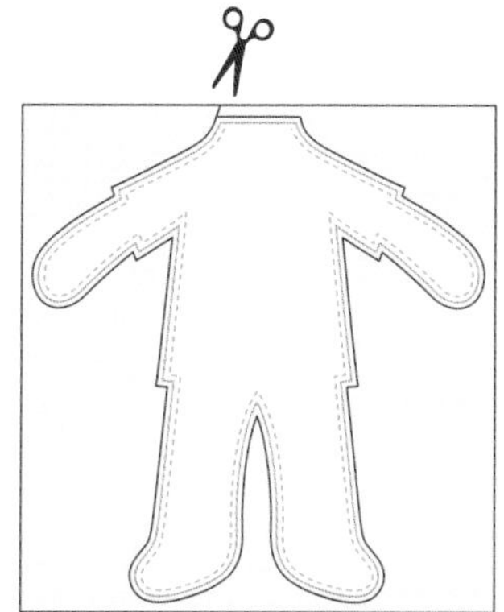

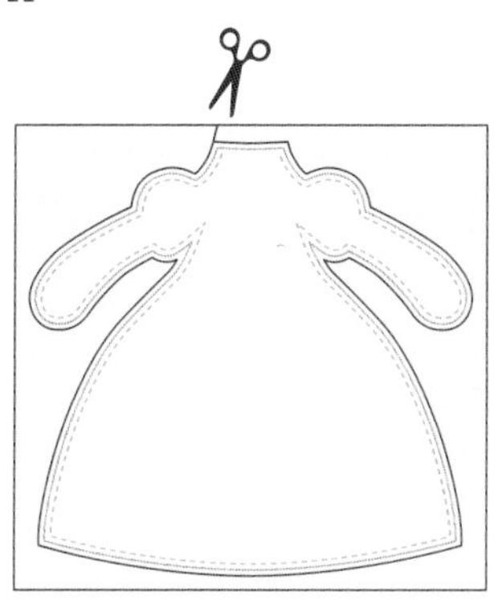

2 INSERT PIPE CLEANER INTO ARMS

RIGHT SIDE | WRONG SIDE

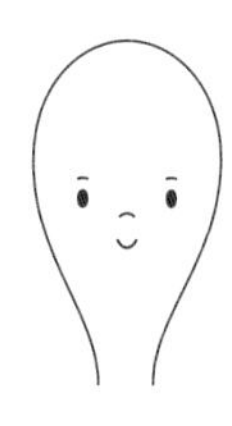

4 INSERT SPOON THROUGH NECK OPENING AND SLIT

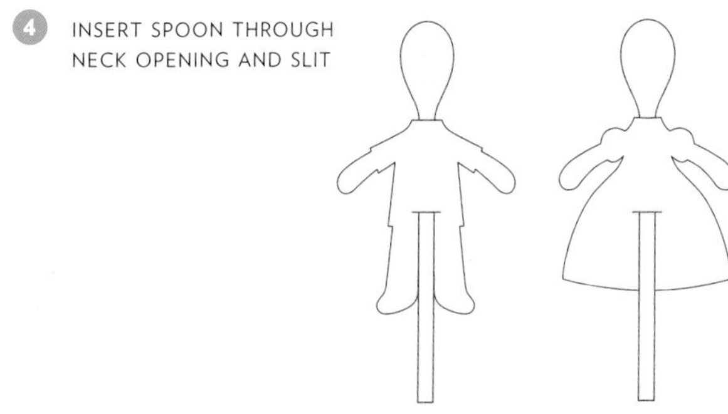

half to make loop and tack stitch the loop to the back of the hair. Repeat for the other braid.

FINISHING

1. Attach Backing Felt

Place Hansel's sewn template right side up on a 7″ x 7″ piece of backing felt and edgestitch it to the backing felt, using a coordinating thread color throughout or changing thread colors to match each section and leaving the top neck edge open (see diagram). Trim the backing to the template's edge. Flip the template over and cut a ¾″ horizontal slit in the backing felt about 3″ below the neck, being careful not to catch the right side of Hansel as you cut. Repeat for Gretel.

2. Add Pipe Cleaner to Spoon

Starting with a 9″-long piece of pipe cleaner, bend about ½″ at each end for Hansel's hands. Tie the center of the pipe cleaner around the spoon's handle to make a center loop and then remove the spoon. Insert the pipe cleaner through the neck opening, bending it to fit as you go; push each end of the pipe cleaner down one of the arms into each hand; and position the center loop right under the neckline of the outfit (see diagram). Repeat for Gretel.

3. Paint Face on Spoon

Place Hansel's hair on his head, and mark facial features on the spoon face with a pencil, using the diagram as a guide. Then remove the hair and, using a small paintbrush and acrylic paint, paint on the facial features. Repeat for Gretel.

4. Dress Up Spoon

Insert the spoon handle down through each template's neck opening, through the pipe-cleaner center, and back out through slit you cut (see diagram). Put Hansel's hair and hat and Gretel's hair in place.

If you leave your spoon puppets as they are, you'll be able to change their outfits. If you want sturdier puppets, use a couple dabs of craft glue to attach the hair and affix the pipe cleaner at the neck of the outfit.

Wee Wonderfuls Basics

To get you started, this section covers the basic materials and methods I use for sewing toys. If you're new to sewing toys, I suggest you begin by following the specific instructions for the projects carefully, but once you feel confident, feel free to experiment. Improvising, asserting your individuality, and following your imagination are what make sewing toys so much fun!

Supplies

You don't need much in the way of supplies to make a toy, but there are many types of fabric, trim, tools, and stuffing available, and your selection will influence the outcome.

FABRIC

Regardless of the project, you always need fabric that will wear well and hold up to stuffing. If the toy is for display only, the fabric doesn't have to be quite as sturdy as if it is for play. For children, choose clean, colorfast or prewashed, nontoxic fabric that feels good next to the skin.

Most toys survive with surface washing alone, but if you want to send a toy through the ringer, or if you fear a print may run or stain if it gets wet (or chewed on), be sure to prewash your fabric. And start with extra yardage if you plan to prewash since washing may cause shrinkage.

When substituting fabrics for those recommended in the book's projects, stick with the same type, that is, knits for knits and wovens for wovens. If you use a knit jersey where a woven cotton is called for—or vice versa—you'll end up with a different type of toy than the one pictured.

The patterns in this book generally provide dimensions in both inches and yards for the fabric you'll need (note that if the fabric called for in a project's Materials list is less than 10″ x 10″, I've called it a scrap and assumed that you'll find it in your fabric stash). The yardage called for will usually exceed the actual amount needed for the project—for instance, I may call for 1/4 yard, but you will only need 9″ x 18″—which saves you from having to do math at the fabric store's cutting table.

You'll also note that sometimes the yardage is listed as a fat quarter. Fat quarters, which quilters often use, measure approximately 18″ wide x 22 1/2″ high and are produced by cutting a square yard of fabric into four squares instead of four rectangles, as it would be at a fabric store. Often handy for small projects, fat quarters are included in the yardage dimensions when relevant in case you happen to be at the quilt shop or have fat quarters on hand. A quilt shop will cut fat quarters for you; most chain fabric stores will not.

SAFETY INFORMATION

The only steadfast rule when sewing handmade toys is to make sure the toys are safe and secure if children are going to play with them. If you are making a toy for a child under the age of three, don't use any detachable pieces like buttons or snaps; instead substitute toddler-safe details and trim, like sewn-on felt instead of buttons for eyes. Use clean, nontoxic materials that will cause no harm even if they end up being chewed on. Sturdily attach limbs, ears, and other extremities and features.

Cotton

Quilting-weight 100% cotton fabric is definitely my go-to fabric when sewing toys because it is durable, doesn't stretch, and is readily available in many wonderful colors and prints. It may seem counterintuitive, but it's much easier to create soft toys from a fabric that does not stretch or give than from a stretchy fabric; this is because stretchy fabric doesn't hold shape well when stuffed.

Woolworth
Woolco
BOIL
SANSIL
RICK RACK
MERCERIZED COTTON
15¢
NO. 413
Tailor Bird

Wool felt and wool
Wool felt is soft, sturdy, all-natural, and warm, and, with its non-fraying edges, is a dream to work with. Pure wool felt and wool-felt blends can be used interchangeably for projects that call for wool felt. Although wool felt is more expensive and not as readily available as acrylic felt, it's definitely worth the cost and effort to find it. During the cold months, fabric stores also carry wool suiting. While not interchangeable with wool felt for parts like eyes or noses that need edges that won't unravel, wool suiting is lovely as a main-body fabric; it is lighter in weight than wool felt, so it is easier to turn right side out. Quilt stores often carry both wool and wool felt in many wonderful colors, and many chain stores carry a small selection of wool felt. There are also many online sources (see Resources, page 167).

Fleece and fake fur
Fleece is soft, warm, very easy to sew, and slightly stretchy. It is not suitable for heirloom-quality toys, but it's an excellent choice for toys that will see a lot of action right now. Fake furs seem to come and go quickly, so if you see something you like, you should grab it. My favorites include acrylic fake fur that looks like antique mohair; soft, fuzzy, loopy fur that makes striking hair; and shaggy felt fur that has a soft, matted feel.

Vintage fabric
Many of my toys and dolls are made from vintage or repurposed fabrics, but I've occasionally made the mistake of creating a toy from a beloved vintage print that was just too threadbare to hold up. Please learn from my mistakes: Only choose used, vintage, or repurposed fabric if it's strong and tightly woven.

OTHER MATERIALS AND TRIM

Trims and bias tape
I tend to embellish most of my toys with trim. Some of my favorites are grosgrain, woven embroidered, and pleated satin ribbons, printed cotton-twill tape, vintage rickrack, and crocheted cotton lace. I also like to encase raw edges with bias tape, which is readily available in various colors and styles.

Buttons
Buttons can be used for eyes, closures, or decoration. I'm always on the hunt for the smallest buttons I can find, and I prefer to use matte, rather than shiny, reflective buttons for eyes; ball buttons make cute eyes, too.

Closures
I like to use Velcro closures for toys for babies. For older kids, big snaps or magnetic snaps work well. When using buttons for closures on toys for kids, make sure that the buttonholes or loops are large enough for small hands to maneuver.

Embroidery floss
For all embroidery, I use six-strand DMC embroidery floss. It is 100% cotton, comes in more than 400 colors, and is fade resistant and machine washable. Floss is also available in linen, perle cotton, angora, and silk. When working with a new type of floss, test it on scrap fabric before incorporating it into your project.

Yarn
For hair and embellishments made with yarn, I favor Brown Sheep Company's Lamb's Pride Worsted, a wool-mohair blend that does not unravel or get too frizzy with wear (see Resources, page 167).

Thread
I generally use 100% cotton or a poly/cotton all-purpose thread in a matching or coordinating thread color; thread is sometimes visible on a toy's stuffed seams, so choose colors accordingly.

TOOLS

Before you get started, make sure you have these tools at the ready: tracing paper, vellum, or cheap printer paper; sharp pencil; chalk pencil; iron-on transfer pencil; measuring tape; fabric scissors; paper scissors; pins; seam ripper; tiny safety pin or bodkin. In addition, you will need the following:

Hand-sewing needles in assorted sizes
Select the one with the smallest possible eye for your project's thread/floss, so that you won't create larger holes than you need to in your fabric. Remember that the higher the number on the needle's package, the thinner the needle.

Chenille needle
You'll need this needle with a large eye for sewing with yarn. A chenille needle is similar to a tapestry needle but has a sharper point.

Doll or soft sculpture needle
A 3″-5″ straight needle used to sew through stuffed doll bodies.

Stuffing fork
Made specifically for stuffing toys, a stuffing fork is a metal stick with a notched end on a wooden or plastic handle. The eraser end of a pencil, a knitting needle, crochet hook, or chopstick all work well, too.

STUFFING

Listed here are the most common types of stuffing. Instead of buying stuffing, you can also cut up fabric scraps.

Fiberfill/Polyfil

Fiberfill is the most readily available and least inexpensive type of stuffing. It is generally made from 100% polyester and is hypoallergenic and machine washable. Fiberfill is dense but very lightweight and airy. Toys stuffed with fiberfill retain their shape well with wear and after washing. There are many different brands. My favorite is Cluster Stuff by Morning Glory (see Resources, page 167). Unlike most fiberfills, it is formed into tiny little clumps (rather than packaged in one big mass), so you don't have to tear off pieces as you go.

Wool

Wool stuffing is lumpy, dense, heavy, and warm to the touch. Toys stuffed firmly with wool have a wonderful antique-toy feel. It wears nicely but isn't machine washable. Some people are allergic to it. Not all stores carry it, so you may need to buy it online.

Cotton

Cotton stuffing is less dense than wool and fiberfill stuffing, so you need to use more of it to get a firm feel. It tends to harden and compact over time and also attracts lint easily. It is machine washable. Not all stores carry it, so you may need to buy it online.

Bamboo

This new addition to the market looks and behaves a lot like cotton stuffing (though it cannot be machine washed) and is eco-friendly and naturally antibacterial. It has a slippery, silky feel, and toys made with it tend to squeak a little bit.

1 Cluster Stuff 2 Polyfil

3 Wool 4 Bamboo

How to Stuff

Stuffing a toy involves building its shape from the inside. The process takes longer than you might expect and cannot be rushed. You can't rearrange stuffing once it's inside a toy, so if you don't like your results, you'll need to pull out all of the stuffing and start over.

The key to successful stuffing is using small quantities of stuffing at a time. To do this, pull small clumps from your main mass and press into the toy evenly and tightly. Stuff the extremities first. Use a stuffing fork (see page 120) or the eraser end of a pencil to work the stuffing into small or skinny spaces, being careful not to push so hard that you poke through the fabric. Once you reach the main body of the toy, you can use bigger clumps. Mold the toy to the shape you want as you work the stuffing into its curves and corners. The amount of stuffing you use will affect how the toy looks and feels.

Firm

Most of the patterns in this book call for stuffing the toy firmly. Firmly stuffed toys hold their shape well and will sit or stand on their own. They should be stuffed very densely so that they're hard and have a taut surface, but not so densely that the seams pop. Once you think you're finished stuffing, try adding just a little more. You may be surprised by how much time and how much stuffing a toy takes.

Floppy

A few of the toys in this book are loosely stuffed, or floppy. Floppy toys are great for babies because they're easy to grab onto and have a wonderful, rag-doll charm. To produce a floppy result, stuff the toy evenly until it has a nice, pleasantly plump feel.

Somewhat flat

Some of the patterns call for stuffing toys so that they're firm but still rather flat. This means amply stuffing the toy but not over-stuffing it so that its shape is contorted. Press the toy flat with your hands during stuffing to keep it from becoming round.

Getting Ready to Sew

Preparing to sew your toy involves tracing and cutting out its pattern pieces and, if applicable, transferring the toy's face template to your fabric.

TRACING PATTERN PIECES

The full-size pattern pieces for all the projects are laid out on the pages at the end of the book and are overlapped because of space constraints. Note that all seam allowances are included in the pattern pieces.

To trace a pattern piece, lay tracing paper or vellum over the pattern sheet, and trace the piece with a sharp pencil as accurately as possible. Trace each piece separately without tracing the overlapping neighboring pattern piece.

Write the name of the pattern piece and the cutting directions on each traced piece. Then trace all pattern markings, such as dots, folds, and facial features.

Some pattern pieces are too big to fit in their entirety on the book's pages, so they have been split. To trace the full-size pattern piece for a split pattern, use a piece of tracing paper large enough to accommodate its size, and begin by tracing the pattern piece's first half or section (noted in gray on the split-pattern layout drawing on the pattern piece). Then align the traced section with the second half or section, matching up the patterns' edges and dashed lines; and repeat the process again if the pattern has more than two sections until you've traced the complete piece (see diagram below).

Some of the projects include a full-size face template with the pattern pieces, which you'll need to transfer to the cut pattern piece or stuffed toy. Sometimes the face template is positioned right on the pattern piece exactly where it belongs. For other patterns, you'll find a separate face template, which you'll need to place on the toy yourself. And, finally, for a couple of projects, you'll find a face template positioned on a pattern edge that's marked to be placed on the fabric's fold. To work with a face template placed on a fold, trace the template's features and also a side of the head, so you'll be able to accurately place the face on your cut pattern piece.

TRACING PATTERN PIECES

TRACING ONE PATTERN PIECE

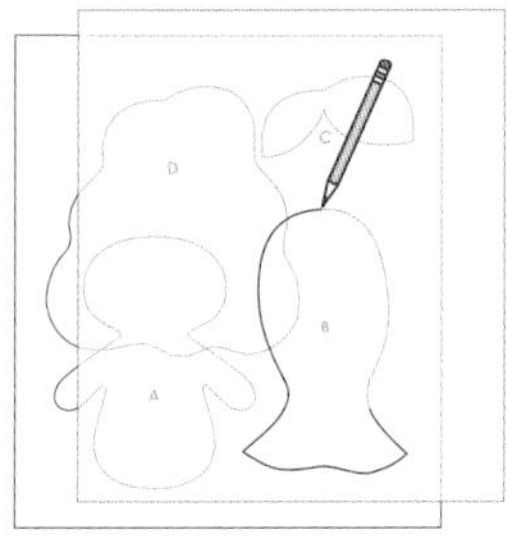

LABELING AND TRANSFERRING PATTERN MARKINGS

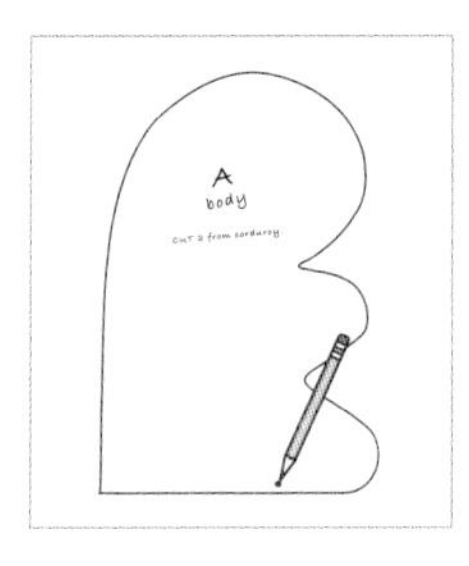

TRACING A SPLIT PATTERN PIECE

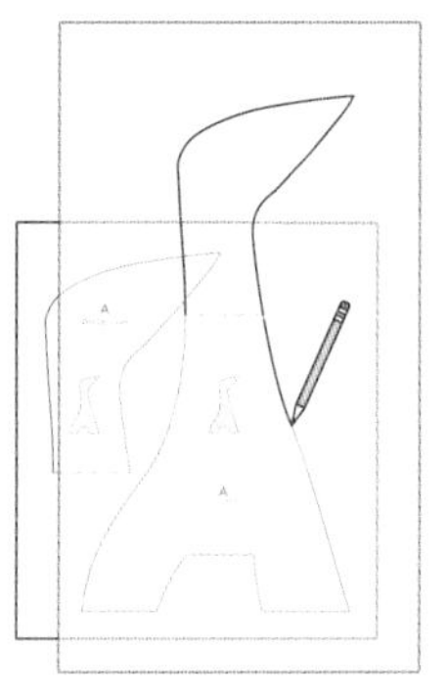

TRACING A FACE TEMPLATE ON THE FOLD

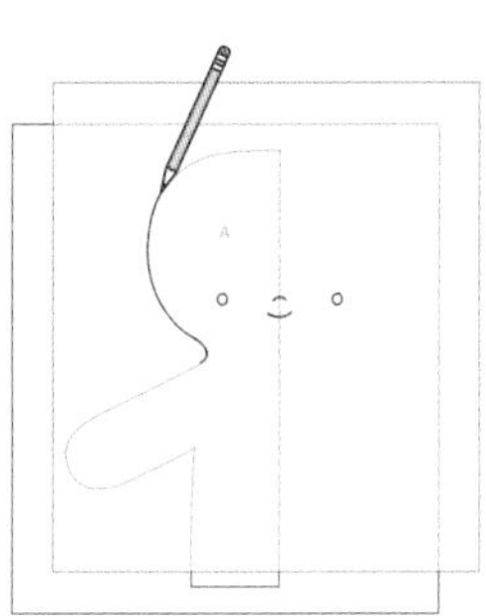

CUTTING OUT PATTERN PIECES

Pin the cut pattern pieces to your fabric and trace around them with a sharp pencil or fine-tip marker. When working with felt, trace around the piece with a chalk pencil. Next cut the fabric on the traced line. If you prefer, skip the tracing step and just cut around the pinned piece, but keep in mind that this may produce inaccurate results that can alter the finished shape of your toy and make pieces more difficult to match up. When working on small pieces, you'll find it much easier to trace first and then cut.

If the grain line is indicated on the pattern piece, make sure to lay the pattern piece so that its marked grain line runs in the same direction as the fabric's grain line, which is always parallel to the fabric's selvedge (the tightly woven edge running along each side of the fabric's length).

On each pattern piece, you'll find cutting directions that may call for cutting that pattern piece once, two or more times, or "on the fold."

For "CUT 1"

Lay the fabric right side up, place the pattern piece right side up on the fabric, and trace and cut out the pattern.

For "CUT 2"

Fold the fabric with right sides together, place the pattern piece right side up on top of the folded fabric, and trace and cut out the pattern. If you're working with a single layer of fabric and need to cut 2 pieces, lay the fabric right side up and cut 1 with the pattern piece right side up, then flip the pattern piece over to its wrong side and cut the second piece.

For "Place on fold"

Fold the fabric with wrong sides together, place the pattern piece right side up with the edge marked "Place on fold" on the fabric's fold, and trace and cut out the pattern.

CUTTING OUT PATTERN PIECES

RIGHT SIDE | WRONG SIDE

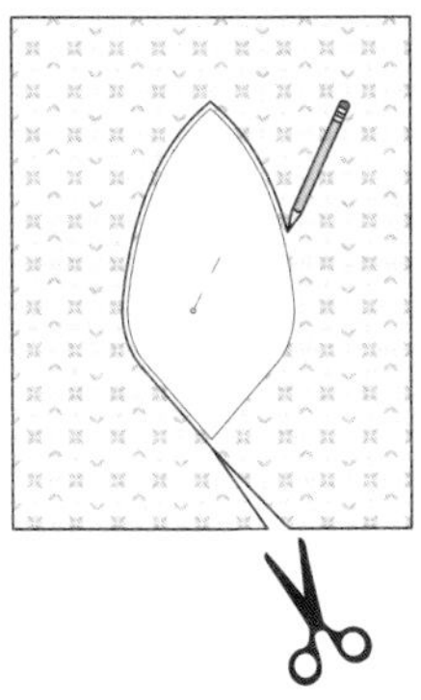

"CUT 2" PATTERN PIECES

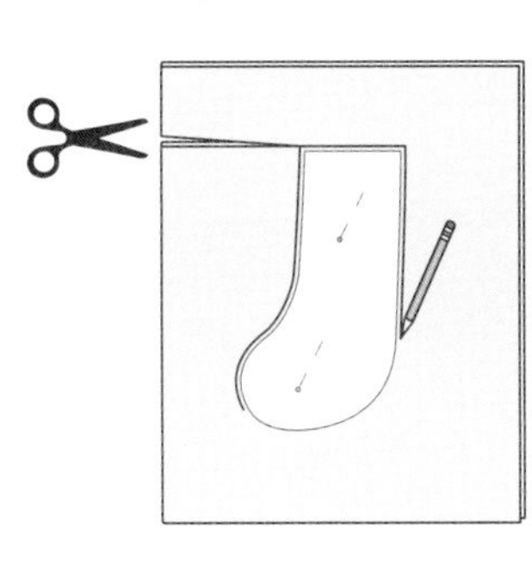

CUTTING A PATTERN PIECE ON THE FOLD

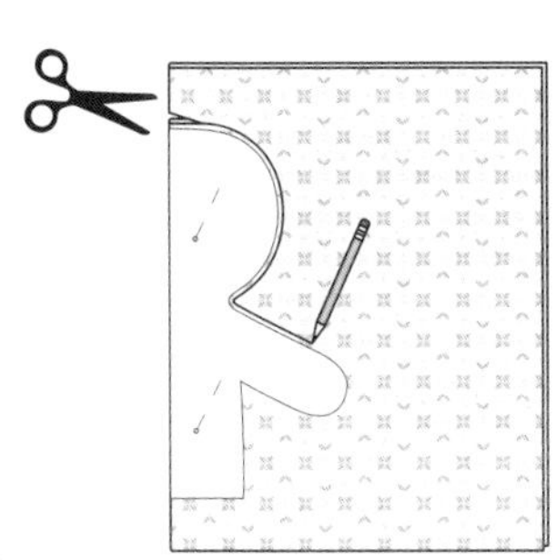

TRANSFERRING FACES TO FABRIC

When I make a toy, I always work on the face last. When I add those little features, the toy becomes a funny little character full of charm and charisma, with its own attitude and quirks. Even when I try to follow a diagram or sketch rigorously, or when I'm trying to make ten dolls exactly the same, they each end up with the slight differences that imbue them with their own distinct, irresistible charm.

Working on the face last is a gutsy strategy because it's very easy to mess up so badly that the toy is ruined, but I don't usually know how I want the face to look until the doll is all filled out. If you're new to making toys, I suggest working on your faces before stuffing the toy so that, if you're unhappy with how it's going and want to start over, all you'll need to do is cut out another head/body piece rather than reassemble an entire doll. But for some toys with facial features that span separate pattern pieces, there's no choice; these toys will need to have their faces put on last.

Below are the two basic methods for transferring a face template: the tracing method, used before stuffing, and the marking method, used after stuffing. The first step for both methods is to trace the face template from the pattern onto tracing paper.

THE MARKING METHOD IS USED TO TRANSFER KATIE KITTY'S FACE TEMPLATE ONTO THE DOLL (SEE PAGE 74).

Tracing method

Tape your traced-paper face template right side up to a window or light box. Then place your fabric right side up over the traced template and trace the template onto the fabric with a sharp pencil. When tracing, keep your marks small so that they'll be easily covered by the embroidery you'll add over them later.

You can transfer the face template either on your already cut-out fabric pattern piece or on a larger piece of fabric. Since embroidering a face is generally a small job, you'll probably find it easy enough to work just holding the fabric in your hands. But if you want to use an embroidery hoop, you'll need to work with an uncut piece of fabric that's large enough to fit your hoop and from which you'll cut the pattern piece afterward. Note, though, that a hoop will crease the fabric, and these creases can be difficult to iron out and may still show if your hoop is smaller than the size of the actual pattern piece.

I don't recommend using disappearing-ink, wash-out, or fade-out markers for marking face templates. I just don't trust that they will always work well, and you may be left with unwanted marks-shadowing your cute little faces. I've found that you can't go wrong with small marks made with a sharp pencil, which won't smear or spread if washed and will remain invisible underneath embroidery.

Marking method

Flip your traced-paper face template over to the wrong side and retrace the features with a chalk pencil. Then lay the template over the doll's stuffed head with the template's chalk side facing the doll. Use pins to poke through the features and transfer bits of the chalk through to the fabric, marking the placement of the facial features.

MAKING YOUR OWN FACES

A great way to experiment with new faces is to cut out little scraps of felt or fabric for the eyes and bits of floss for the eyebrows, nose, and mouth and lay them out on the head. When you're happy with what you've got, mark lightly behind the positioned scraps with a sharp pencil. I've always found that the most successful faces with the broadest appeal have simple features; small, widely spaced eyes; and small, minimal lines for the mouths, eyebrows, and noses. But this is definitely a matter of personal taste, so experiment until you're satisfied.

Basic Sewing Terms and Techniques

Below are brief explanations of some of the key terms and techniques used in the patterns in this book. If a technique is new to you, I suggest practicing it on a fabric scrap before using it in your project.

Clipping and notching

Clipping and notching curves and points on the wrong side of a sewn piece helps the piece turn correctly to the right side and lie flat. To clip inward curves, notch outward curves, or clip points and notch underarms, snip small triangular shapes through the seam allowances up to, but not into, the seam line stitches (see diagrams below).

Darts

Darts are sewn to give three-dimensional shape to a flat piece of fabric. On our pattern pieces, a dart is represented by a large V-notch cut out of the edge of the piece. Trace and cut around all dart notches when cutting out pattern pieces. To sew a dart, fold the edges of the dart's notch with the fabric's right sides together, and sew along the dart's edge with a standard 1⁄4″ seam allowance.

Gussets

A gusset is a fabric panel added to build three-dimensional shape into a toy, like the shaded gusset in the diagram below.

Stitch length

Because stuffing can put a lot of strain on a toy's seams, set your machine to a shorter stitch length to sew all seams to be stuffed: 10 to 12 stitches per inch for sewing on lightweight cotton and 12 to 15 stitches per inch for medium- and heavyweight fabrics.

MACHINE STITCHES

I sewed most of the projects in this book by machine, but they all can be sewn by hand (if you have the time and patience), using a small running stitch or backstitch. If you want to machine-sew your projects, a basic sewing machine is all you need. In addition to the standard straight stitch and zigzag stitch, below are descriptions of the machine stitches you'll need for the projects in this book.

Backstitch

To prevent seams from unraveling, sew a backstitch at the beginning and end of a seam by taking a few stitches in reverse. Alternatively, drop the machine's feed dogs—or set the stitch length to zero—and sew a few stitches in place at the beginning and end of the seam (raising the feed dogs or resetting the stitch to its regular length afterward).

Edgestitch and topstitch

Edgestitching and topstitching are both stitching lines sewn from the right side of the fabric at a given distance from an edge or seam. Edgestitching is sewn 1⁄8″ from an edge or seam, while topstitching is sewn 1⁄4″ or more from that edge or seam.

Gathering stitch

To create gathers, set your machine for a basting stitch (the longest stitch length) and sew two parallel lines along the edge to be gathered. Do not backstitch at the beginning or end of the stitching line, and leave long thread tails to pull up the gathers.

BASIC SEWING TECHNIQUES

CLIPPING CURVES

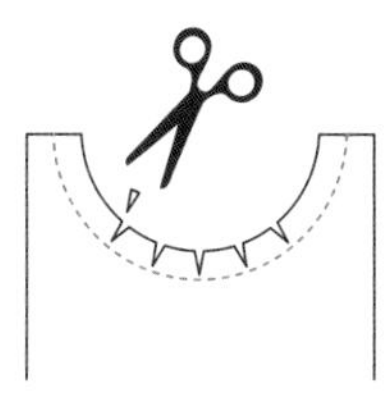

NOTCHING CURVES

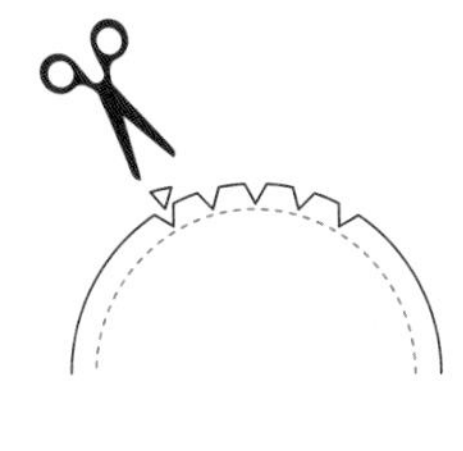

CLIPPING POINTS

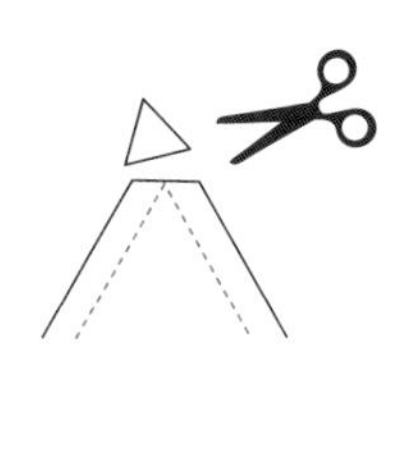

NOTCHING UNDERARMS

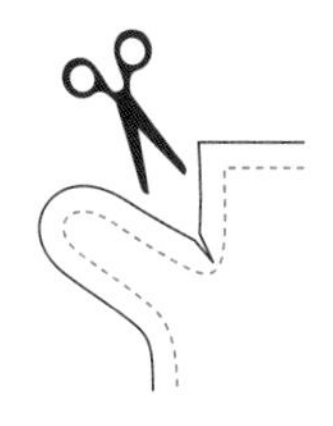

GUSSET

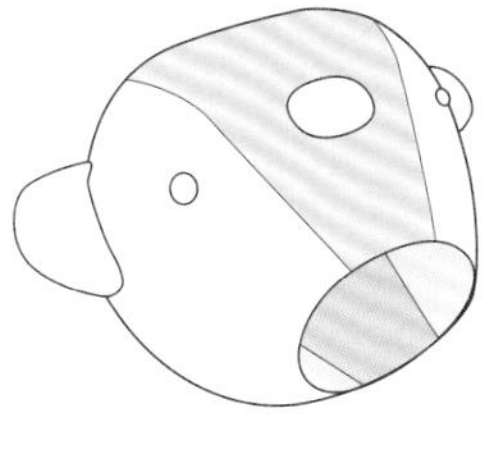

RIGHT SIDE | WRONG SIDE

GATHERING STITCH

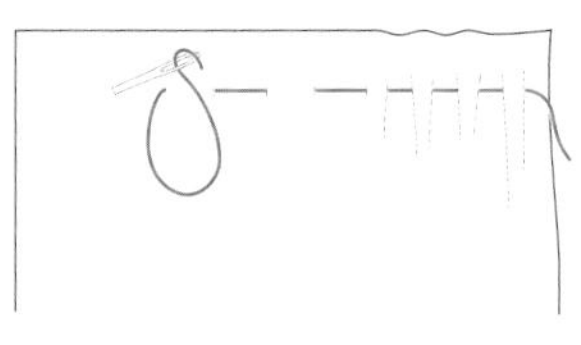

LADDER STITCH CLOSING

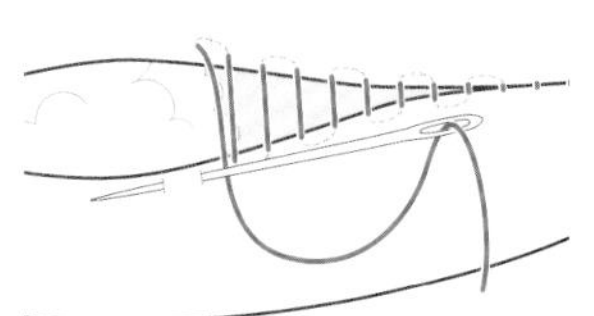

LADDER STITCH JOINING

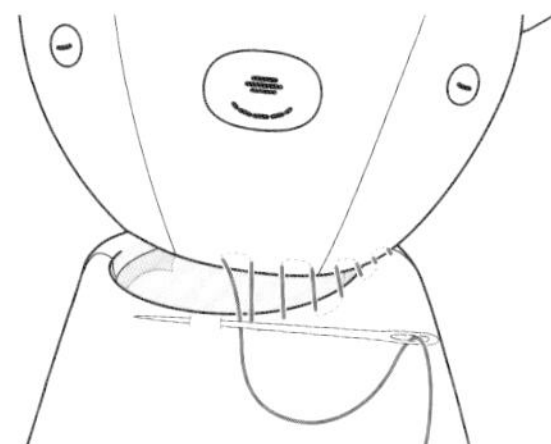

TACKING STITCH

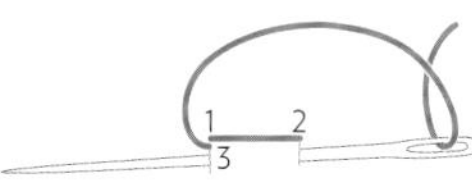

WHIPSTITCH

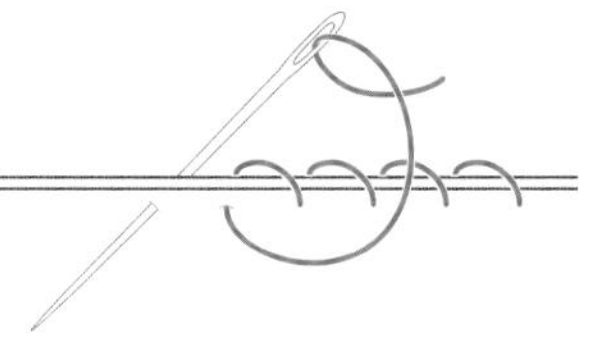

HAND STITCHES FOR CONSTRUCTION

For all hand-sewing with thread, use a doubled, knotted thread. Even when sewing a project by machine, there is usually some construction that must be completed by hand.

Gathering stitch

Sew a line of loose, evenly spaced running stitches (see page 128) along the edge to be gathered without knotting the thread and leaving long thread tails at each end to pull up and create gathers.

Ladder stitch

This stitch is used to close openings invisibly after stuffing a toy and to join two stuffed parts together. Always use matching thread when working the ladder stitch to keep stitches as invisible as possible. After knotting off, bury the thread tails (see page 128) in the stuffed body.

For closing an opening, work the stitch as shown in the diagram above, lacing the opening's sides together firmly, stitching just on the seam line itself, and tucking in the opening's two raw edges as you sew.

For joining two separate parts (for example, for attaching a head to the body), take a small straight stitch just on the seam line on one part; then stitch directly below the first stitch into the adjoining part, again just on the seam line. Next stitch ¼″ or so to the left onthe body and then take a small stitch directly above where the needle emerged, sewing just on the head's seam line. Continue stitching in this pattern, keeping the stitches aligned and consistently spaced, and tug on the thread every three or four stitches to pull it taut and draw together the two parts being joined. Since there's no thread on the surface to get worn, the join will be strong and durable.

Tacking stitch

A tacking stitch anchors fabric, trim, or yarn in place. Sew a tacking stitch by taking one or more small stitches in the designated spot.

Whipstitch

Use this stitch to join folded or hemmed edges, join abutted felt edges, or sew closed an opening. But note that, unlike with a ladder stitch, these joins will be visible. Work this stitch on the very edge of the fabric, about ⅛″ from it, and slant your needle as you sew to produce slanted stitches or keep it upright for straight stitches.

EMBROIDERY STITCHES

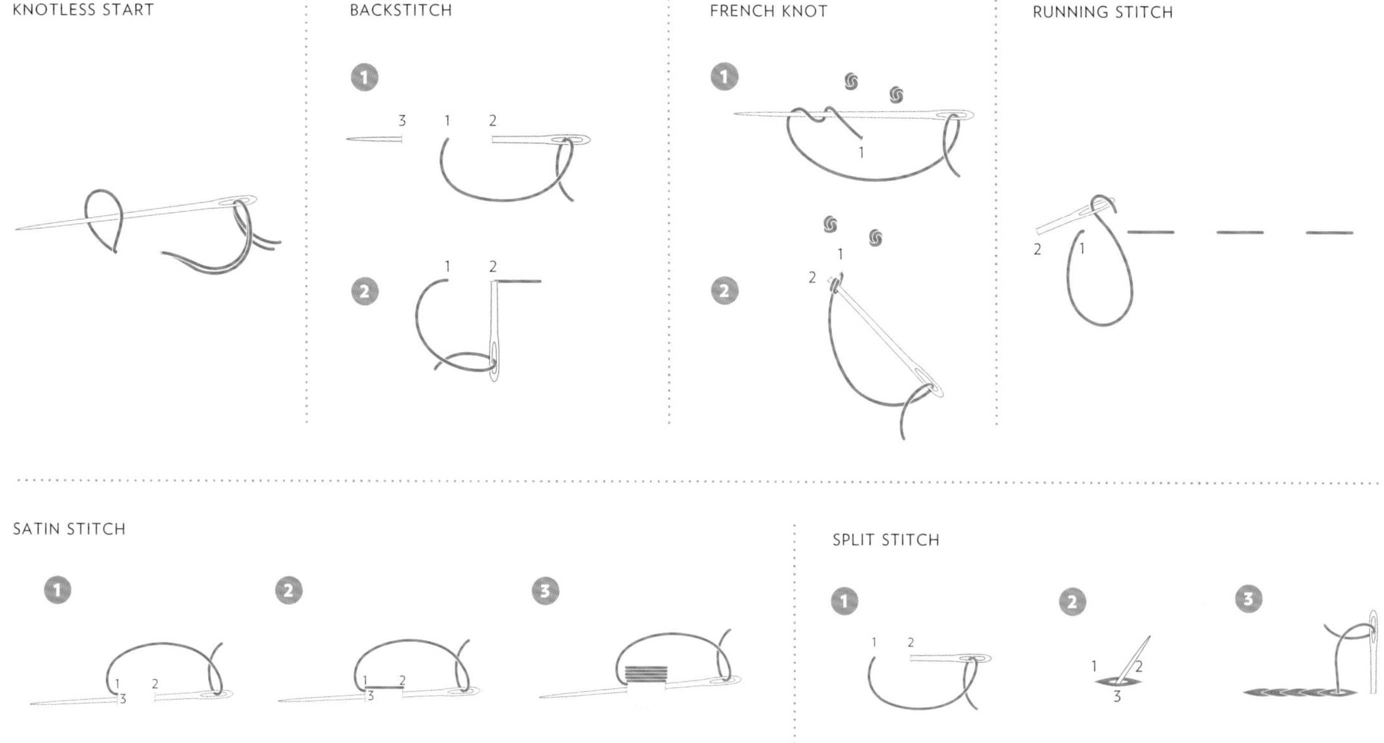

EMBROIDERY STITCHES AND TERMS

For embroidering faces and for construction stitching in some projects, you'll use embroidery floss, which is made of six separate strands that are twisted together. The pattern directions will state how many strands to use for each instance of embroidery. To separate floss, cut the length of floss you'll need; pull the threads into two groups, with the number of strands you need in one and the rest in the other; and pull gently to separate the strands down the length of the floss. When embroidering with floss, do not double the floss. Also note that you can either knot the floss to start sewing or embroidering or, if you're embroidering on a stuffed surface, you can hide the knots (see page 128), or use what's called a knotless start (see below).

Knotless start

To use a knotless start with embroidery floss to start embroidering the face on a stuffed head, begin with half as many strands as called for in the pattern directions so that you have the correct number needed after folding. If the directions call for an odd number of strands, round the number up by one strand. To work a knotless start, fold your length of floss in half and thread the loose floss tails through your needle. Take a tiny, 1/16" stitch in your fabric, but don't pull the floss all the way through; instead pull the needle through the folded loop (see diagram above), and pull the floss taut.

Backstitch

Make a short stitch, pulling the needle up at 1 in the diagram above, inserting it at 2, and bringing it out one stitch ahead at 3. Repeat as needed, working from right to left (or vice versa if you're left-handed).

French knot

Bring the needle up and, holding the thread taut with one hand, wind the thread somewhat tightly around the needle two or three times (or more depending on the size of knot you want). Insert the needle right next to where it came out, still holding the thread wraps tight, and draw needle to the wrong side, forming a knot.

Running stitch
The most basic of hand stitches, a running stitch is formed by sewing a series of short, evenly spaced stitches. Try to keep the stitches and the spaces between them the same consistent length (see diagram, page 127).

Satin stitch
Use this stitch to produce a series of neat, even, parallel stitches that are worked closely together to fill in an outlined shape (see diagram, page 127).

Split stitch
Use this stitch to draw a shape or facial features and work it by taking a short stitch (from 1 to 2 in the diagram on page 127) and bringing the needle back up at the midpoint (3) to split the thread. Repeat, working left to right (or vice versa if you're left-handed). Don't worry about an even split if you're working with an uneven number of strands of floss.

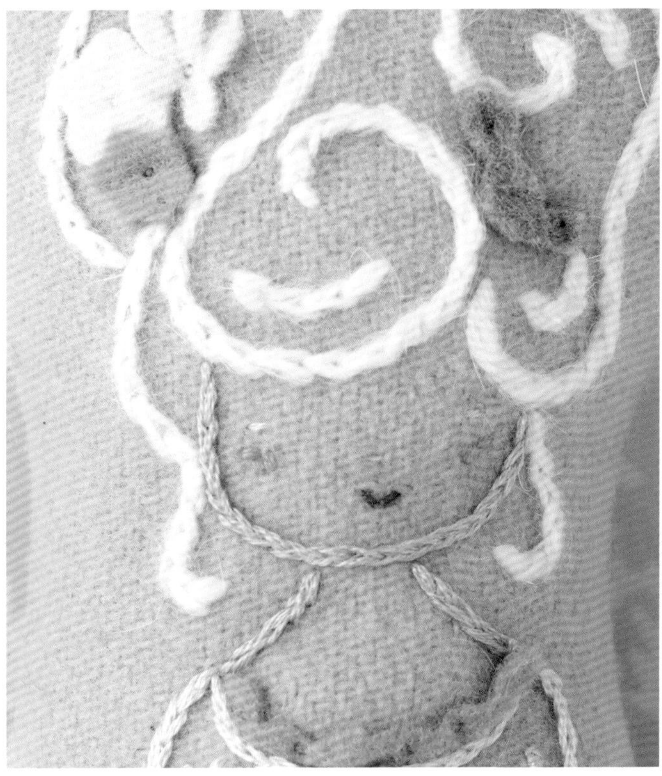

SPLIT STITCHES AND BACK STITCHES ARE USED TO EMBELLISH MARIE ANTOINETTE (SEE PAGE 20).

Finishing

Finishing a project neatly isn't difficult but makes all the difference. Below are two key finishing techniques you'll want to use.

Burying thread tails
After knotting off embroidery or hand-sewing, insert the needle (pulling the ends of the thread along with it) into and through the toy's stuffed body. Clip the remaining thread tails close to the body as they emerge on other side and "knead" the body until any remaining tails are sucked into the toy.

Hiding knots
If you're embroidering or hand-sewing on an already stuffed toy, you can hide knots in inconspicuous spots, for example, inside yarn hair, under felt pieces like eyes, or inside seams. To do this, pull the needle up on your last stitch through your chosen hiding spot and knot off the thread, tucking the knot into that same hiding spot, then bury thread tail (see above). Another way to avoid knots altogether is to use a knotless start (see page 127) to begin embroidery.

Care and Repair

A well-loved toy may need to visit the "emergency room" at some point for patching up. In most cases, split seams or lost stuffing can be repaired, and clothes and accessories can be patched or resewn. And since children love to be involved in repair activities, this can be a great chance for a first sewing lesson.

For washing, I recommend surface washing only, if possible. If you've used machine-washable, colorfast, or prewashed fabric and washable stuffing, you can send the toy through the washing machine and dryer on a gentle cycle, but keep in mind that it may not fare as well as you would like. I always embrace wear and tear on toys, since the most battered are often the most loved.

Wee Wonderfuls Pattern Pieces

Evelyn Inchworm

(see page 9)

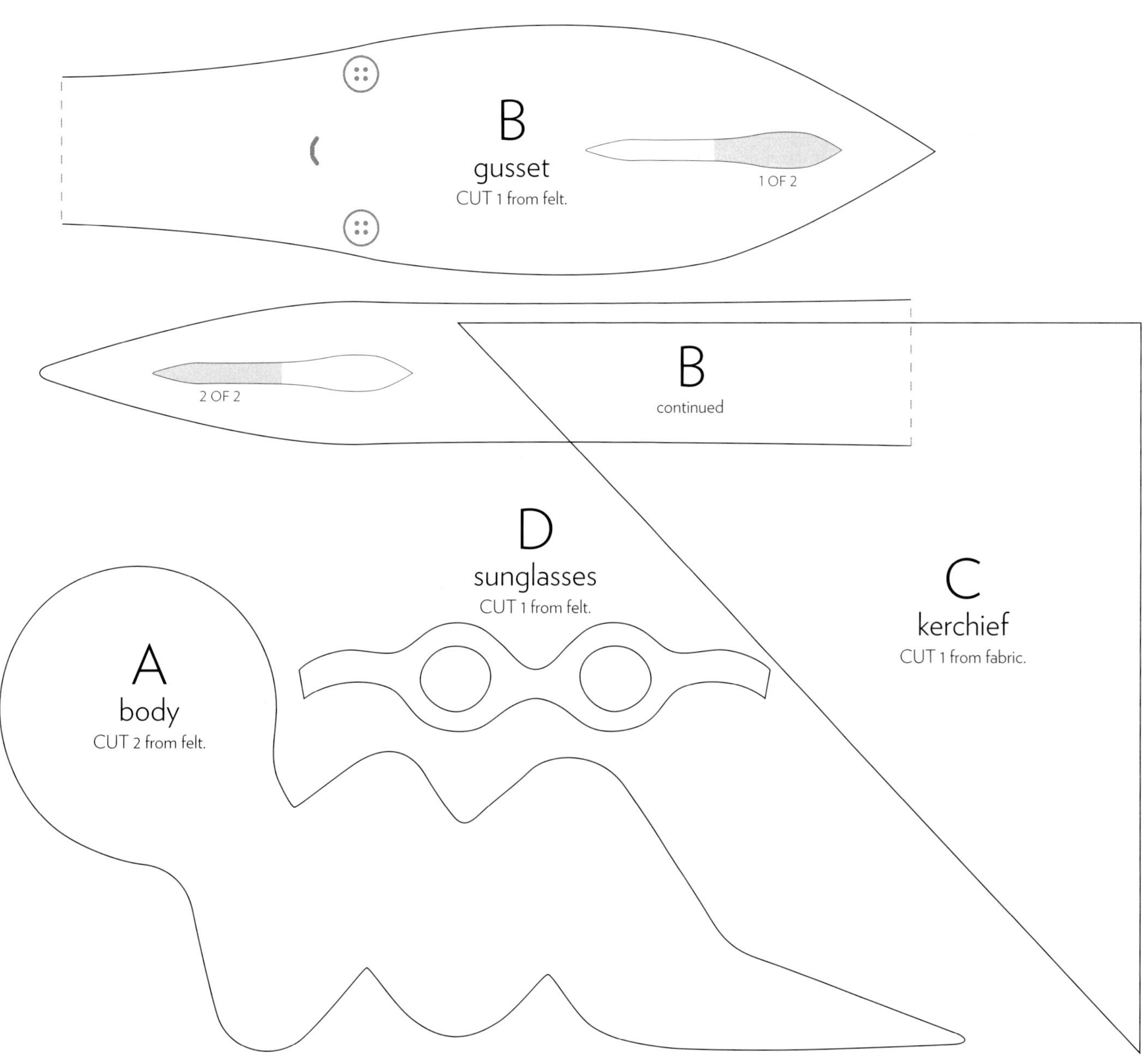

Pixie

(see page 13)

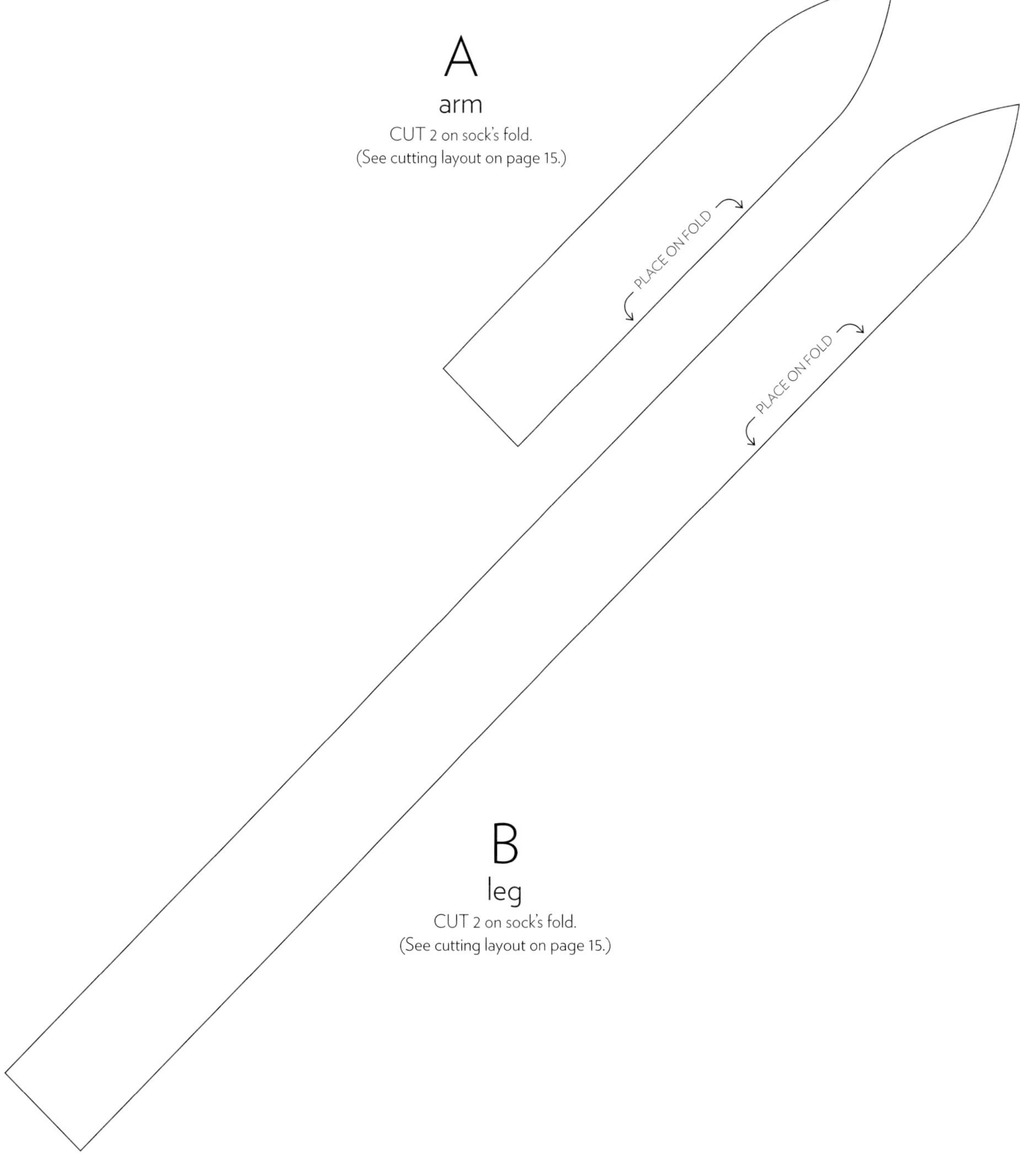

Koji

(see page 17)

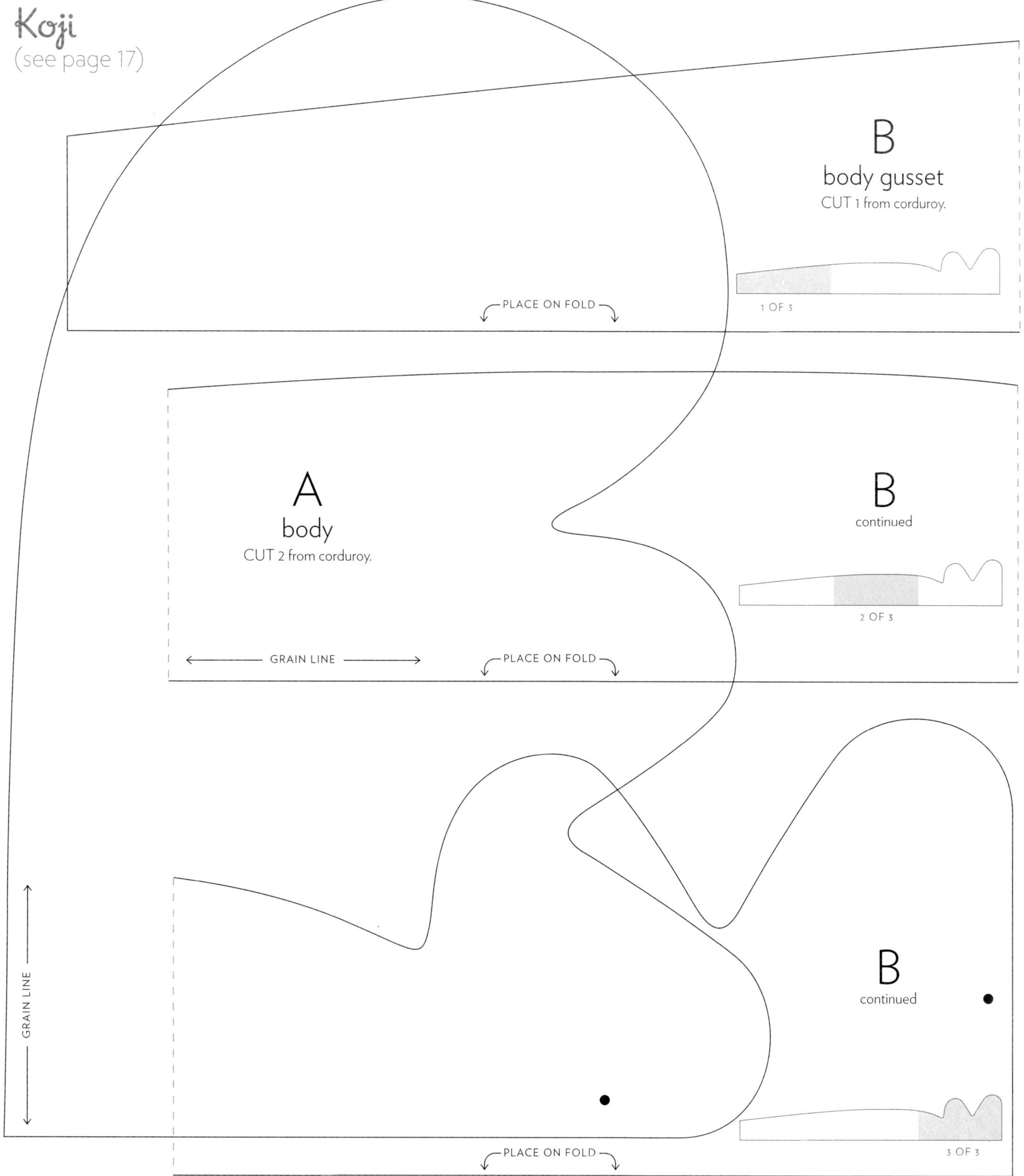

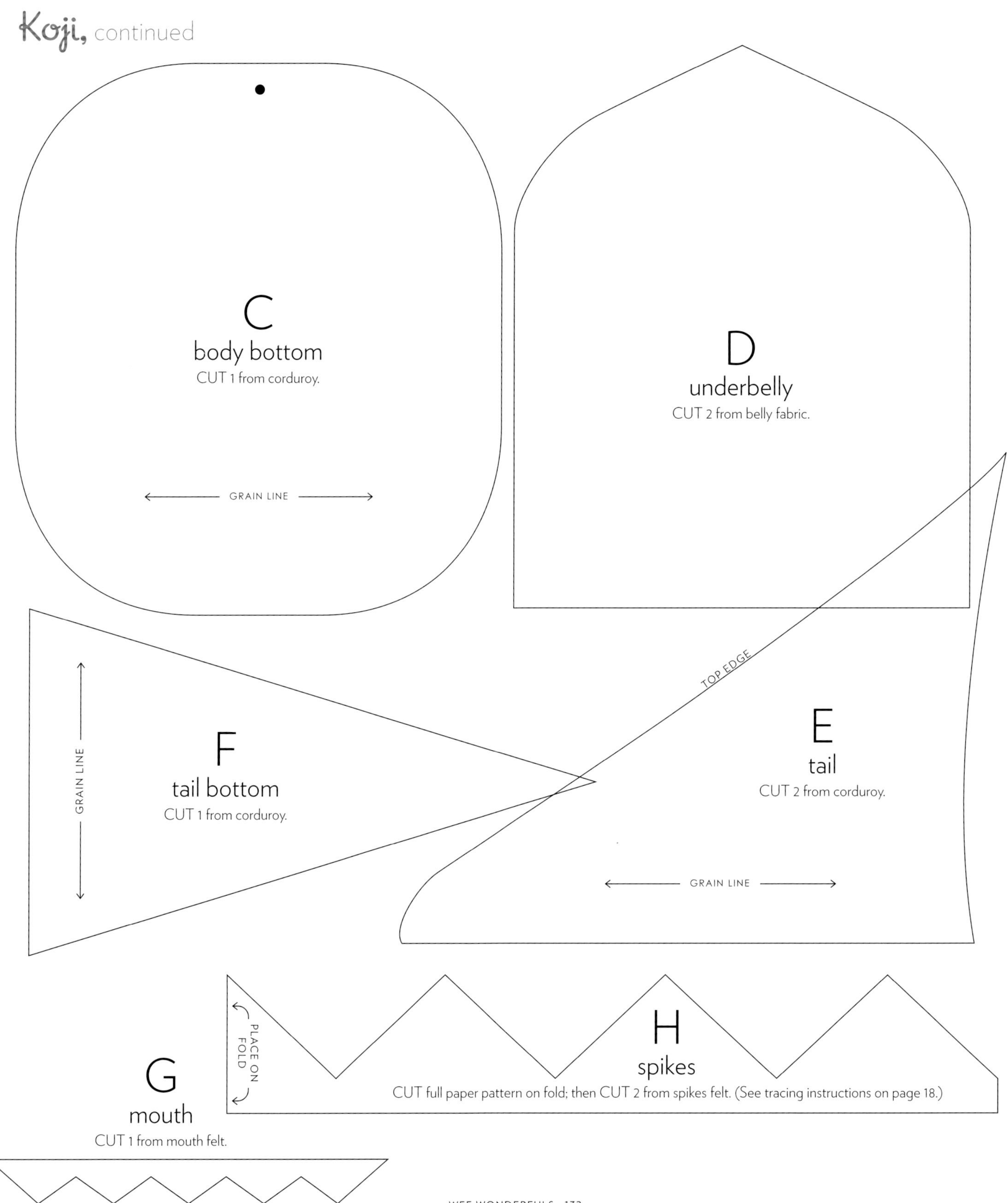
C
body bottom
CUT 1 from corduroy.
GRAIN LINE
D
underbelly
CUT 2 from belly fabric.
TOP EDGE
E
tail
CUT 2 from corduroy.
GRAIN LINE
F
tail bottom
CUT 1 from corduroy.
GRAIN LINE
PLACE ON FOLD
H
spikes
CUT full paper pattern on fold; then CUT 2 from spikes felt. (See tracing instructions on page 18.)
G
mouth
CUT 1 from mouth felt.

Marie Antoinette

(see page 21)

1 OF 2

2 OF 2

Margot

(see page 25)

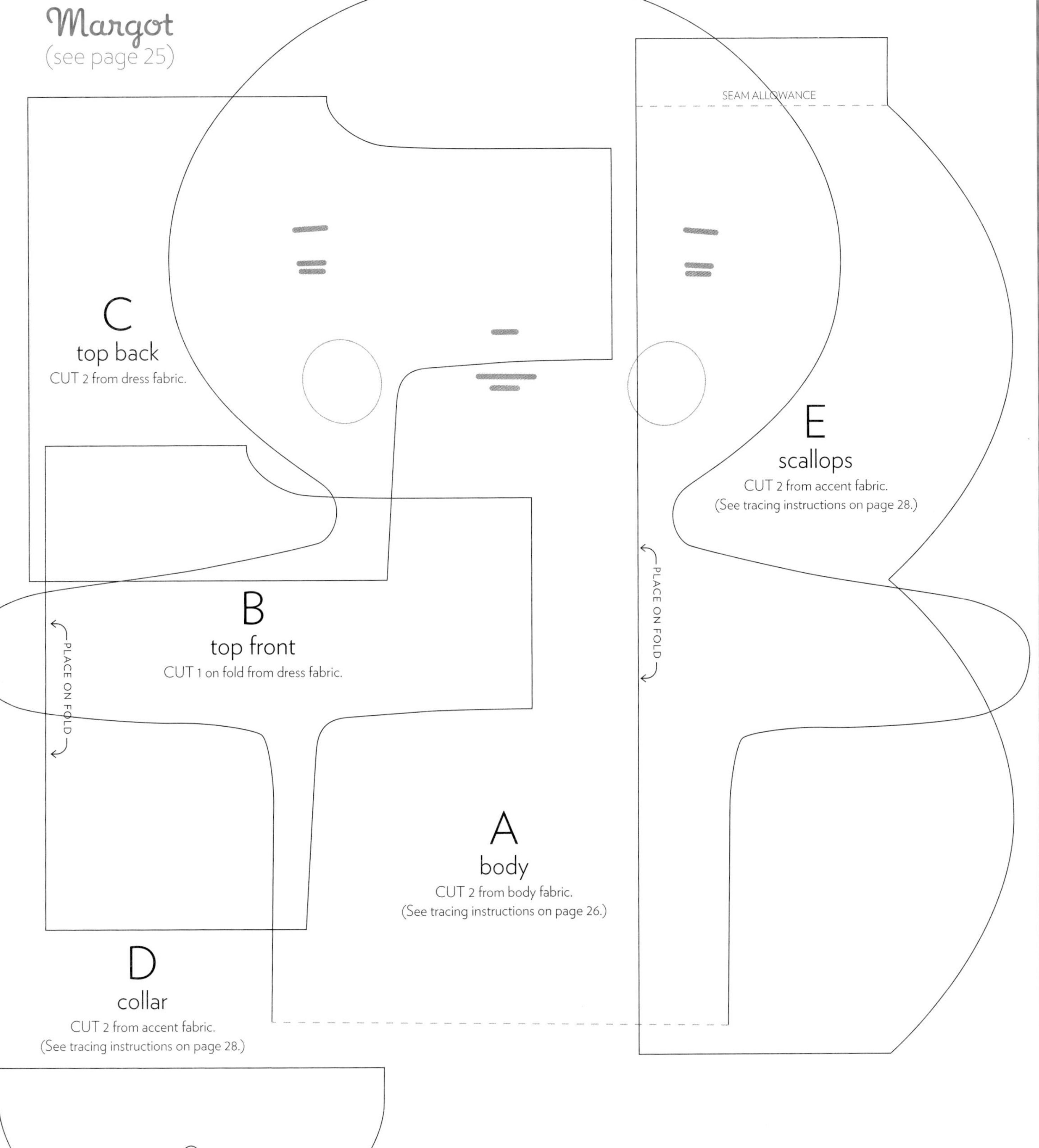

Betsy (see page 31)

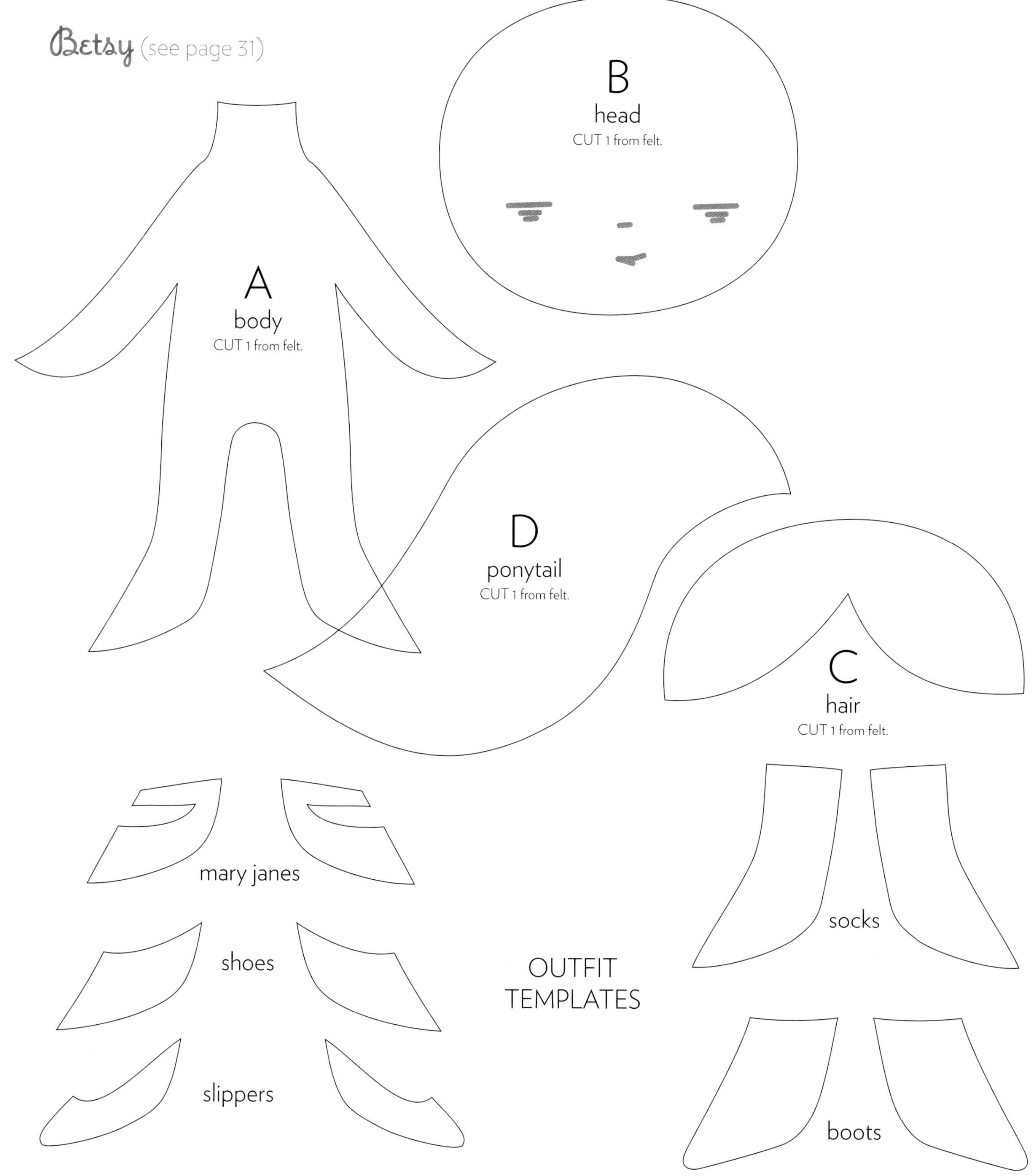

OUTFIT TEMPLATES

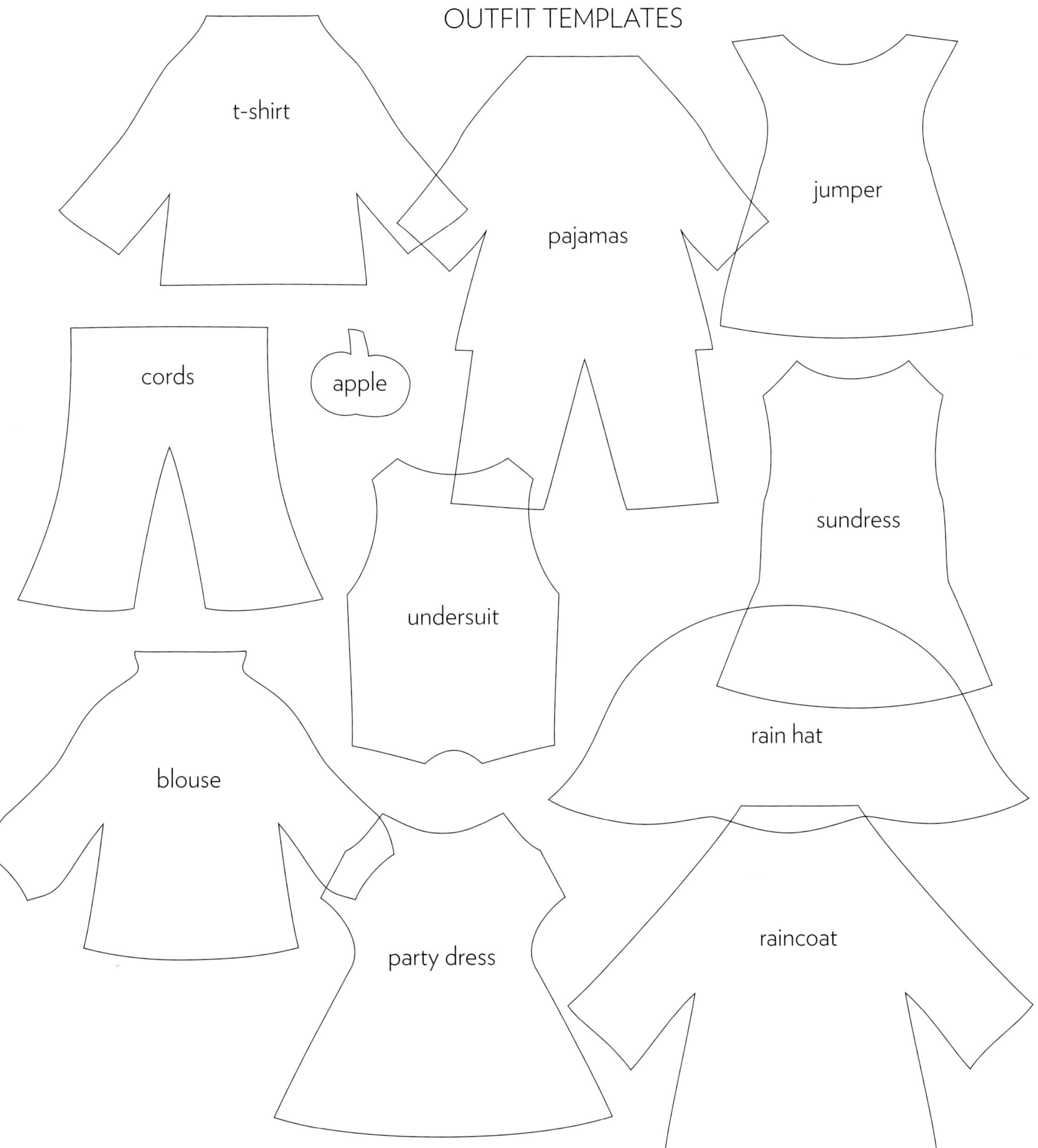

Mermaiden

(see page 37)

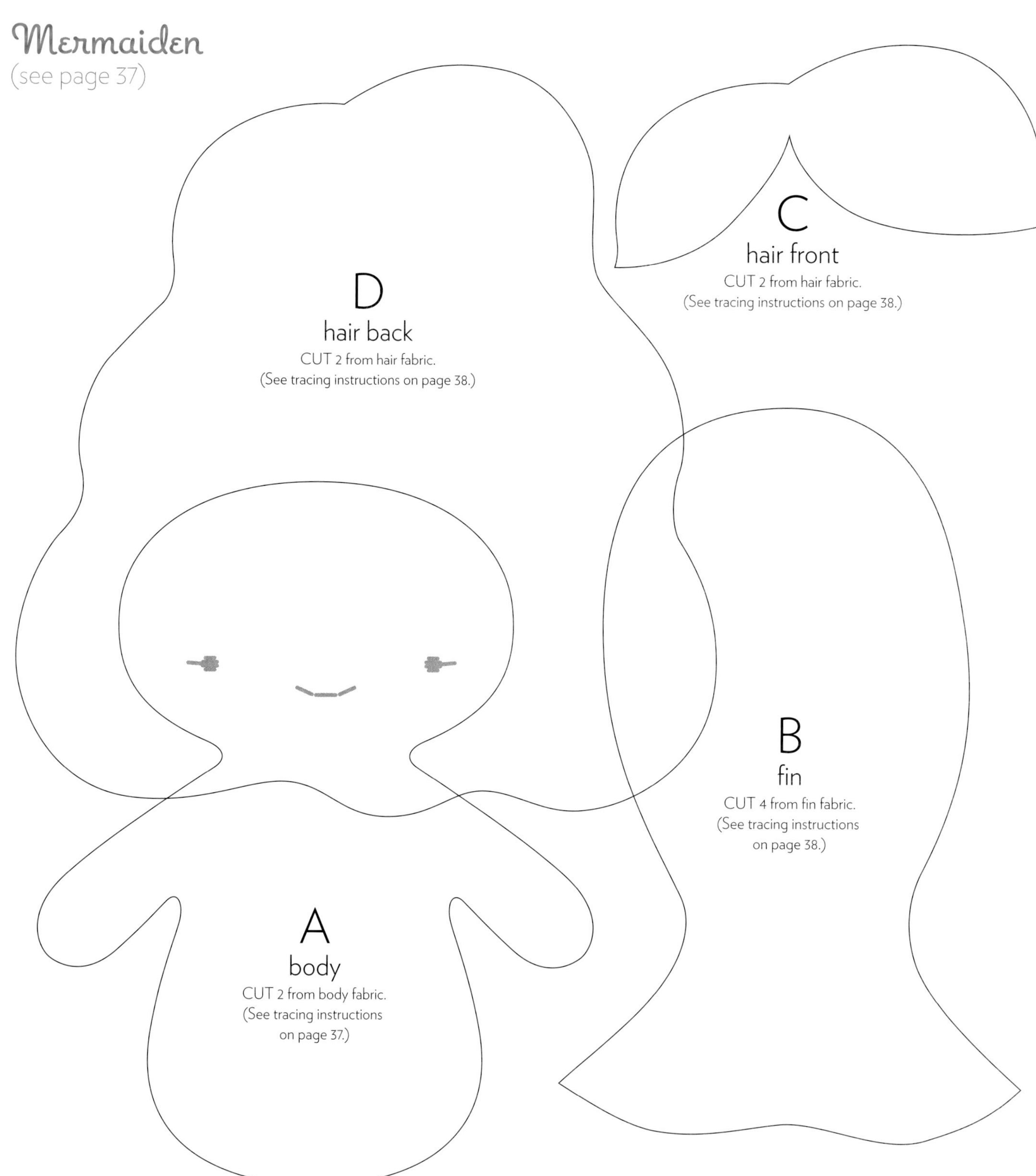

Ellie Bag

(see page 41)

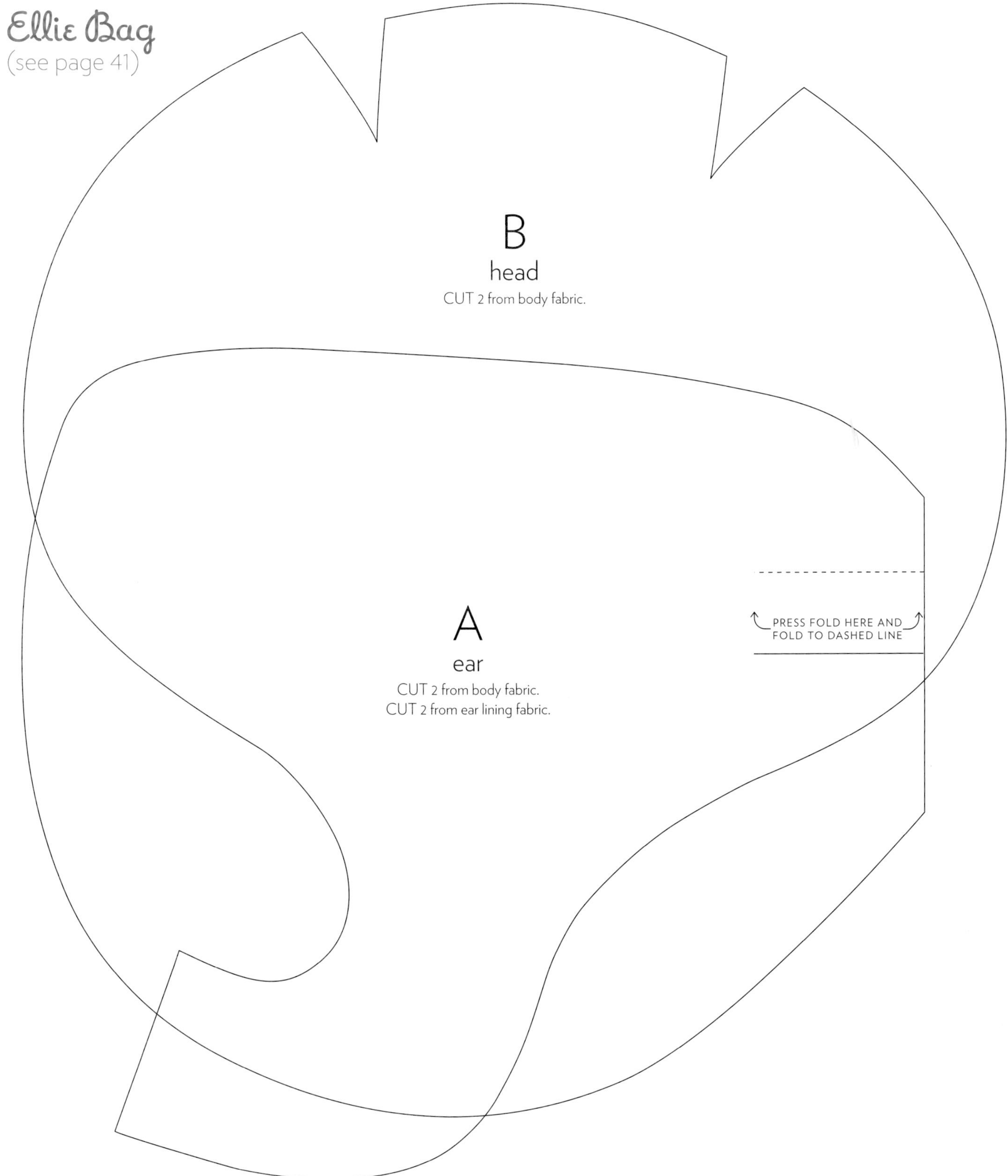

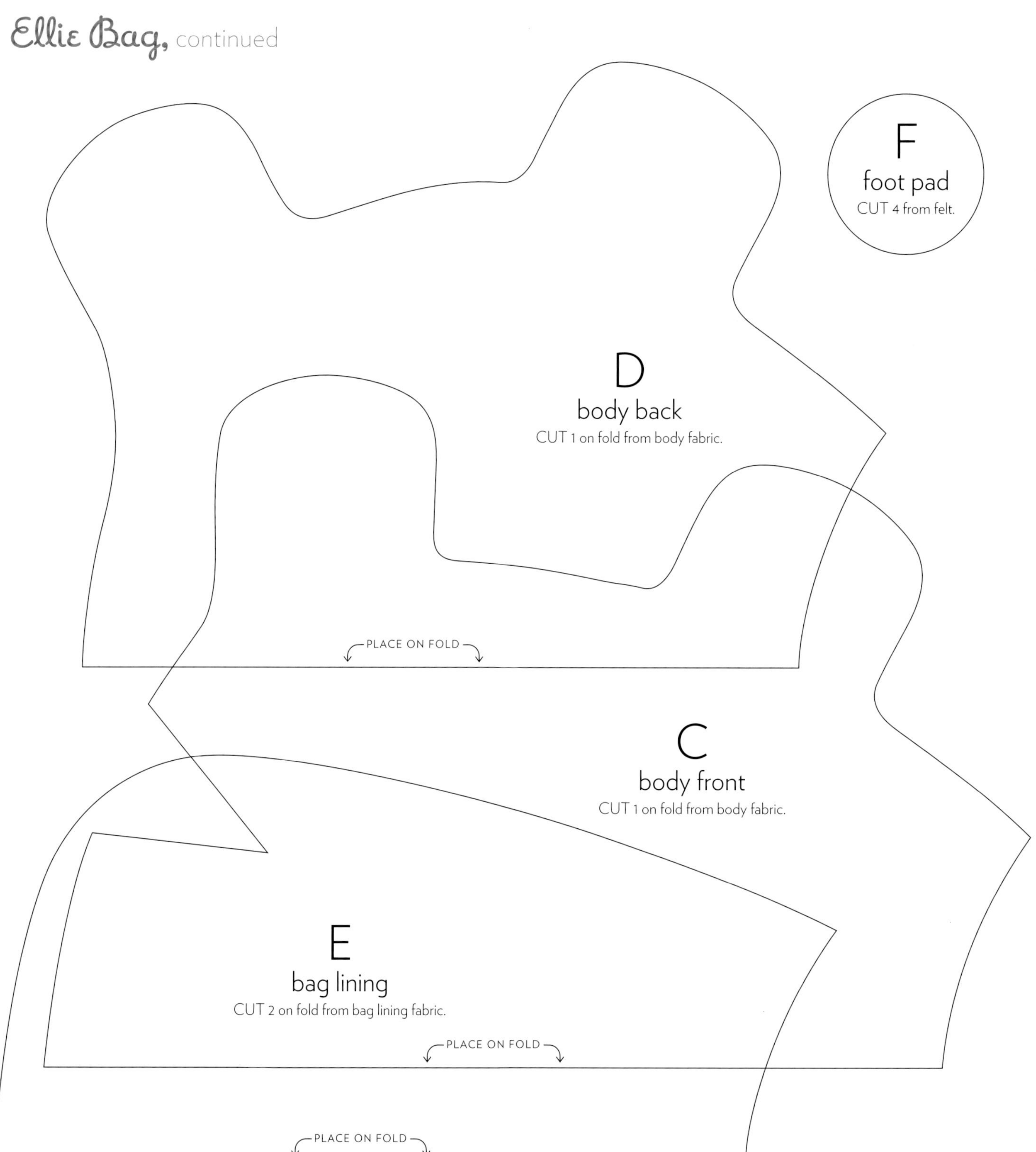
F
foot pad
CUT 4 from felt.
D
body back
CUT 1 on fold from body fabric.
PLACE ON FOLD
C
body front
CUT 1 on fold from body fabric.
E
bag lining
CUT 2 on fold from bag lining fabric.
PLACE ON FOLD
PLACE ON FOLD

Panda Buns

(see page 45)

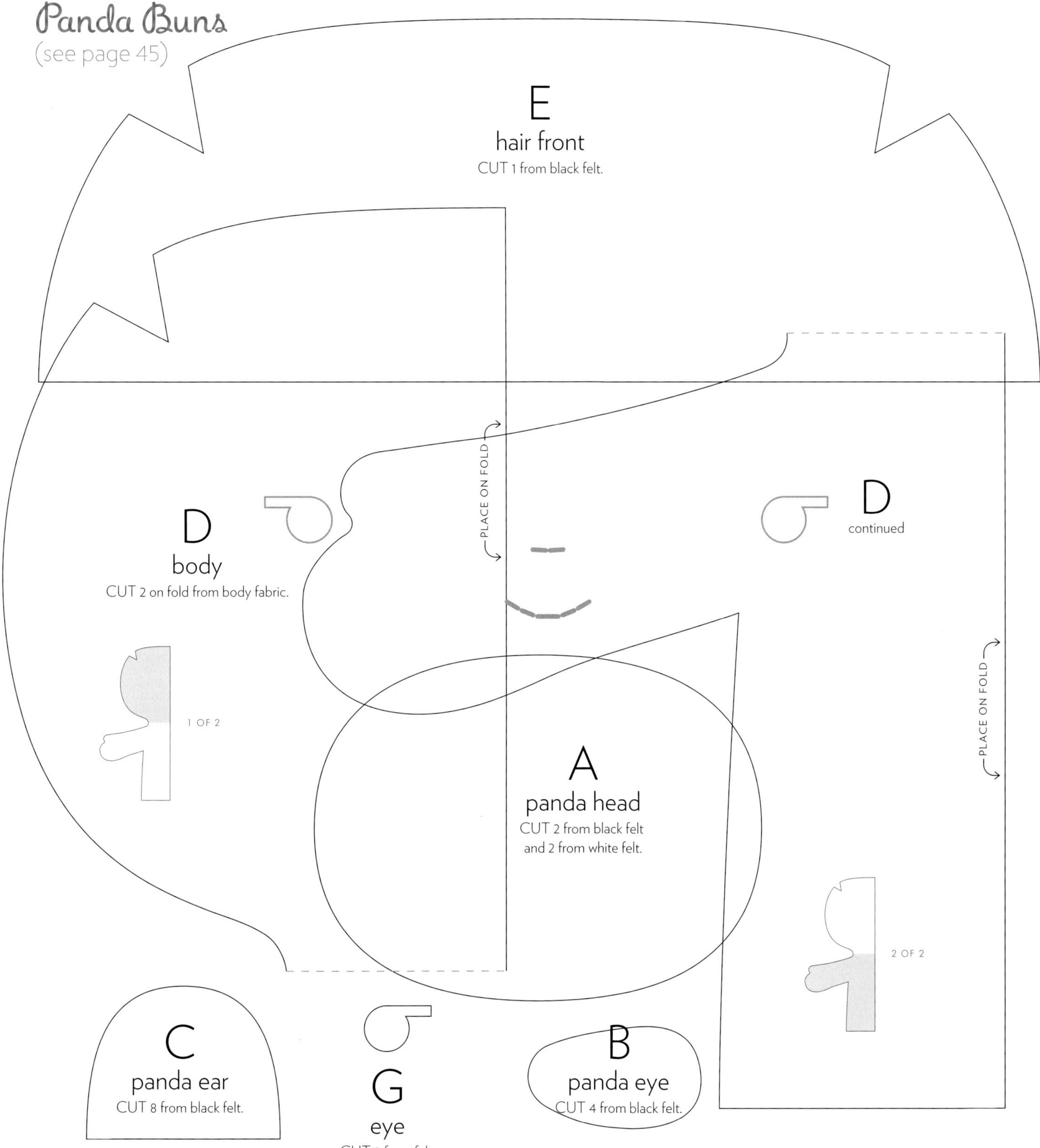

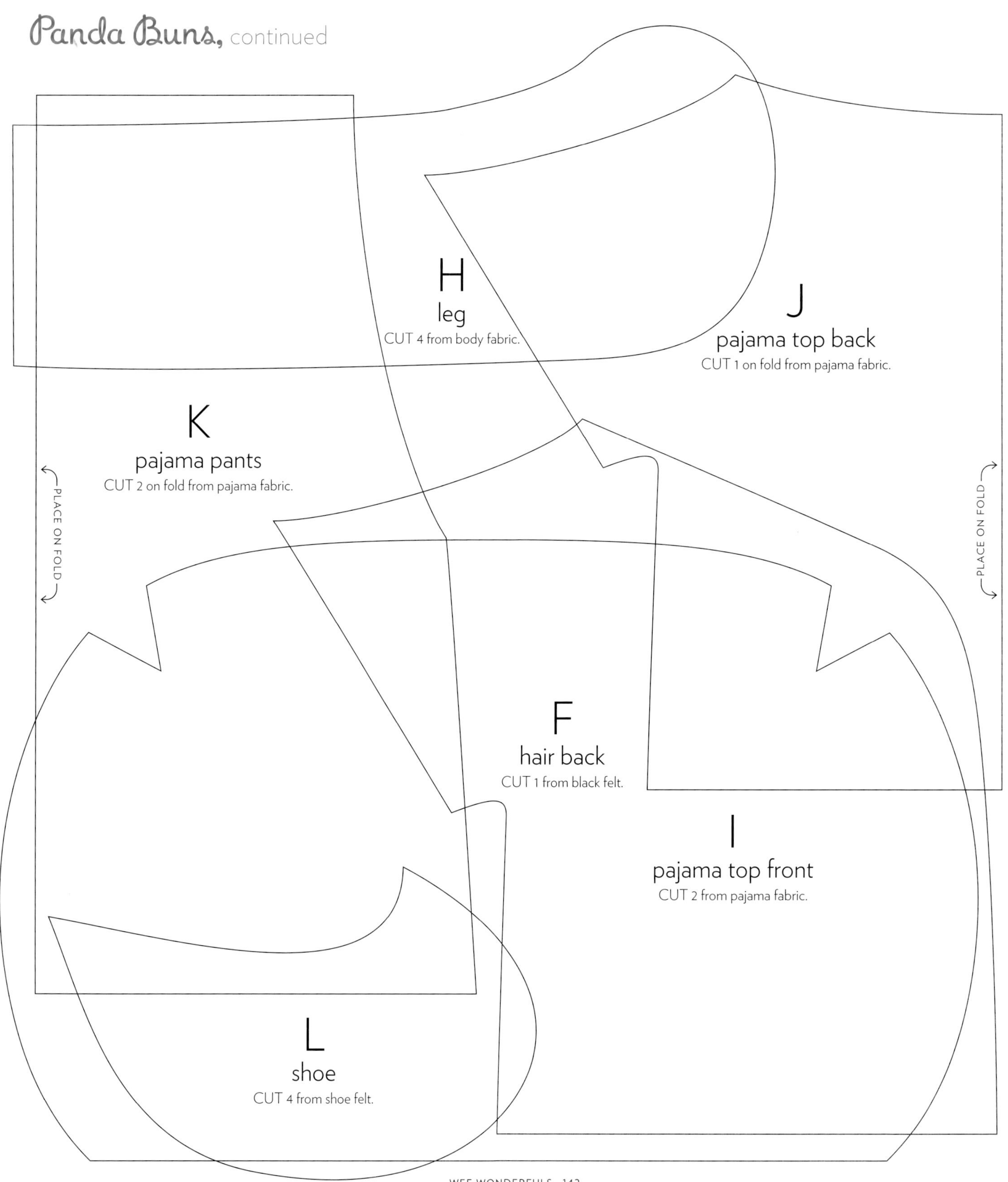
H
leg
CUT 4 from body fabric.
J
pajama top back
CUT 1 on fold from pajama fabric.
K
pajama pants
CUT 2 on fold from pajama fabric.
PLACE ON FOLD
PLACE ON FOLD
F
hair back
CUT 1 from black felt.
I
pajama top front
CUT 2 from pajama fabric.
L
shoe
CUT 4 from shoe felt.

Wee Town Trolley (see page 49)

D
back door
CUT 1 from door felt.

E
side door
CUT 4 from door felt.

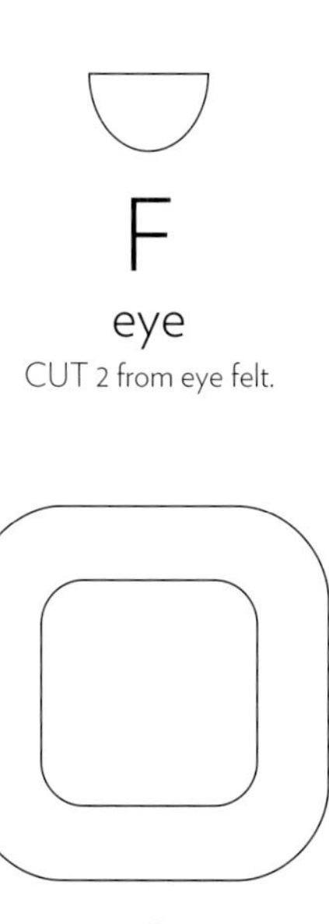

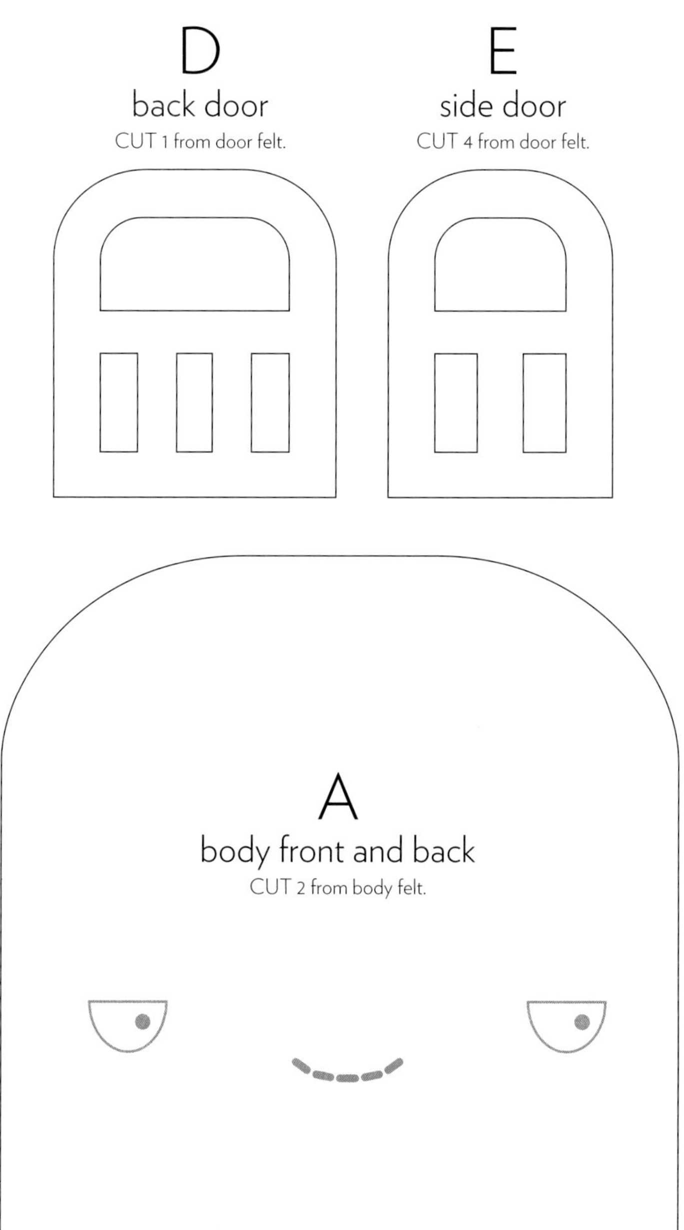

Sleepover Pals (see page 53)

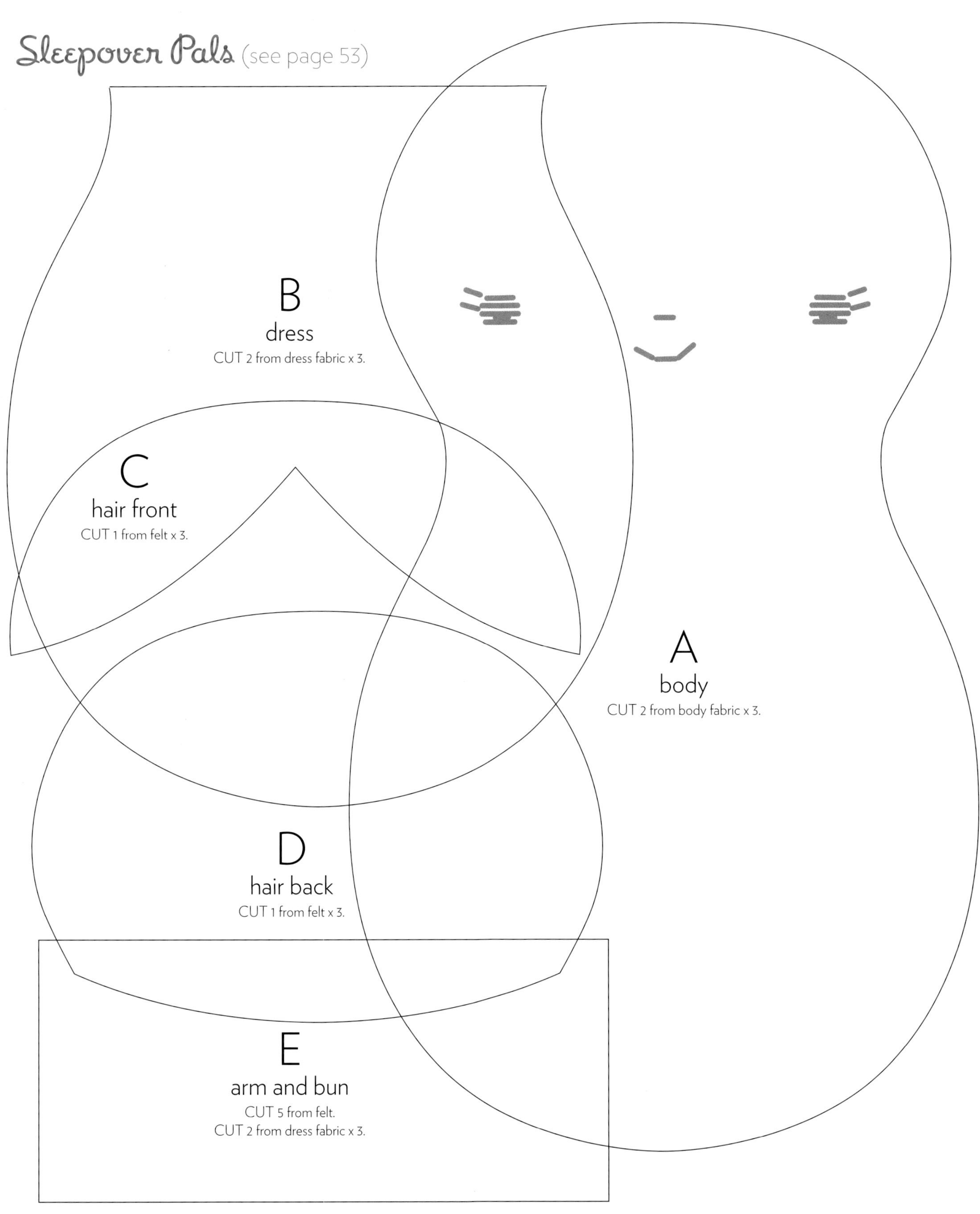

Eddie

(see page 57)

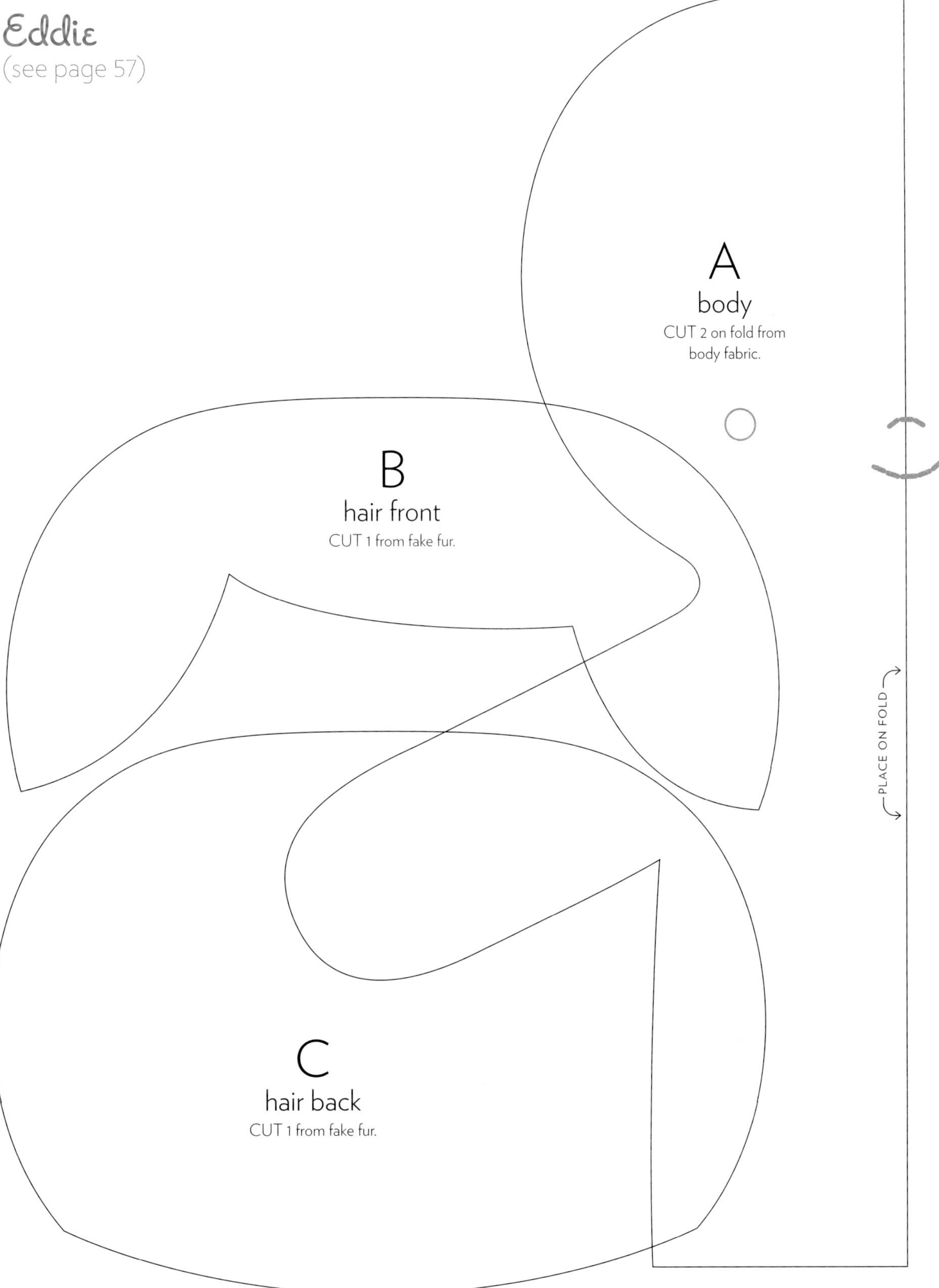

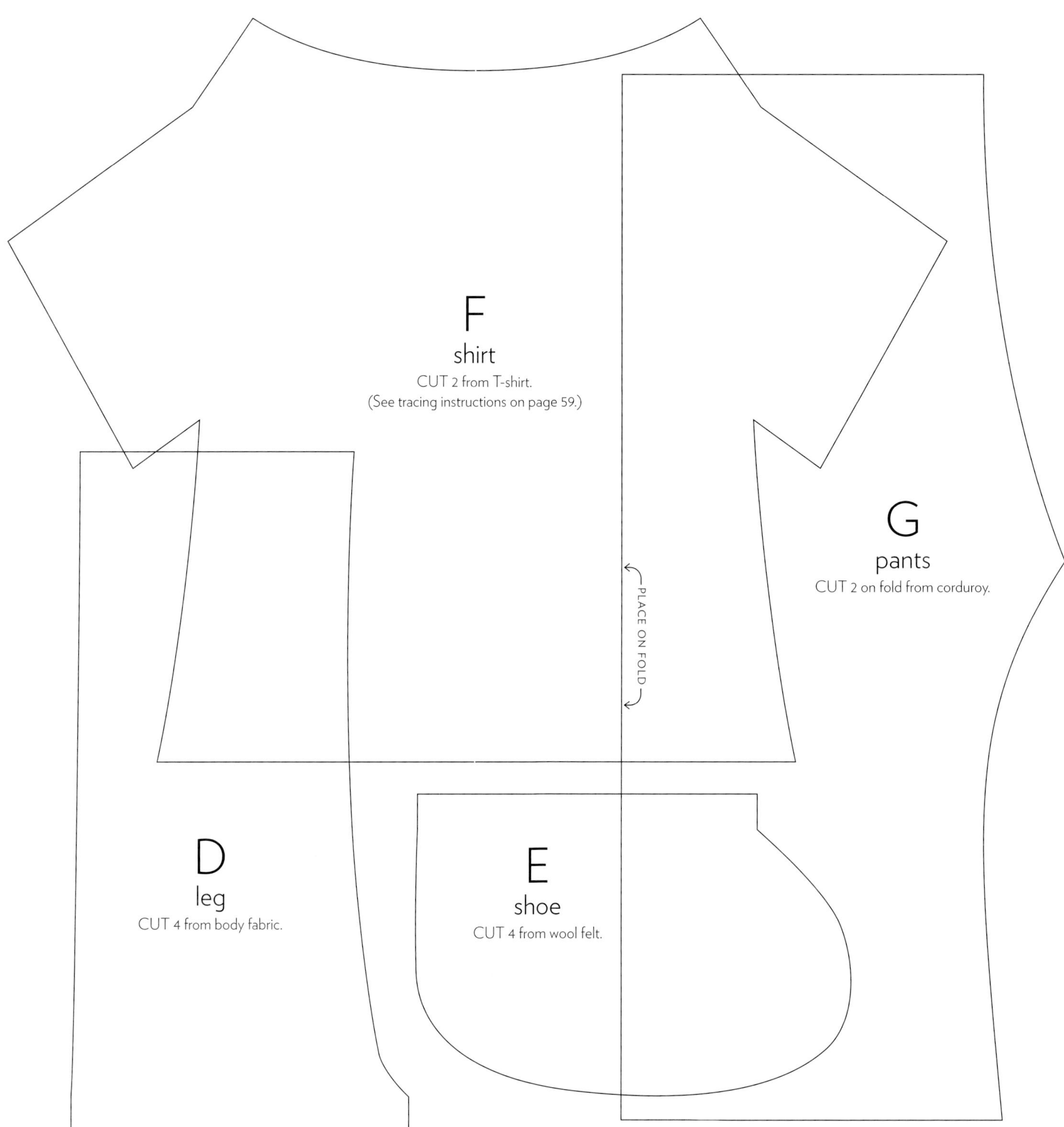
F
shirt
CUT 2 from T-shirt.
(See tracing instructions on page 59.)
G
pants
CUT 2 on fold from corduroy.
PLACE ON FOLD
D
leg
CUT 4 from body fabric.
E
shoe
CUT 4 from wool felt.

Tag-a-Long Doll (see page 61)

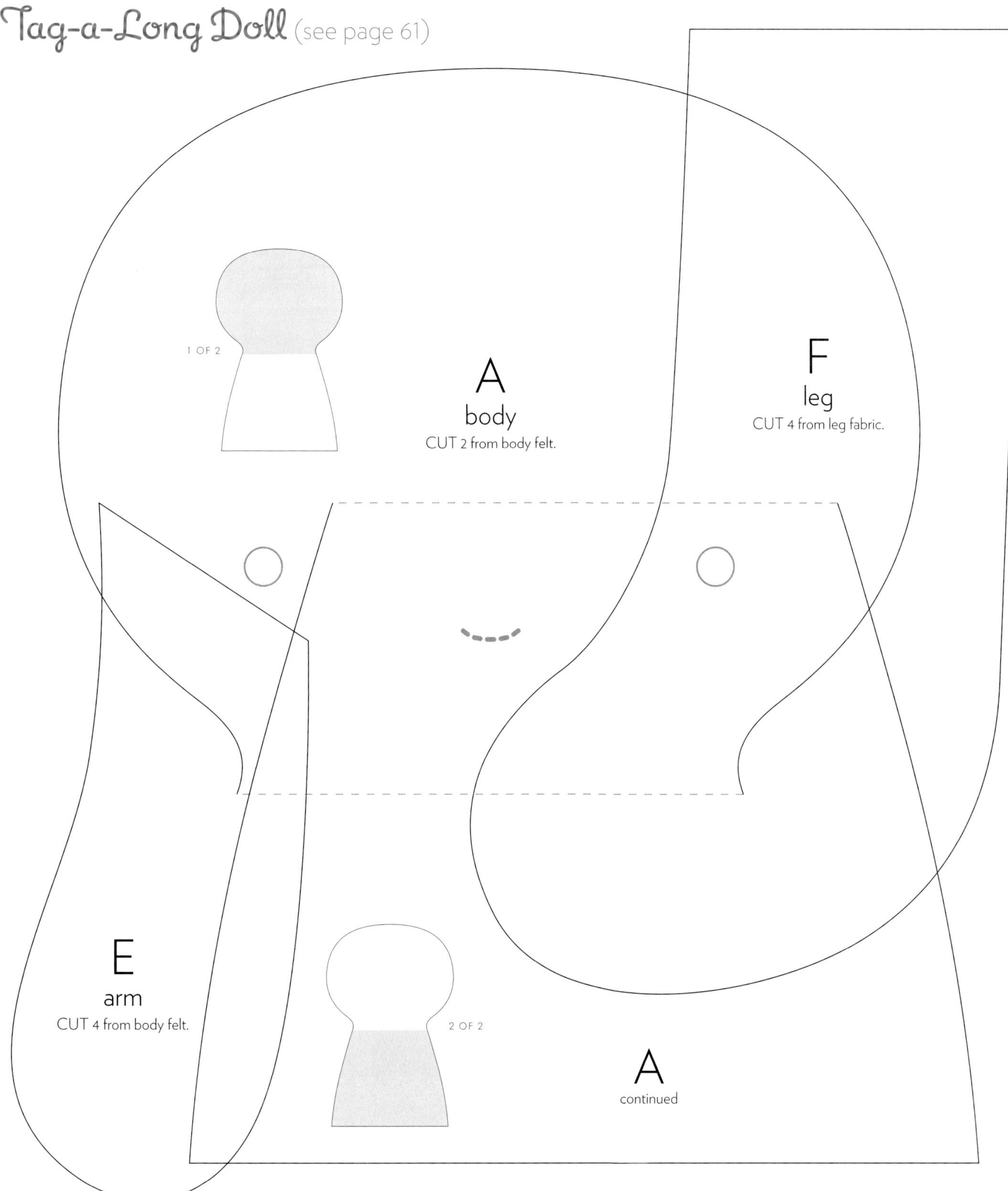

Tag-a-Long Doll, continued

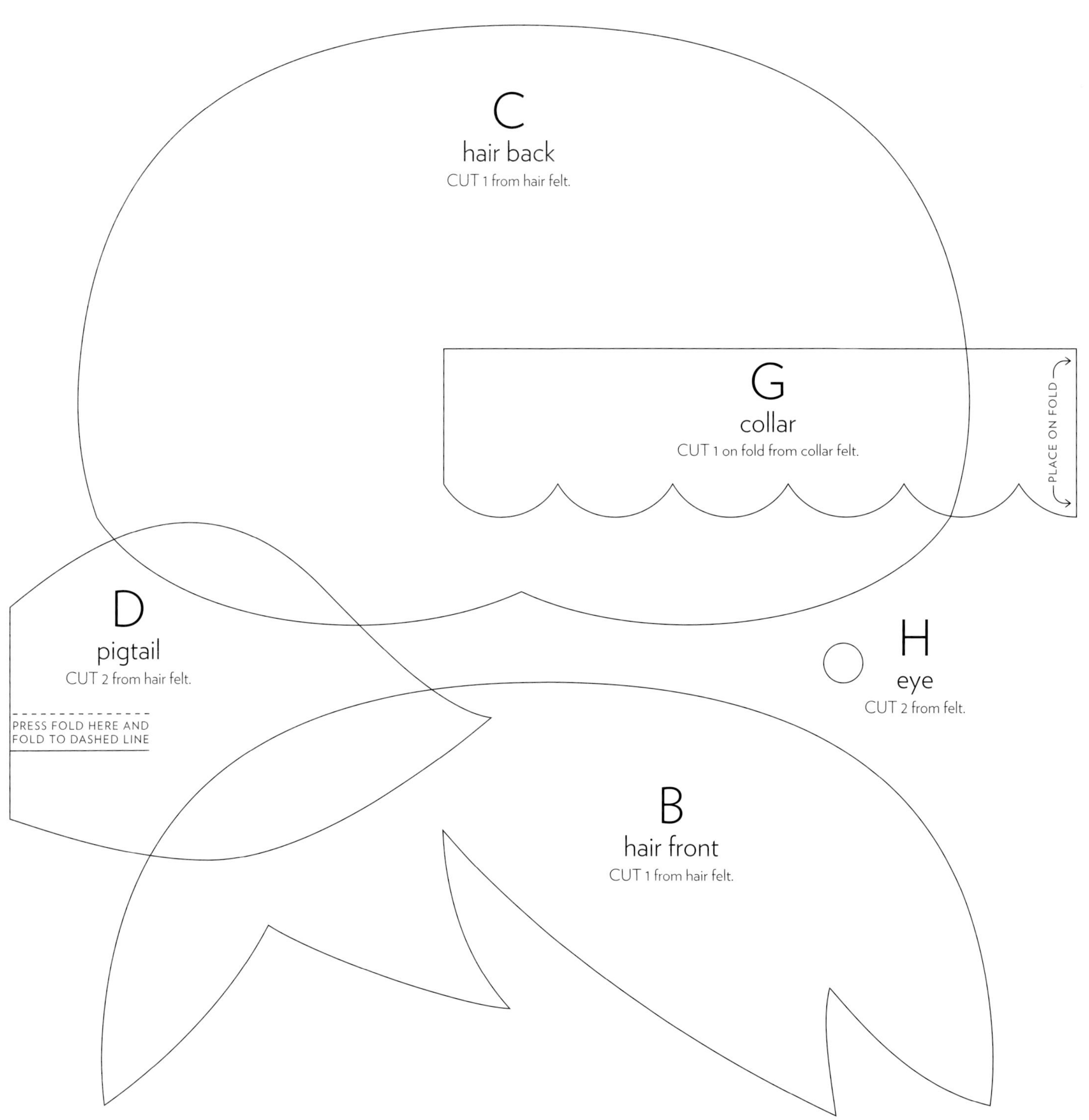

I Heart You (see page 67)

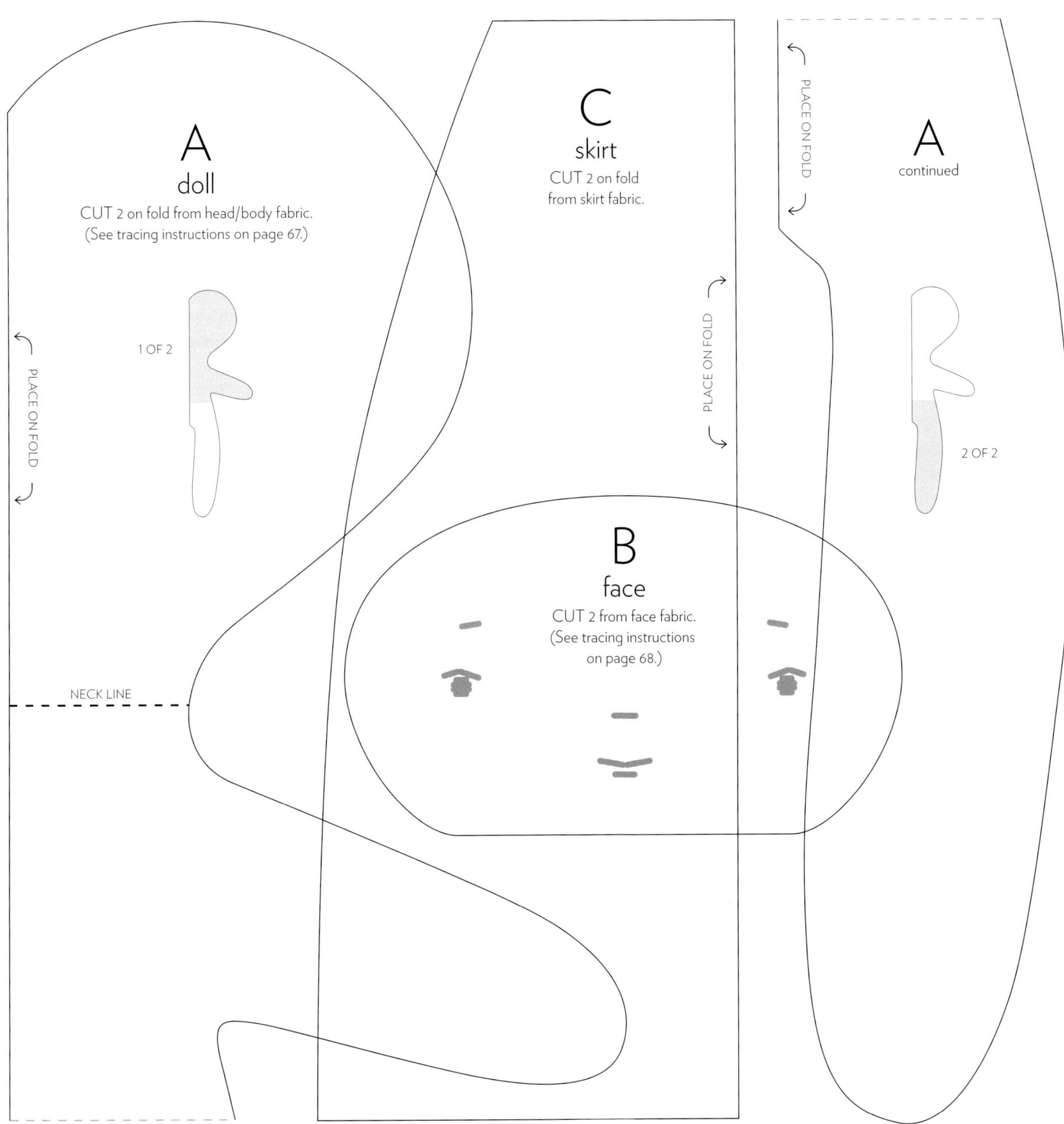

Wes, the Baby Giraffe

(see page 71)

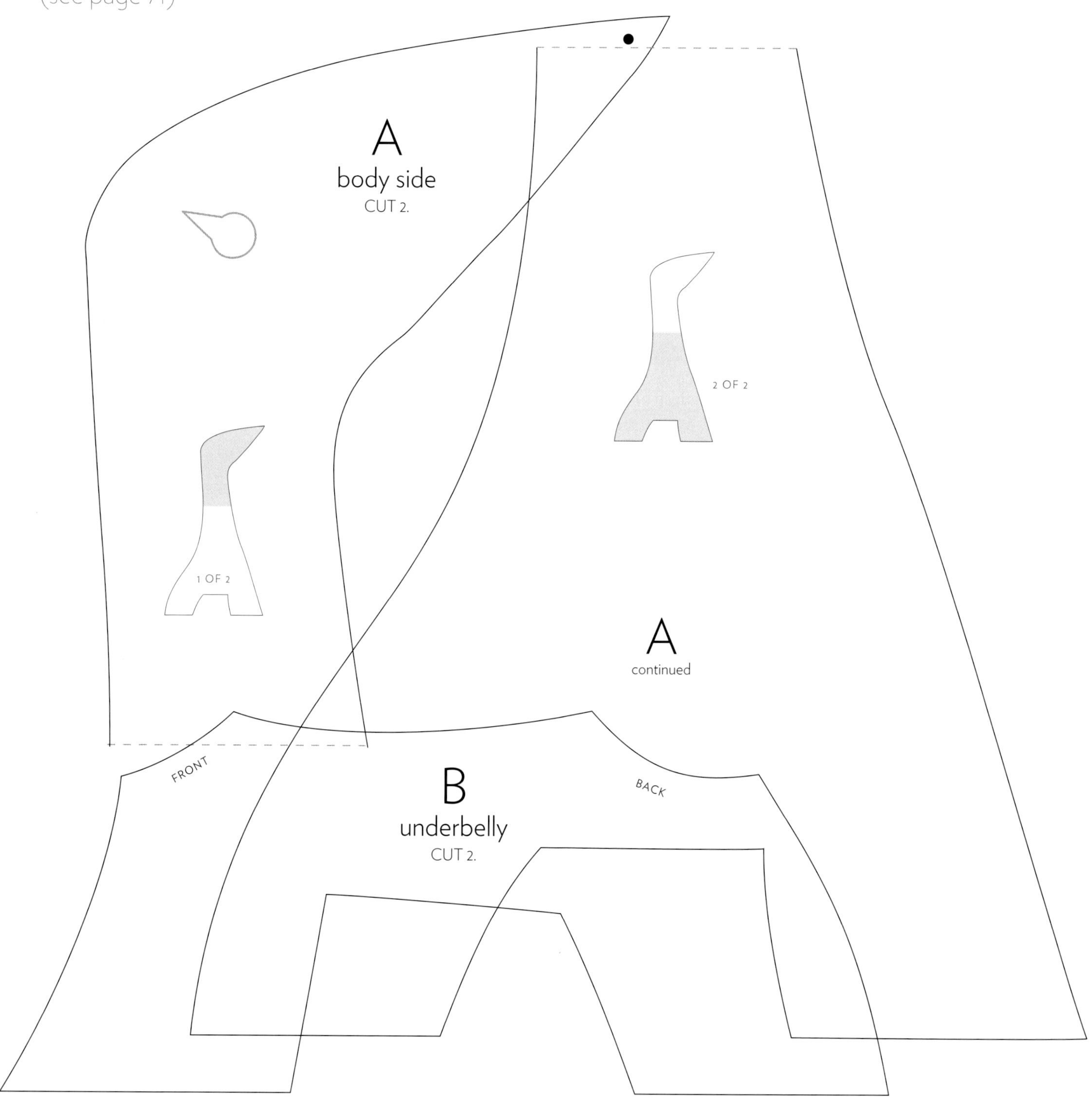

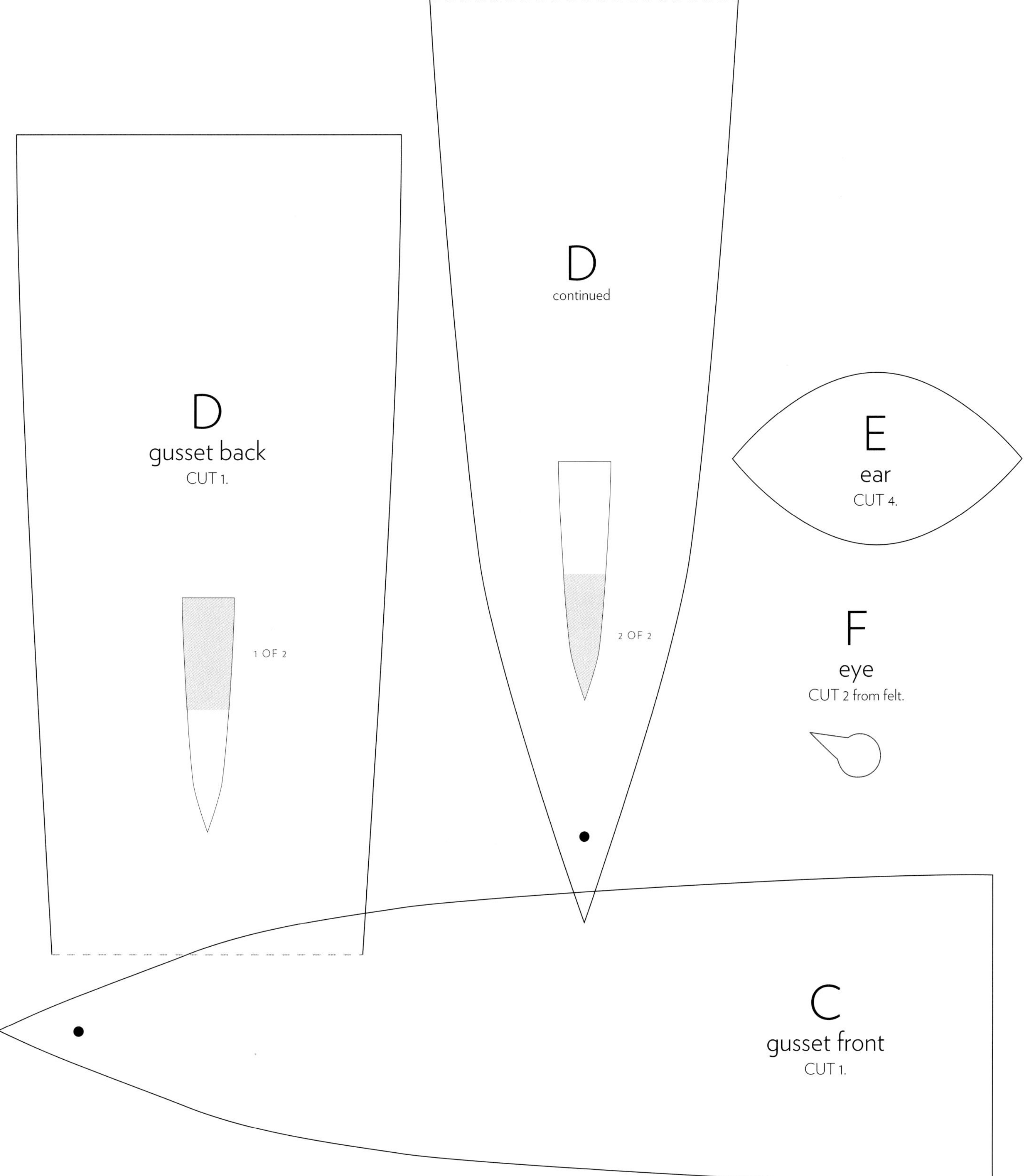
D
continued
2 OF 2
D
gusset back
CUT 1.
1 OF 2
E
ear
CUT 4.
F
eye
CUT 2 from felt.
C
gusset front
CUT 1.

Katie Kitty (see page 75)

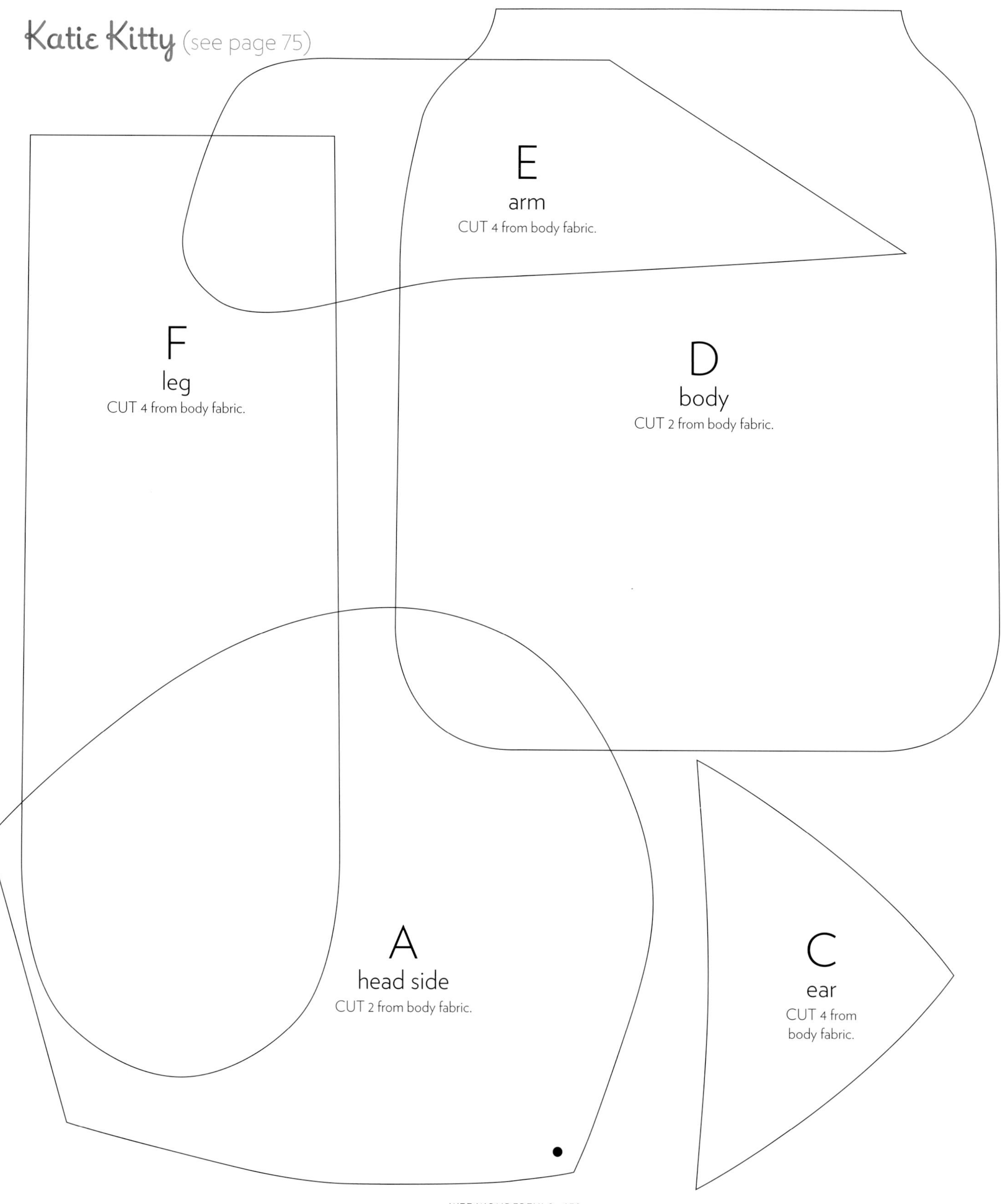

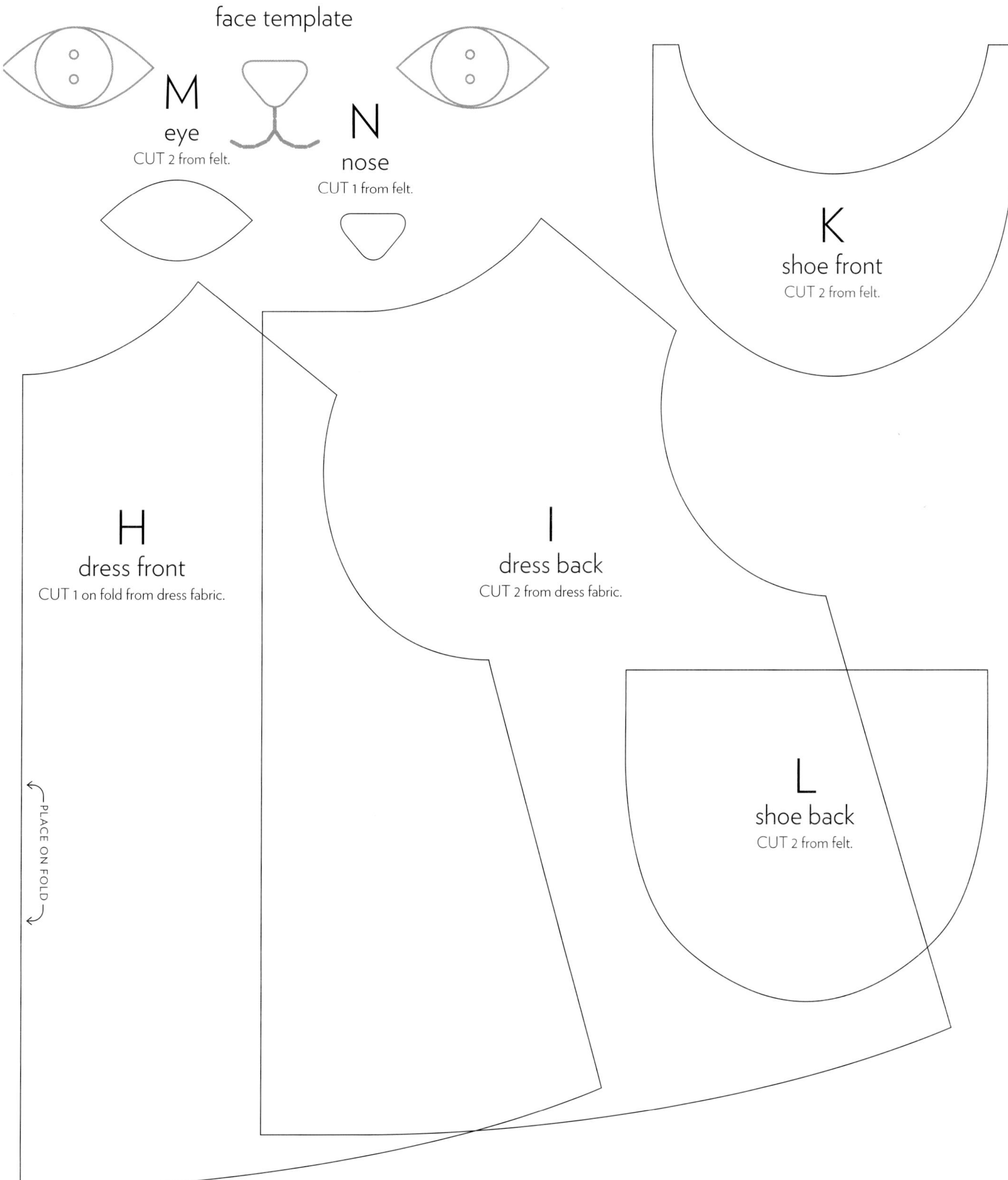
face template
M
eye
CUT 2 from felt.
N
nose
CUT 1 from felt.
K
shoe front
CUT 2 from felt.
H
dress front
CUT 1 on fold from dress fabric.
PLACE ON FOLD
I
dress back
CUT 2 from dress fabric.
L
shoe back
CUT 2 from felt.

Katie Kitty, continued

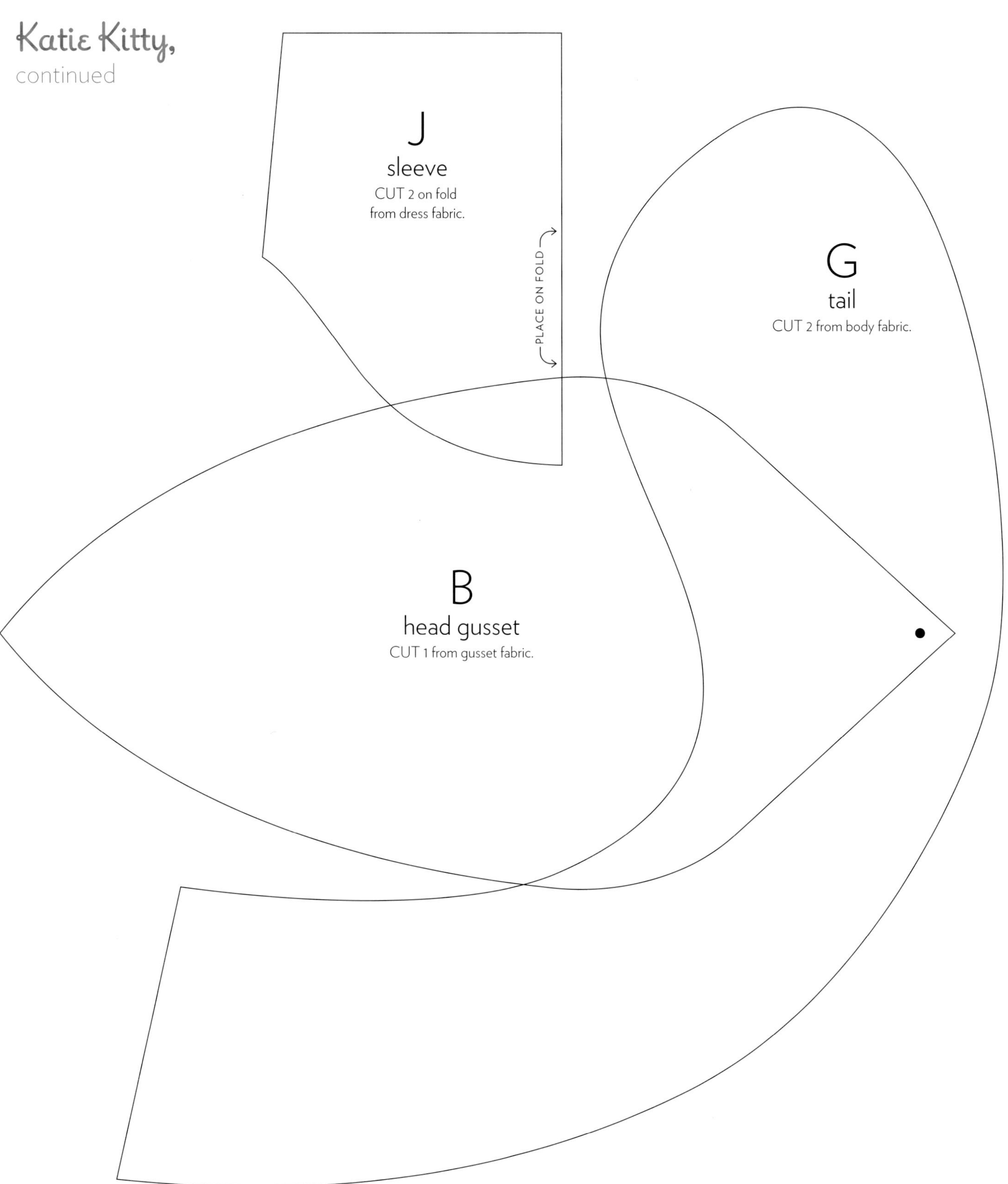

Melvin and Marian (see page 79)

Note: Cutting directions are for one bear.

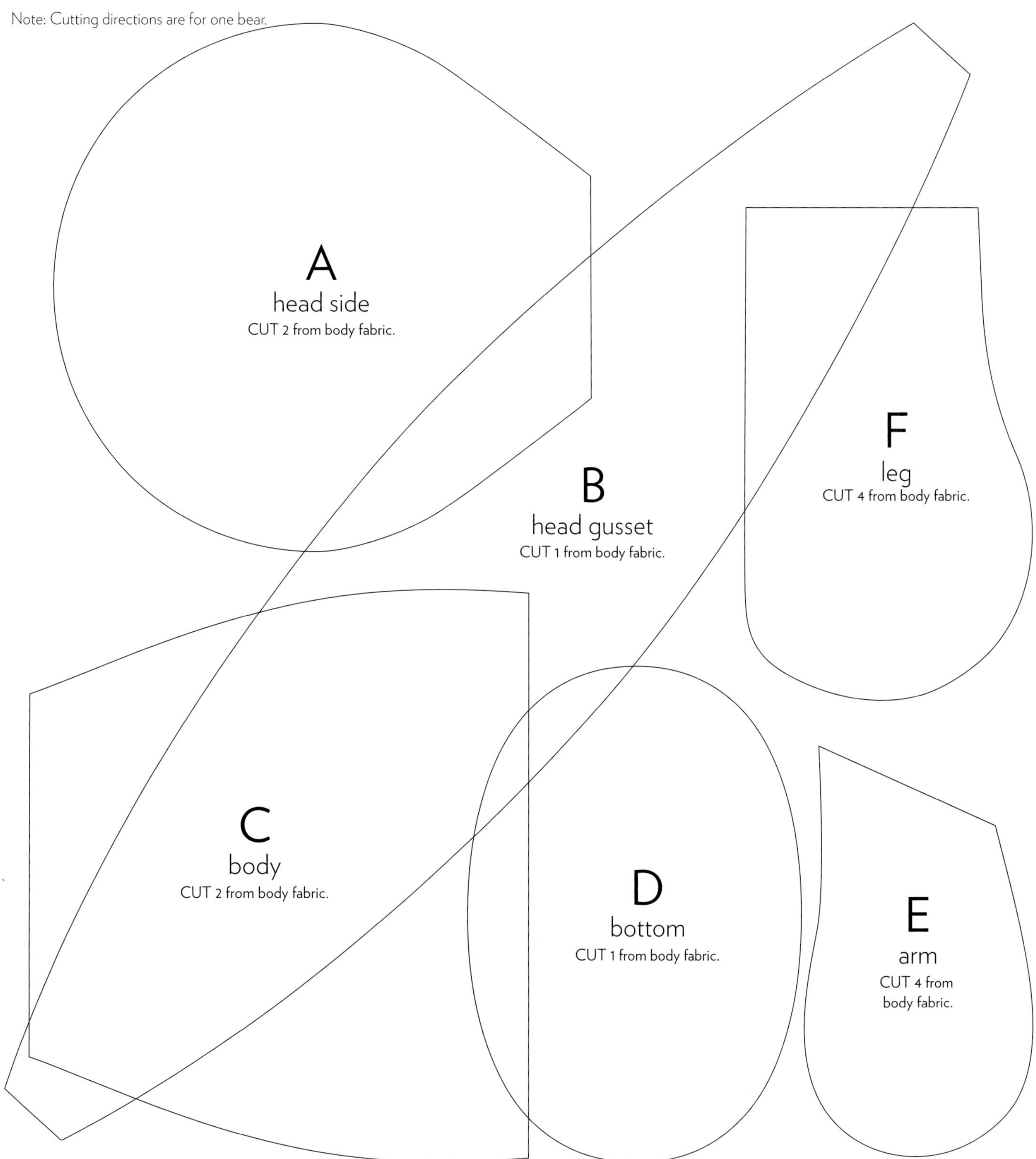

Melvin and Marian,
continued

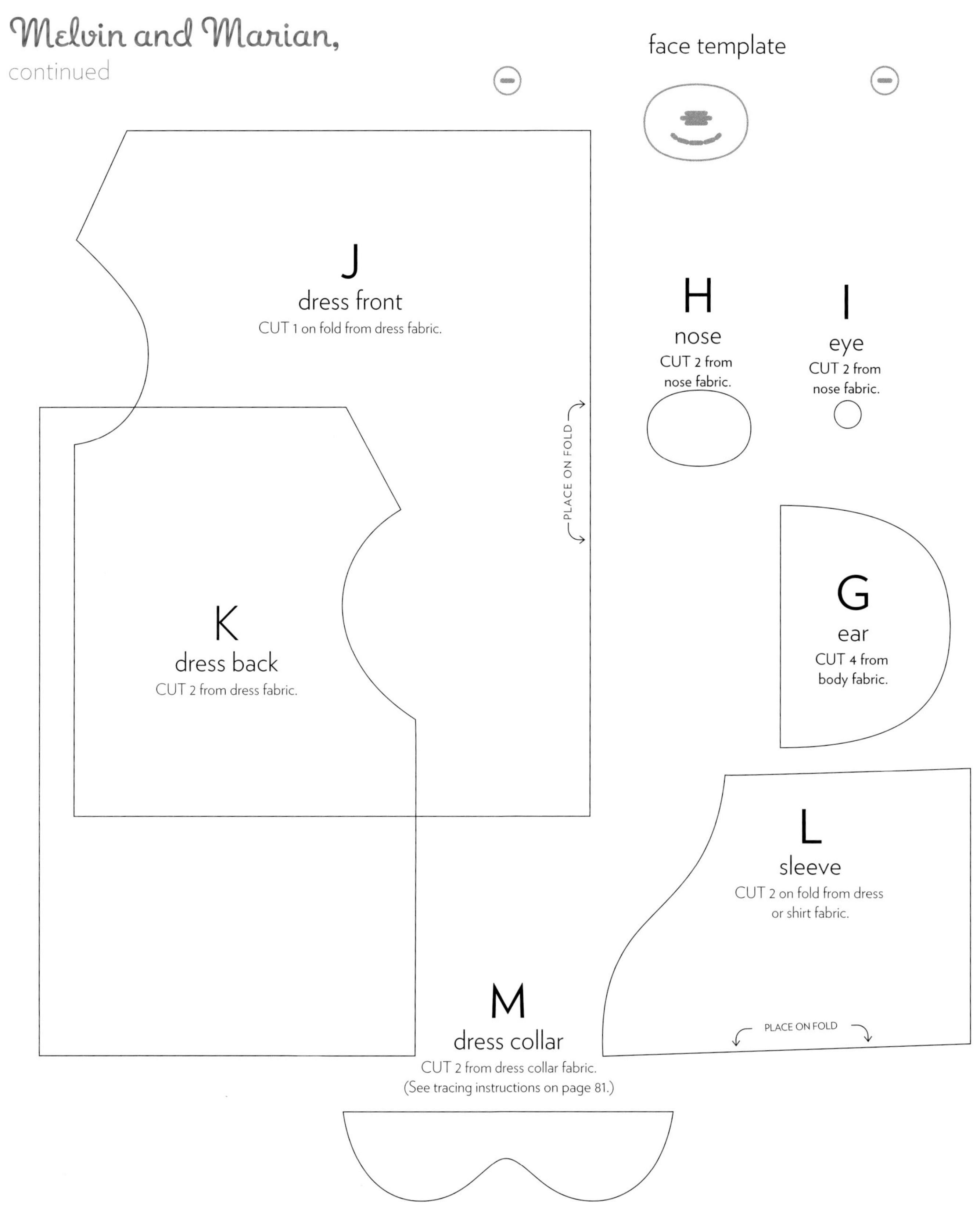

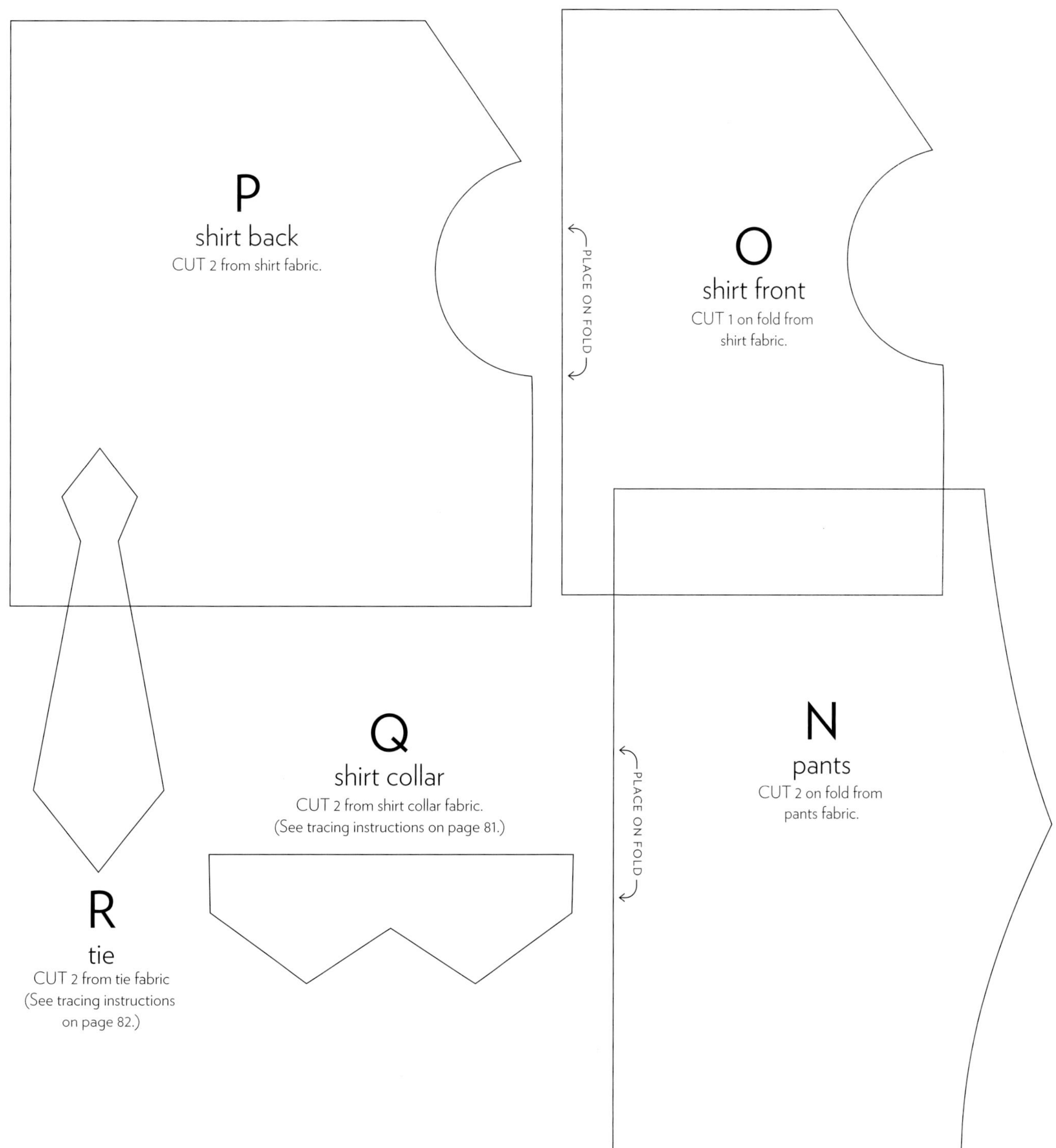
P
shirt back
CUT 2 from shirt fabric.
O
shirt front
CUT 1 on fold from
shirt fabric.
PLACE ON FOLD
R
tie
CUT 2 from tie fabric
(See tracing instructions
on page 82.)
Q
shirt collar
CUT 2 from shirt collar fabric.
(See tracing instructions on page 81.)
N
pants
CUT 2 on fold from
pants fabric.
PLACE ON FOLD

Bjorn Bjornson

(see page 85)

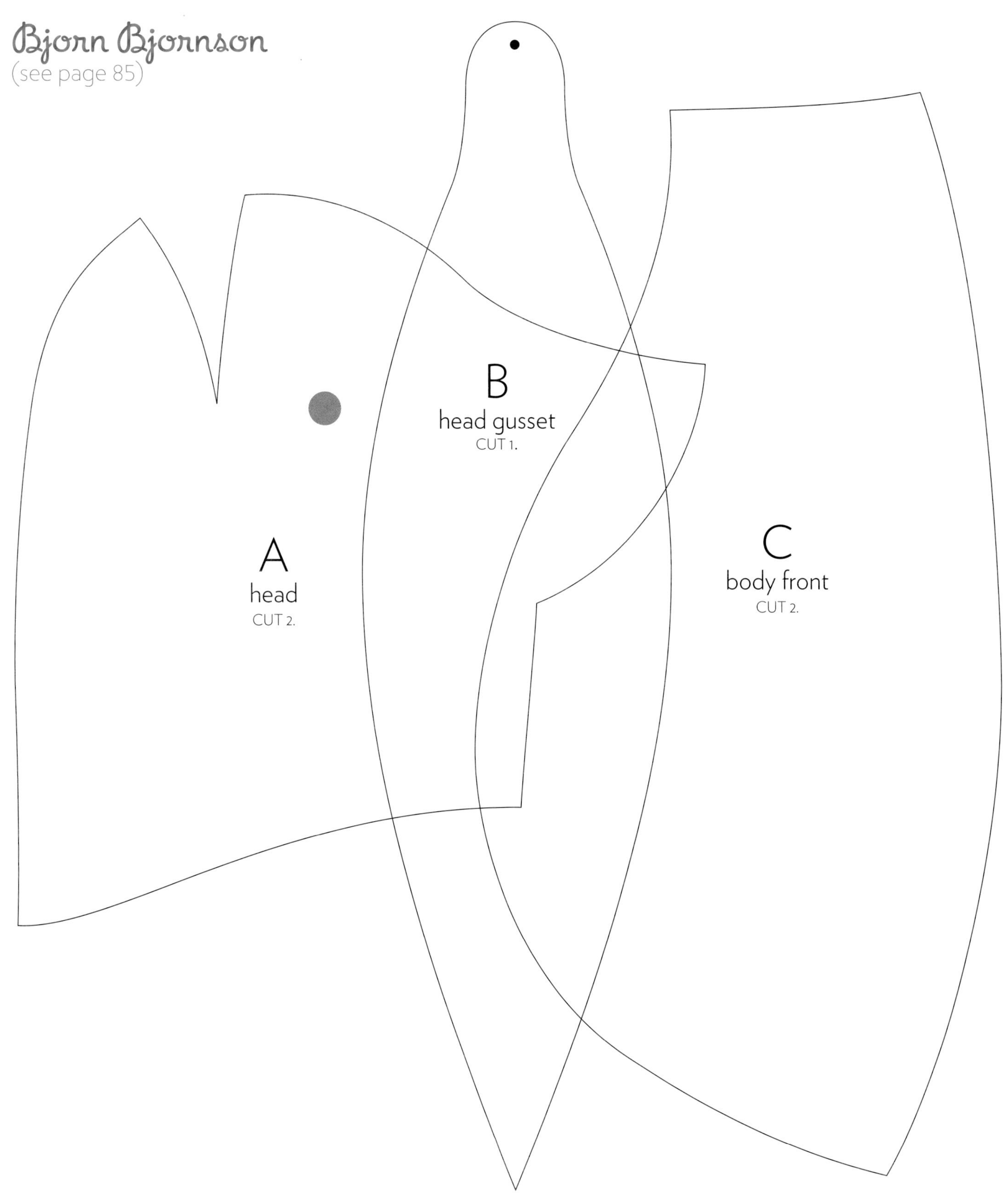

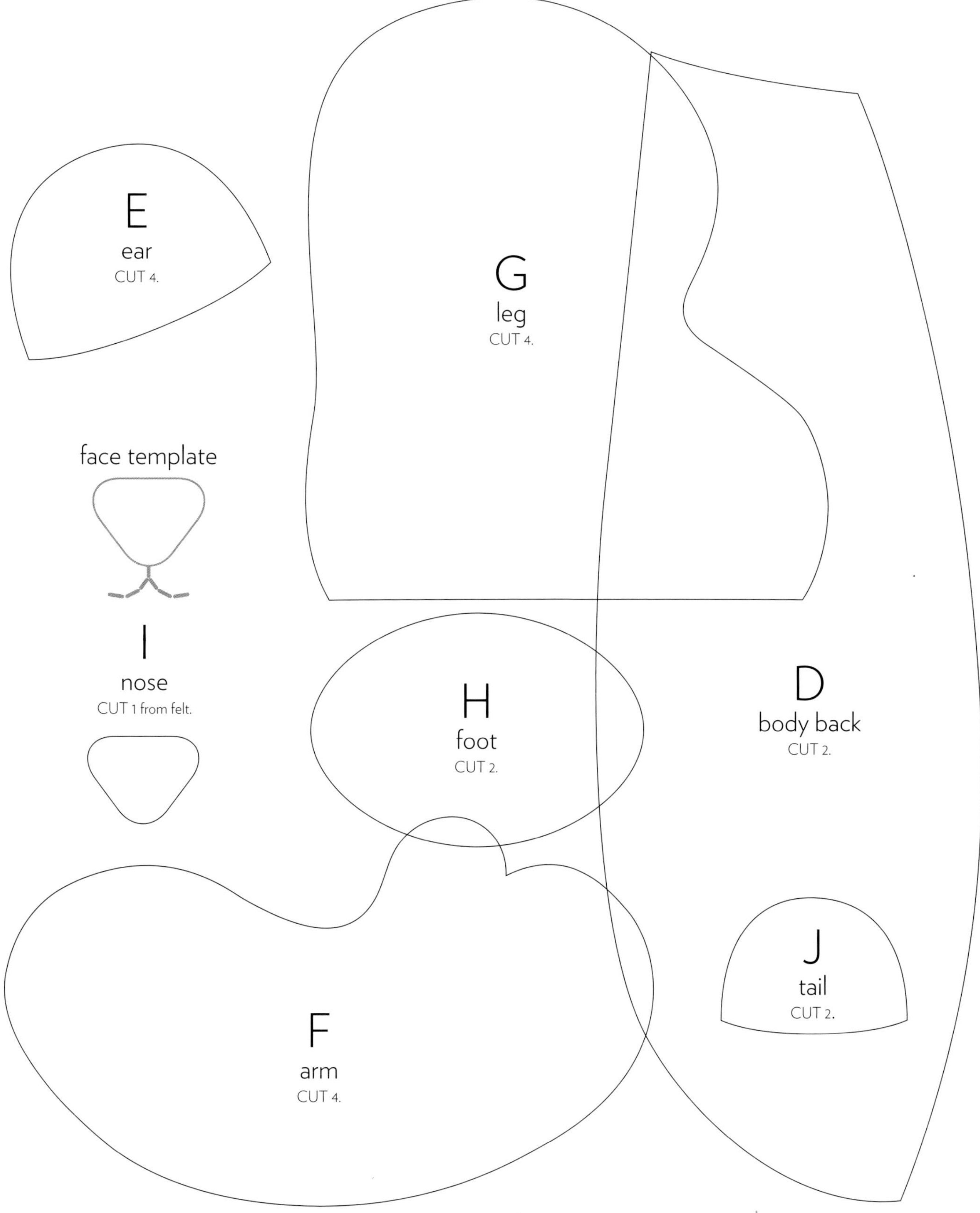
E
ear
CUT 4.
G
leg
CUT 4.
face template
I
nose
CUT 1 from felt.
H
foot
CUT 2.
D
body back
CUT 2.
J
tail
CUT 2.
F
arm
CUT 4.

Little Miss Storybook

(see page 89)

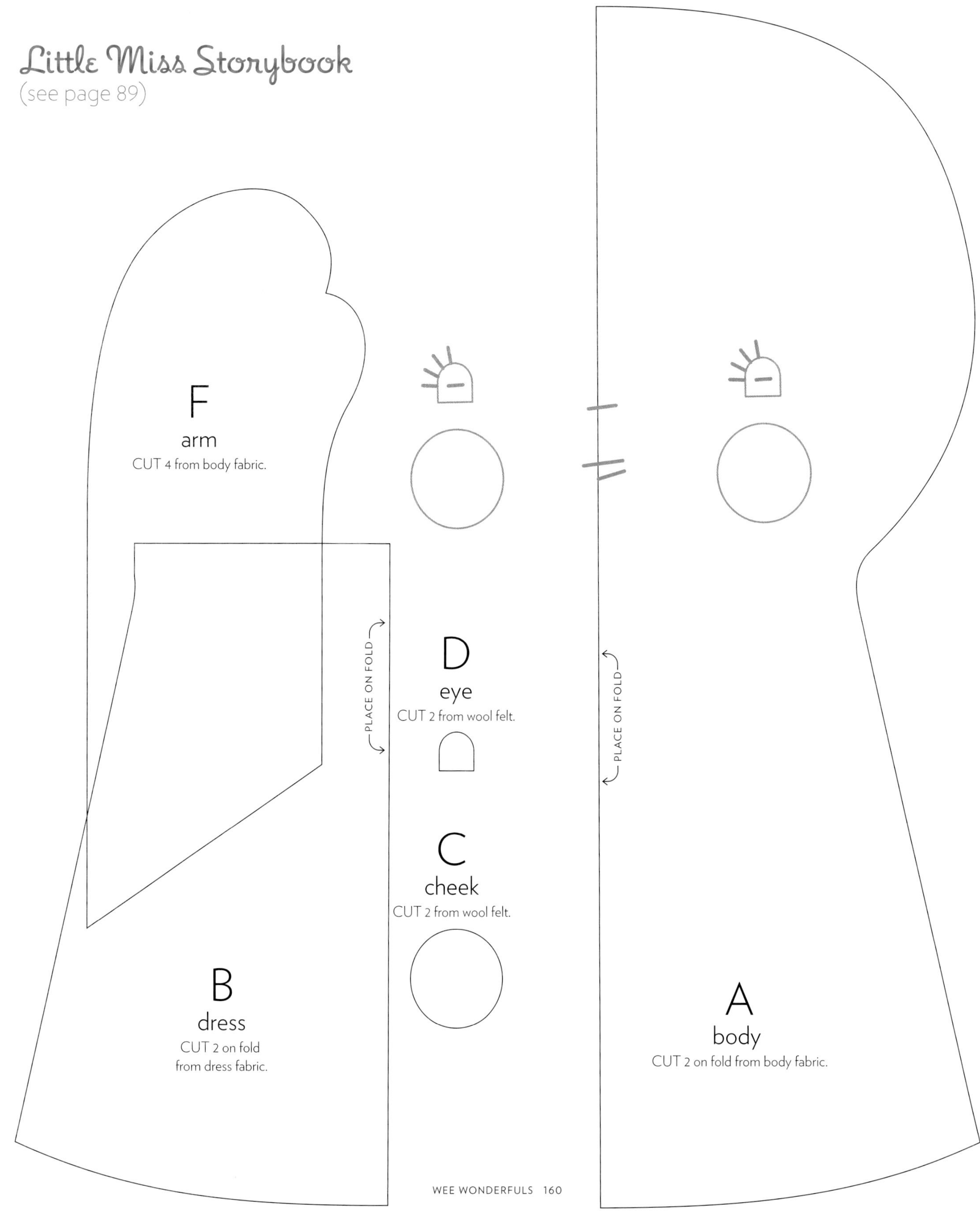

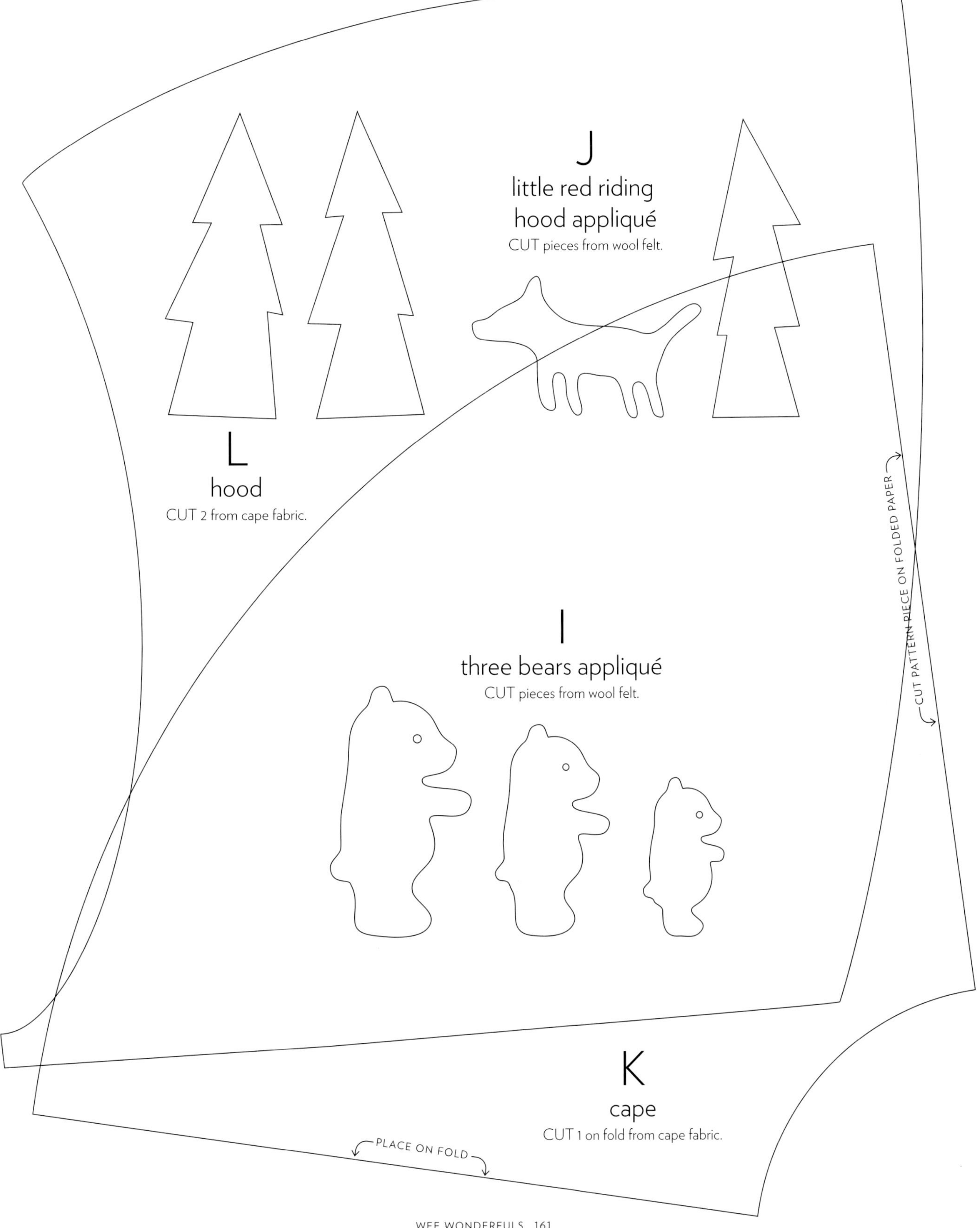
J
little red riding
hood appliqué
CUT pieces from wool felt.
L
hood
CUT 2 from cape fabric.
CUT PATTERN PIECE ON FOLDED PAPER
I
three bears appliqué
CUT pieces from wool felt.
K
cape
CUT 1 on fold from cape fabric.
PLACE ON FOLD

Little Miss Storybook,
continued

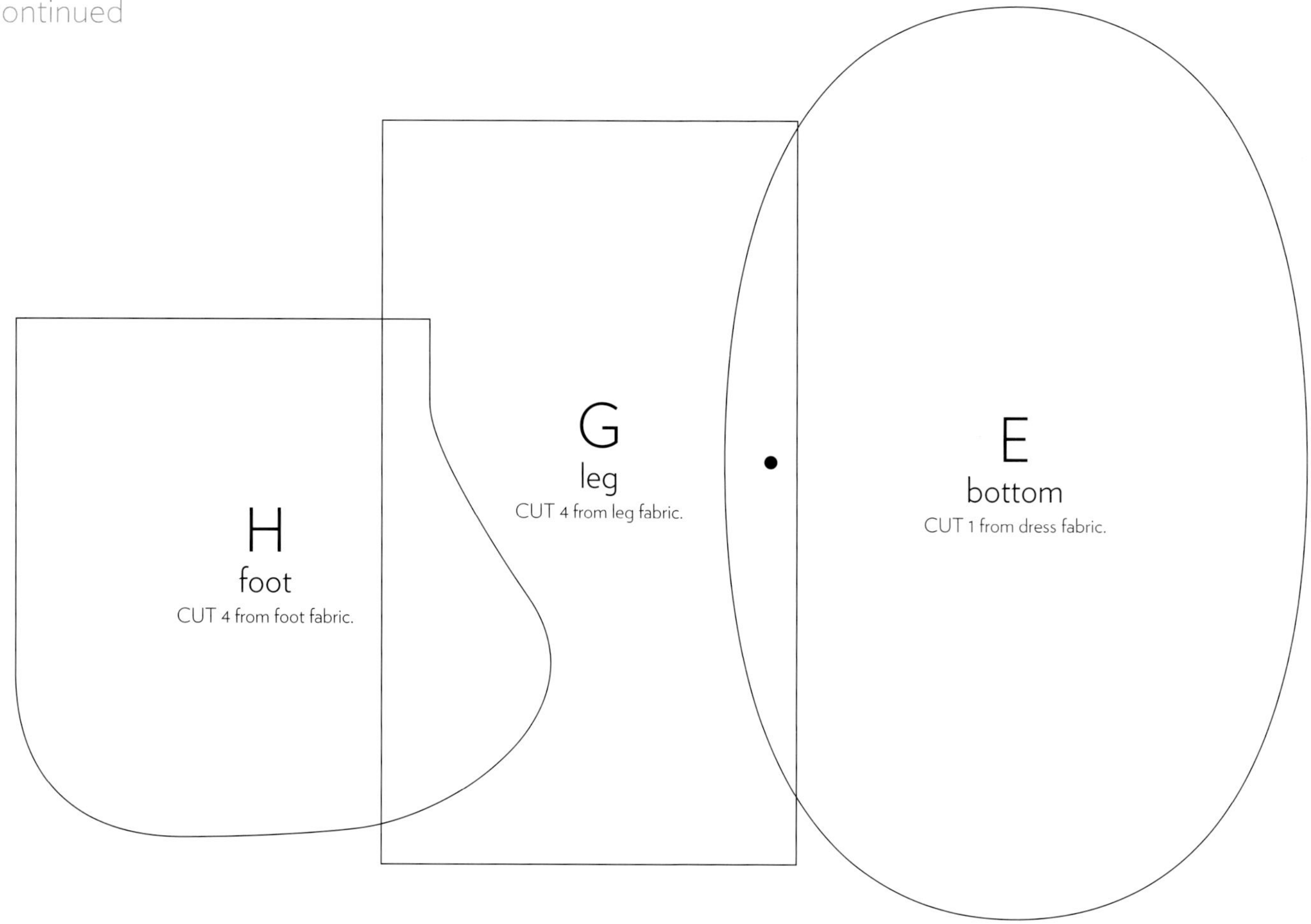

H
foot
CUT 4 from foot fabric.

G
leg
CUT 4 from leg fabric.

E
bottom
CUT 1 from dress fabric.

Doxie Necklace
(see page 95)

A
body
CUT 2 from body fabric.
(See tracing instructions on page 95.)

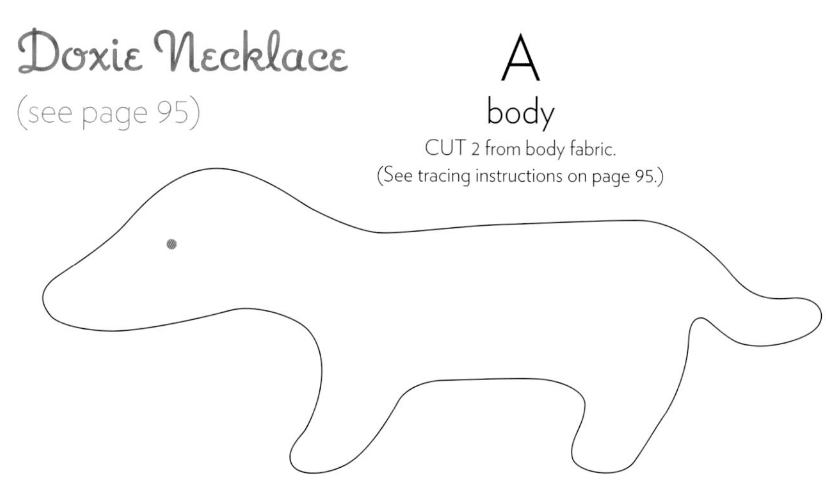

B
ear
CUT 4 from body fabric.
(See tracing instructions on page 95.)

Patchwork Penny (see page 99)

A
head
CUT 2 from body fabric.

E
boot
CUT 4 from boot fabric.

D
leg
CUT 4 from body fabric.

C
arm
CUT 4 from body fabric.

F
eye
CUT 2 from eye felt.

B
body/dress
CUT 2 from dress fabric.

Bonneted Baby

(see page 105)

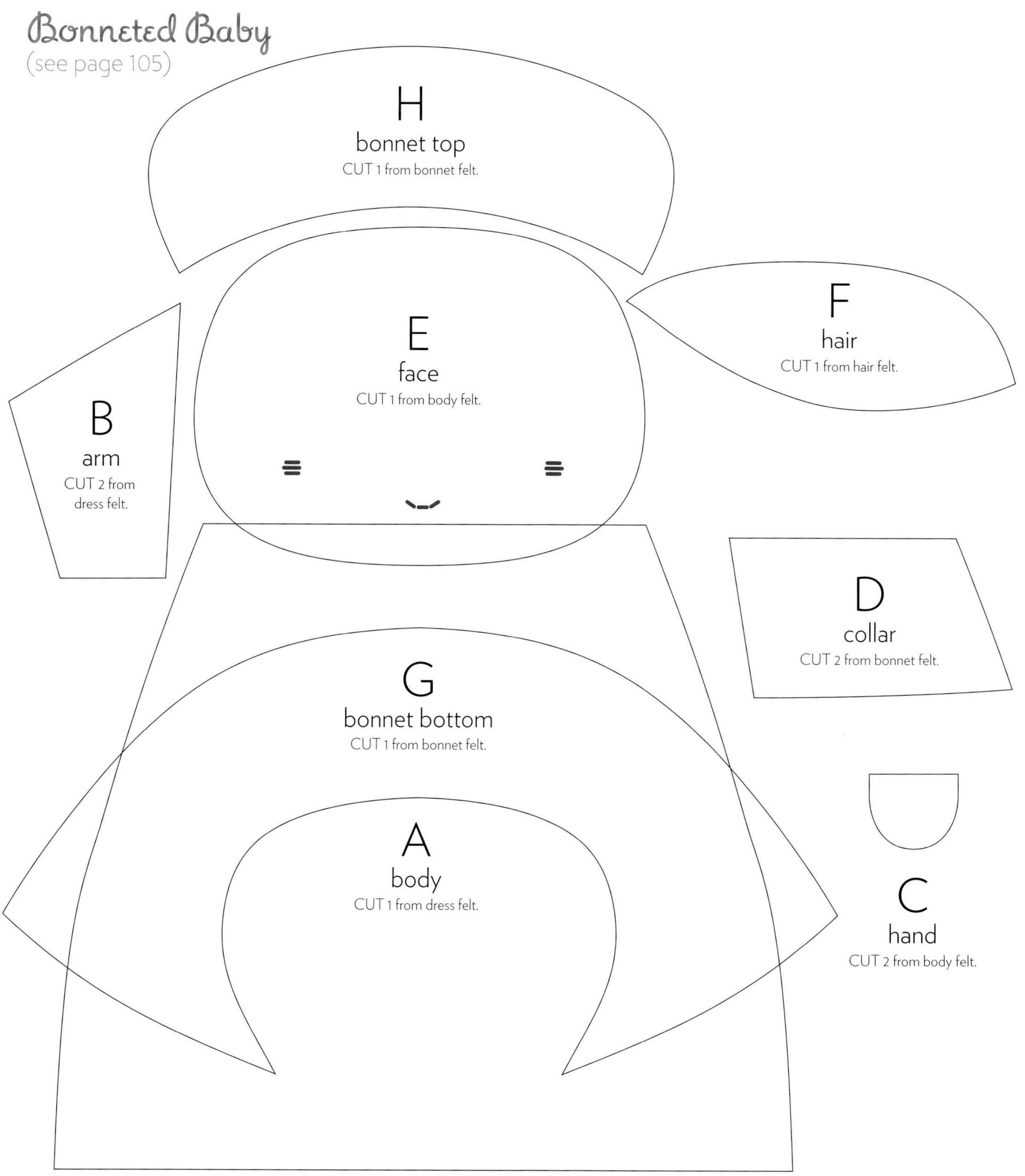

Hansel and Gretel (see page 113)

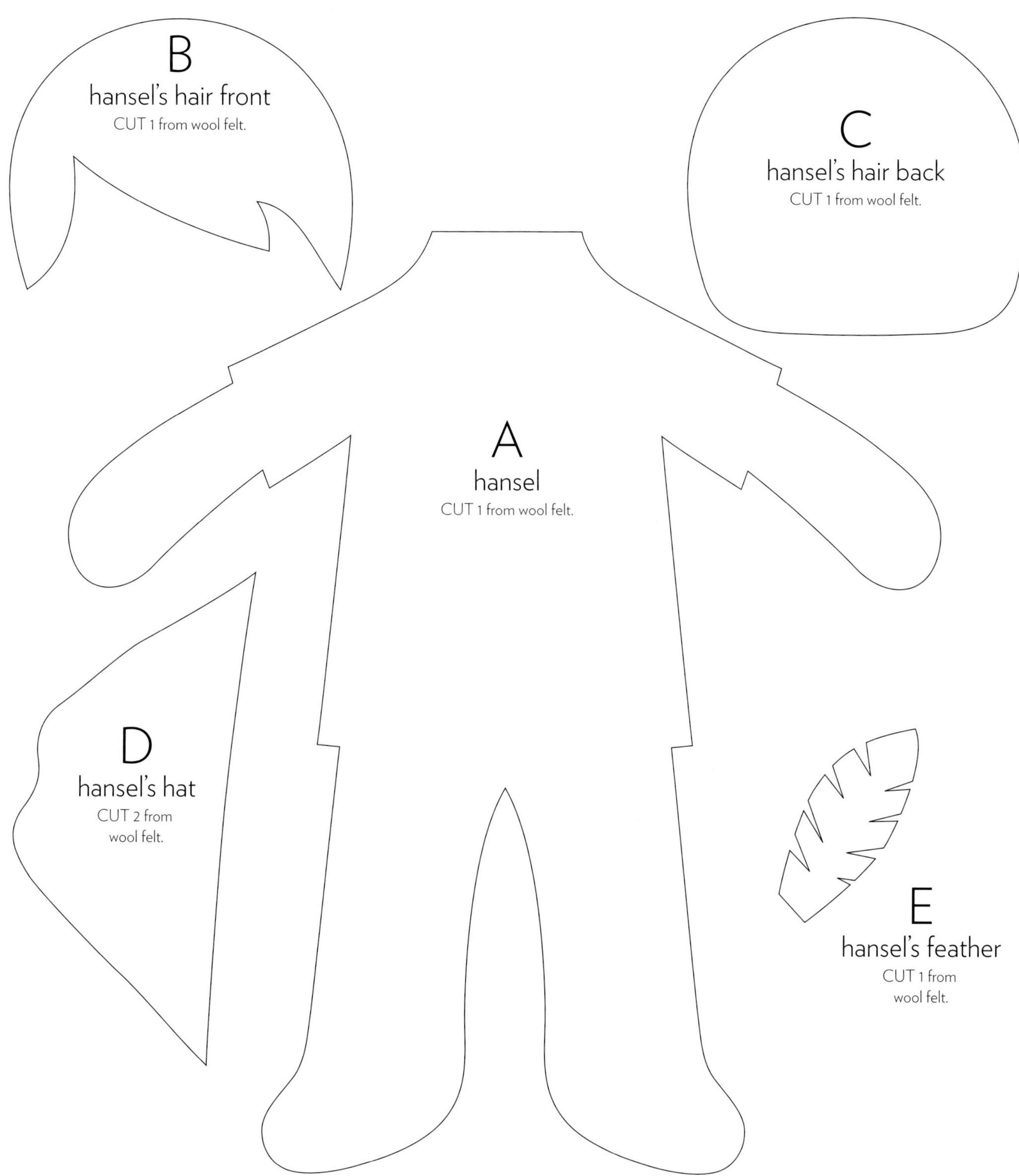

Hansel and Gretel,
continued

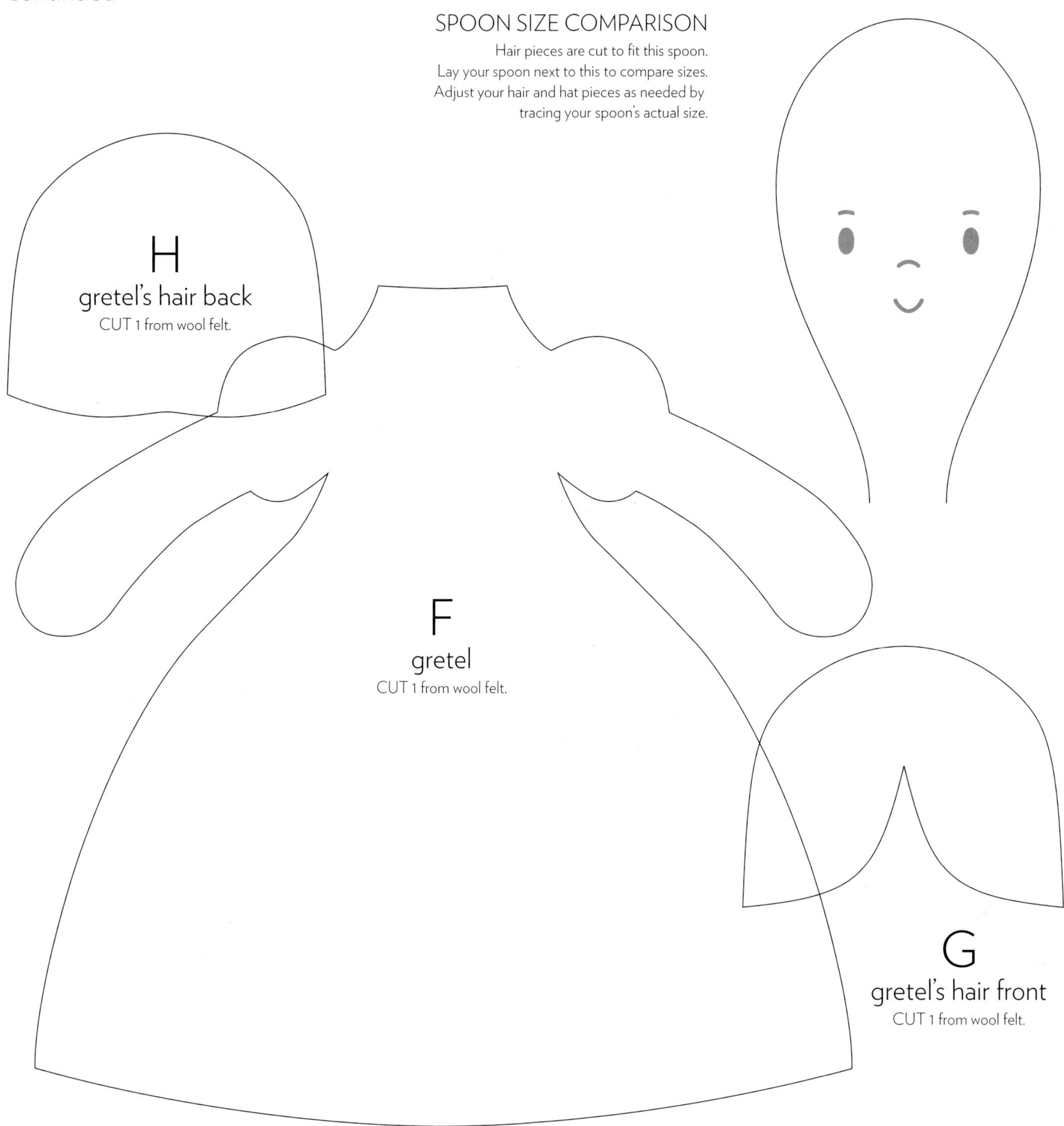

Resources

The materials and tools used to make the projects in this book are generally available at fabric and craft stores nationwide. If you cannot find what you are looking for locally, try these sources:

A CHILD'S DREAM COME TRUE
214 Cedar Street, Suite A
Sandpoint, ID 83864
(800) 359-2906
www.achildsdream.com
info@achildsdream.com
(Wool felt, felt beads, and wool stuffing)

BROWN SHEEP COMPANY, INC.
100662 County Road 16
Mitchell, NE 69357
(800) 826-9136
www.brownsheep.com
(Lamb's Pride yarn)

CLUSTER STUFF BY MORNING GLORY
(800) 406-4080
Available at Hobby Lobby stores
www.hobbylobby.com
(Stuffing)

EQUILTER
5455 Spine Road, Suite E
Boulder, CO 80301
(877) 322-7423
www.equilter.com
service@equilter.com
(Huge selection of fabric, great place for flannel solids)

FAT QUARTER SHOP
P.O. Box 1544
Manchaca, TX 78652
(866) 826-2069
www.fatquartershop.com
Kimberly@FatQuarterShop.com
(Designer fabric and fat quarter bundles)

GAIL WILSON DESIGNS
420 Grout Hill Road
South Acworth, NH 03607
(603) 835-6551
www.gailwilsondesigns.com
email@gailwilsondesigns.com
(Doll-making supplies)

HOBBY LOBBY
www.hobbylobby.com
(fabric, stuffing, and supplies)

JOANN FABRIC AND CRAFTS
www.joann.com
(fabric, stuffing, and supplies)

M&J TRIMMING
1008 Sixth Avenue
New York, NY 10018
(800) 965-8746
www.mjtrim.com
info@mjtrim.com
(Trim and ribbon)

MATATABI
www.matatabi.etsy.com
(Japanese fabric and sewing books)

NEARSEA NATURALS
P.O. Box 345
Rowe, NM 87562
(877) 573-2913
www.nearseanaturals.com
info@nearseanaturals.com
(Cotton and wool stuffing)

THE NEEDLE SHOP
2054 W. Charleston Street
Chicago, IL 60647
www.theneedleshop.net
info@theneedleshop.net
(Designer fabric)

PINK CHALK FABRICS
P.O. Box 11551
Bainbridge Island, WA 98110
(888) 894-0658
www.pinkchalkfabrics.com
customerservice@pinkchalk-fabrics.com
(Designer and Japanese fabric)

PURL PATCHWORK
147 Sullivan Street
New York, NY 10012
(800) 597-7875
www.purlsoho.com
(Designer and Japanese fabric, wool felt, and yarn)

RAINBOW GALLERY
7412 Fulton Avenue, Unit 5
North Hollywood, CA 91605
www.rainbowgallery.com
email@rainbowgallery.com
(Angora floss and other unique threads and floss)

REPRODEPOT FABRICS
www.reprodepot.com
help@reprodepot.com
(Japanese and reproduction fabrics)

SEW, MAMA, SEW!
P.O. Box 1127
Beaverton, OR 97075
(503) 380-3584
www.sewmamasew.com
(Modern cotton fabric)

SEWZANNE'S FABRIC
(888) 620-8382
www.sewzannesfabrics.com
(Children's fabric)

WEEKS DYE WORKS, INC.
1510-103 Mechanical Boulevard
Garner, NC 27529
(877) 683-7303
www.weeksdyeworks.com
contact@weeksdyeworks.com
(Wool bundles and fibers over-dyed by hand)

WEE WONDERFULS
P.O. Box 1136
Wheaton, IL 60187
www.weewonderfuls.typepad.com/wee_wonderfuls/store/
hillarylang@gmail.com
(My online shop)

Acknowledgments

ALL MY THANKS TO TIM, WITHOUT WHOM THERE WOULD BE NO BOOK. I WOULD LIKE TO THANK: MY FAMILY, ESPECIALLY LIFESAVERS GRANDMA AND AUNT KATIE. CAROL, RACHEL, BETSY, AND JEN FOR THEIR ENCOURAGEMENT, AID, AND ADVICE. SARAH, ALICIA, KIM, CLAIRE, AND ROSA, MY FELLOW BLOGGERS AND ALLIES, WHO HAVE INSPIRED ME TO KEEP AT IT ALL ALONG. ALL THE AMAZING CRAFT BLOGS THAT FILL MY OVERSTUFFED BLOGLINES AND GET ME THROUGH THE DAY WITH THEIR TALENT AND CREATIVITY. AMY, YOU TROUBLEMAKER. MY GENEROUS VOLUNTEER PATTERN TESTERS FOR THEIR TIME AND ATTENTION TO DETAIL. MY EDITOR, MELANIE FALICK, FOR...WELL, EVERYTHING. THE SUPERSTAR TEAM AT STC—CHRIS TIMMONS, TECH EDITOR; SARAH VON DREELE, GRAPHIC DESIGNER; AND LIANA ALLDAY, EDITOR—FOR THEIR TIME AND CONSIDERABLE TALENTS. MY PHOTOGRAPHER, JEN GOTCH, FOR MAKING EVERYTHING GORGEOUS. AND FINALLY MY KINDRED SPIRITS—THE READERS AND SUPPORTERS OF WEE WONDERFULS. IT'S YOU I HAVE TO THANK FOR THE WORD "TOYMAKER" APPEARING ON MY BUSINESS CARD.

THANK YOU!